CANOE COUNTRY

▼ ▼ ▼ ▼ ▼ ▼ ▼

AN EMBATTLED WILDERNESS

by

David Backes

NorthWord

PRESS, INC

Box 1360 • Minocqua, Wisconsin 54548

CANOE COUNTRY

Published by
NorthWord Press, Inc.
Box 1360, Minocqua, WI 54548

Designed and Illustrated by Mary Shafer
Cover Photo by Michael J. Furtman
ISBN 1-55971-112-4

For a Free Catalog describing NorthWord's line of
nature books and gifts, call 1-800-336-5666

Library of Congress Cataloging-in-Publication Data

Backes, David.
    Canoe country: an embattled wilderness / by David Backes. --
1st ed.
        p.   cm.
    Includes bibliographical references.
    ISBN 1-55971-112-4 : $12.95
    1. Boundary Waters Canoe Area (Minn.) 2. Conservation of
natural resources--Minnesota--Boundary Waters Canoe Area. I.
Title.
QH76.5.M6B33 1991
508.7767--dc20   91-3060
                                                          CIP

DEDICATION

To Jeanne V. Backes

and in memory of Gilbert F. Backes,
who introduced me to the canoe country,
taught me to fish,
and treasured the following verse:

Forests are made for weary men,
That they might find their souls again;
And little leaves are hung on trees,
To whisper of old memories;
And trails with cedar shadows black,
Are placed there just to lead men back
Beyond the pitfalls of success,
To boyhood peace and happiness.

— Mary Carolyn Davies —

CONTENTS

ACKNOWLEDGMENTS

I am happy to thank those who helped me during the course of this project. First, I would like to thank John Ross, who led my committee of academic advisors during my doctoral work at the University of Wisconsin-Madison. He strongly encouraged me to pursue the PhD at a time when I otherwise might not have seriously considered doing so. He was generous with his time, and provided excellent criticism.

I also wish to thank my other committee members: Bud Jordahl, Steve Vaughn, John Fett and Gretchen Schoff. Jordahl and Vaughn, who joined Ross as the committee's readers, provided helpful suggestions throughout the writing process.

Among those current and former UW faculty members whose courses and individual attention helped me decide the content and form of this book, three deserve special mention: Tom Bonnicksen, Paul Boyer, and Yi-Fu Tuan.

Many others contributed to this book in various ways. I would like to thank those organizations and individuals in the Ely area who helped provide information: Border Lakes Outfitting Co., Burntside Lodge, Camp Charles L. Sommers Canoe Base, Camp Van Vac, the Ely Chamber of Commerce, Mark Heywood, Elizabeth Olson, Sigurd T. Olson, Tom Stillman, and the Vermilion Interpretive Center.

I would like to thank Gordon Peters of the U.S. Forest Service in Duluth, and Floyd Henniger of the Minnesota Department of Natural Resources in St. Paul.

The excellent staff of the Minnesota Historical Society Research Center deserves recognition. Special thanks should go to Dallas Lindgren, Ruth Ellen Bauer, Ruby Shields, Steve Nielsen and Frank Glotz.

The cost of doing research would have been prohibitive without the help of those who provided inexpensive lodging in the St. Paul area. I am very grateful to Bob and Lol Ballsrud, Len and Lorraine Hertz, Denny Caneff and Reenie Marrinan.

The people at NorthWord Press, Inc., have been unfailingly friendly and hard-working. Special thanks to Tom Klein, the publisher, and to Mary Shafer, who designed the layout and illustrations.

Schooners to Rich Hoops, Curt Meine and Gerry Walter, whom I joined on regular excursions to the 602 Club to trade apocryphal anecdotes of academia.

Finally, and most importantly, I want to thank my wife, Judi, for her love, friendship, and never-failing support, and my children, Heidi, Timothy, and Jennifer, for bringing much joy into my life.

GUIDE TO MAPS

PREFACE

Northwest of Lake Superior on the Ontario-Minnesota border is a land that represents nature's defiance of modern engineering. In an area less than half the size of New Jersey, maps show at least five thousand lakes and interconnecting rivers, carved out of ancient bedrock by the last Ice Age glaciation. It took many thousands of years, but appears to be the work of a harried planner — the waterways are wildly twisted, jumbled, thrown down helter-skelter as if the glacier was in a hurry to move on to bigger things.

There is no making sense of it. If the maps were in black and white, and all of the labels removed, this tiny portion of North America called the Quetico-Superior would appear to be an elaborate Rorschach test. And perhaps that is what it really is. Those who travel through it see the same landscape, but it means something different to each person. Its meaning has less to do with any objective characteristics of the land than it does with the subjective characteristics of the individual's mind. Some people find its meaning in the rollicking call of a loon, others in the steady, downward tug of a walleyed pike at the end of a fishing line. Some people find it only in solitude and silence, while others find it in the unspoiled scenery they view from their motorboats.

The Quetico-Superior consists of Quetico Provincial Park in Ontario and, in Minnesota, of the Boundary Waters Canoe Area, part of the Superior National Forest. Altogether, it contains more than three million acres devoted to wilderness recreation. For more than seventy years, people have been expressing their visions of this area in magazines, newspapers, books and pamphlets. Radio, television and film also have played a role. Along with all of this publicity has come a lot of conflict over the area's proper use. Probably no other wilderness area in the United States can match the BWCA in the number of court battles fought and amount of legislation passed. For this reason, the BWCA often has set precedents for wilderness management in other parts of the country.

Quetico Park has seen less conflict than its neighbor, partly because the Quetico has always been completely government-owned. Also, there was no good Canadian access to the park until the mid-1950s, so, other than loggers and poachers, few Canadians went there. Before 1965, conflict over its use usually was related to conflict over the BWCA.

The history of political efforts to preserve the Quetico-Superior was first documented in 1977 by R. Newell Searle, in *Saving Quetico-Superior: A Land Set Apart* (St. Paul: Minnesota Historical Society Press). He focused on the work of a small group of Americans, the Quetico-Superior Council, who worked to get the United States and Canada to sign a treaty creating an international wilderness area. The story began in the 1920s, with the formation of the Council, and ended in 1960 when, instead of a treaty, the two nations exchanged letters that promised cooperation in the area's management. In the process, Searle described in detail the battles over preserving the portion now called the BWCA.

Although this book covers a longer time period — 1920 through 1980 — it inevitably touches upon many of the same issues and people covered by Searle. But our purposes differ. Searle's book presented a blow-by- blow, behind-the-scenes description of each canoe country conflict, as seen from the perspective of conservationists. He made little effort, however, to put this detailed political history into context. In other words, he left a central question largely unexplored? What was it about American culture that drew large numbers of diverse people to this watery wilderness? This question, in turn, leads to others: How did people perceive the Quetico-Superior? What did it mean to them? How did the meanings they attached to it affect the ways in which they used it? Why did some perceptions or images of the Quetico-Superior become socially and politically influential?

This book attempts to answer these questions. It focuses on people's <u>ideas</u> about the canoe country, and the mass media's role in spreading these ideas. It largely ignores the insider details of the various conflicts as documented by Searle, and instead focuses on the public debate and the clash of images.

Besides putting the area's history into context, this book gives attention to a number of previously neglected topics. Foremost is its analysis of the role of mass communication in the canoe country's history. For example, it examines in detail the ways in which the local tourism industry promoted the area. It also gives much more attention than previous works to Sigurd Olson's role in developing local tourism and in preserving the wilderness. This book is the first to examine the practice of fish stocking and the introduction of smallmouth bass, and their impact on tourism and the Quetico-Superior ecosystem. It also shows how evolving technology, such as the changes in outboard motors and canoes, affected the ways in which people used the area.

When we think about the relationship between society and nature, we tend to focus on the things *people* do that affect the environment. We tend to forget that the land itself affects our perceptions and actions. In an attempt to present a more holistic perspective, this book uses three central concepts: environmental, perceptual, and political boundaries.

Environmental boundaries are the natural processes and elements that limit the kinds and quality of relationships people can have with the land. For example, iron mining can occur only in places where geological conditions had produced iron ore. Natural processes also determine the quality, distribution, and amount of the ore.

Perceptual boundaries are the walls of our world views, built out of beliefs, attitudes, values, and faith. They determine the meanings we attach to a place such as the Quetico-Superior, and limit the culturally acceptable uses for that place.

Political boundaries are implied by the lines on a map that represent the geographical jurisdiction of a government or government agency; they consist of the accompanying legal limits to the agency's decision-making power, and of the policies created within those limits.

Changes in any one of these boundaries leads to changes in the others; this book will show how they interacted in the Quetico-Superior.

ᴥ ᴥ ᴥ

I first visited the Quetico-Superior region in 1962, at the age of five. On our way back to Wisconsin from a trip to the Canadian Rockies, my parents, my three older siblings and I stopped at a small northeastern Minnesota city named Ely; my father wanted to search for a quiet family resort on a lake teeming with fish. All I remember is a seemingly endless drive along a narrow collection of potholes and gravel known as the Fernberg Road.

We found what can only be described as Fishing Paradise: a resort with beautiful, comfortable log cabins, situated on a lake surrounded by miles of spruce, fir, and jack pine; home-cooked meals served family style in the main lodge; a sand beach; and, of course, fish. Lots of fish. Smallmouth bass, largemouth bass, northern pike, walleye pike, lake trout, rainbow trout, bluegill, perch. We came back every summer for many years, and eventually my parents built their own cabin in the area.

During those years we fished many times within the BWCA, sometimes on overnight trips, but usually on day trips, and always with an outboard motor. I was not aware of the tremendous battles being waged over this form of transportation, or of the philosophical issues involved. My main memory of those childhood trips is the tremendous joy I felt each time we got out onto the water; I remember the wind on my face and the sweep of the shores; and I remember humming in tune with the outboard motor — a child's mantra of peace and freedom.

As I reached adulthood my needs changed, and so did my perceptions. I grew to prefer paddles to outboards, although I continued to join my father for motorized day trips. I also learned about the long history of conflict over the area's management, and differed with my family over the 1978 legislation that made the BWCA a designated wilderness and led to the demise of the resort we all had loved.

Not long after that I moved to the area, became a reporter for the *Ely Echo,* and saw the bitterness many local citizens felt toward wilderness restrictions in both the BWCA and Quetico Park. For example, a miner friend of mine who loves to canoe and fish has been virtually shut out of the Quetico because competition for permits requires planning a trip months in advance, while the mine gives him short notice of when he can take off.

From such experiences I grew to dislike the blind hatred that wilderness preservationists and their local opponents often inflict upon each other. Wilderness enthusiasts find it easier to justify their stance if they imagine local citizens are greedy and narrow-minded, with no legitimate economic worries relating to wilderness management. Local citizens who oppose wilderness restrictions find it easier to justify their stance if they portray the wilderness preservationists as wealthy, power-hungry outsiders looking for a private playground, who don't care whose rights and livelihood get trampled in the process. I hope this book shows that people on both sides often are well meaning, with legitimate concerns, and that they even have something in common — a deep attachment to this rugged land known as the Quetico-Superior.

CHAPTER 1
WILDERNESS BOUND

*Our Dinner Table was a hard Rock, no Table Cloth could
be cleaner and the surrounding Plants and beautiful Flowers
sweetening the Board. Before us the Waterfall, wild, romantic, bold.... The Wildness of the Scene was added to by the
melancholy white headed Eagle hovering over our Board.*

— ***Nicholas Garry (1821)*** [1]

In the beginning there was space. Only space — for there were no
people to give the land meaning. During the course of
several billion years, mountains rose and fell without ever
having been climbed, life-forms evolved and disappeared without ever
having been named, and the seasons came and went without ever
having been memorialized in poetry.

Perhaps twenty times the northern hemisphere was inundated with
ice, thousands of feet thick, gouging lake and stream beds in granite
and greenstone. Each time, after fifty thousand or one hundred
thousand years the ice would melt, and the hemisphere would have up
to twenty thousand years of warmer weather. The retreating glaciers
would leave new watersheds, with new configurations of lakes and
streams that would be filled with new complexes of plants and animals.

Perhaps twenty times this happened, and the last was no different from
the first, except in the nature of one of the beasts that moved in the lee
of the ice. As with all animal species, this one was genetically ordained
to specialize in a lifestyle that enhanced its survival. For most, the
genetic adaptation that distinguishes them from other species restricts
them to certain kinds of behaviors and to certain kinds of places. But
this two-legged creature that followed the ice had developed an
adaptation that expanded its geographical boundaries to coincide with
the boundaries of its rapidly-growing mind. The adaptation was

culture; Homo sapiens was the cultural animal.[2]

With the arrival of humans, land became more than space. The cultural animal does not possess an instinctual mechanism that organizes the world into a neatly-coded system; it depends upon the learning processes of its mind to create a meaningful order out of experience.[3] Space, once experienced, acquires meaning. It becomes place.[4]

The ice-free land of the North became a series of places as the first people established themselves there about nine thousand years ago: home places, food-gathering places, ceremonial places and more. Some settled at the edge of an inland sea, one of the largest bodies of fresh water the world has ever known, where they hunted mastodon and other large animals.[5] The glacial sea disappeared during the course of four thousand years. As it shrunk, a lake nearby to the east became the world's largest. The people who settled at the edge of this lake mined copper for several thousand years, hammering it into spear points, knives, fish gorges and jewelry.[6]

Connecting the great lake to a remnant of the glacial sea was a vast network of smaller lakes, rivers, and muskeg bogs. The land it wound through was rugged and rocky, full of glacier-strewn boulders and punctuated with outcrops of ancient bedrock. Near the great lake, a largely eroded mountain range crossed the land. To the east of the range, all waters drained into the great lake; to its west, they drained toward the remains of the glacial sea. The fourteen thousand square miles of territory bound by these westward-draining waters is known today as the Rainy Lake watershed.

The descendants of the mastodon hunters and copper miners eventually came to call themselves Dacotah, which means "Friends." They adapted themselves to the Rainy Lake watershed during eight hundred years of unusually dry, warm weather, when many fires swept over the mixed conifer and deciduous forest. Fire was a key environmental boundary during this period. It limited the size and distribution of the conifers and opened large sections of land, ensuring ideal habitat for moose and caribou. The Dacotah built hide-covered tepees and

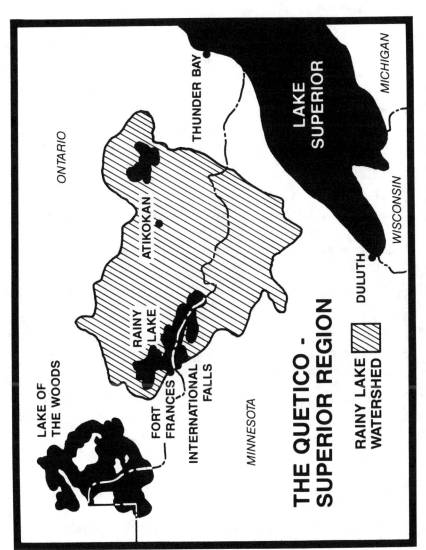

Figure 1 - *Present day Quetico-Superior Region, showing the Rainy Lake watershed area.*

depended on the large animals for food. They also built hide-covered boats and heavy dugouts, but they traveled the watershed's labyrinth of lakes and rivers as little as possible. Their eyes were on the open-land hunting grounds.[7]

During the time of the Dacotah, but far across the world, there lived water-traveling adventurers from several cultures. They called themselves Francois, Espan'ol and British. Although they spoke different tongues and declared different allegiances, these Easterners shared a Christian world view, with its linear perspective of time that focused their attention on the future. It was the sixteenth century in Europe, and the future lay beyond the Atlantic horizon in the direction of the recently-discovered New World.

On September 7, 1535, three ships flying the banner of the Fleur de Lis entered a river known to the natives as Hochelaga. It led, they told the captain, to a place called Canada. Jacques Cartier and his crew of 110 men became the first to spend a winter in New France. Twenty-five of them died of scurvy.[8]

The Rainy Lake watershed was part of New France, but the Dacotah did not know that; more than a century passed before the French arrived there. When they did, they were responding to pressure from the British over control of the fur trade, the critical economic factor behind both nations' imperialist intentions.

New World economy was predicated upon Old World scarcity. It simply cost too much to transport back to Europe anything that still could be found in Europe without difficulty. At the end of the sixteenth century, the beaver was nearly gone from the Old World. Its pelt made hats of the highest fashion, and demand was much greater than supply. The way to New World fortune was through the fur trade.

Success in the trade depended upon convincing natives to trap; they had the expertise and the labor supply. It did not take long. Every European explorer who reached the northeast coast in the early seventeenth century reported that the natives were anxious to trade.[9]

In return for beaver skins, the Europeans gave knives and hatchets with metal blades, brass and copper pots, needles and thread, beads, and woven fabrics.

Historians often have described the introduction of European technology as a cataclysmic event, and there is no question that traditional subsistence practices became easier and methods changed. But the real explosion occurred in the natives' minds. Until the fur traders arrived, the natives' perceptual boundaries — the walls that enclosed their world view — had limited their images of the beaver to the practical, eat-and-wear kind, or to the realm of myth, which said that beavers once had been people, but had been changed into animals, and that someday the "little men of the woods" would be changed back in reward for their hard work. But the fur traders turned the beaver into money, with which the natives could buy European goods.[10] When the beaver became cash, a mental wall crumbled, and a world view irrevocably changed. Every watershed became a savings and loan, and the natives began withdrawing furs at an alarming rate.

Beaver populations plummeted. The animal's ability to reproduce, limited by such environmental boundaries as genetic makeup, disease, and the types and amounts of available food, could not keep up with human predation. The beaver, in turn, acted as an environmental boundary to the natives; there could be no trapping on a given piece of land once the fur-bearing animals were gone. Tribes faced a choice of giving up the fur trade or moving to new land. They could not give up the trade. They had become dependent upon Europe for wool to replace the skins they once had worn, and they had become accustomed to the trade goods they received. Europe demanded fur. As the beaver declined, therefore, tribes began pushing against ill-defined territorial boundaries, and intertribal warfare increased. Both factors led to a westward movement that by the late seventeenth century reached the Rainy Lake watershed.[11]

The heaviest fighting began in 1649, when a federation of tribes called the Iroquois, supplied by Dutch traders with guns and ammunition, moved into Huron territory south and east of present Georgian Bay.

With their superior weaponry and military acumen, the Iroquois forced the Hurons to flee within a year; as many as eight thousand starved. During the next fifty years more than half a dozen tribes followed the waterways west to escape from the Iroquois.

The removal of the Hurons forced the French also to head west. The Hurons had been their allies, and had acted as middlemen to control nearly all of the currently merchantable beaver in New France. The French, who also had suffered greatly in warfare with the Iroquois, had to go west or lose the fur trade entirely to the British and the Dutch, both of which were on better terms with the Iroquois federation. By 1662 the French were conducting business at Keweenaw, on the south-central shore of the great lake that bordered the territory of the Dacotah. The French named it Lac Superieur, or "Upper Lake."

French explorers may have reached the east end of Lake Superior as early as 1623, while the British still were huddled at Jamestown and other coastal settlements. They definitely reached the lake by 1641. In September of that year two Jesuit priests, Charles Raymbault and Isaac Jogues, arrived at its thundering, eastern outlet, which they named Sault de Sainte Marie. There they met a tribe that soon would play a major role on the Rainy Lake watershed. The Jesuits called them Saulteurs, "People of the Rapids." They called themselves Anishinabe, "Human Beings."

The Anishinabe were among the peoples forced west of Lake Huron by the Iroquois. They found safety and abundant resources at the east end of the lake they called Kitchigami, the "Big Sea Water," and their numbers increased to such an extent that they soon spread west along both the north and south shores of the lake. Many had reached the west end by the 1670s, and some entered the Rainy Lake watershed. The Dacotah quickly took up weapons against the outsiders, and they became bitter enemies. The victor eventually was determined by two factors beyond the control of either side: the fur trade and the climate.

The French fur trade expanded dramatically late in the seventeenth century, much faster than demand. Consumption in France averaged forty thousand to forty-five thousand pounds of fur from 1675 to 1687, but trappers increased their average supply from about ninety thousand pounds to one hundred forty thousand pounds. But with the best beavers trapped out, much of the increase was in lower quality skins, which hurt the popularity of the fur at a time when smaller hats and substitute furs were gaining favor. Meanwhile, Great Britain was expanding its involvement in the fur trade, and the added pressure to the beaver populations worked to the advantage of the British. The British woolen industry was more efficient than that of the French and was able to give the increasingly dependent natives superior cloth at a price lower than the French could ask.

The British also gained a geographical advantage. In 1670, the Crown awarded the Hudson's Bay Company a charter that gave the company claim to all the territory containing streams that drained to Hudson Bay. This included the Rainy Lake watershed, and almost 40 percent of modern Canada — land that also was claimed by the French. An environmental boundary made Hudson Bay the key to the fur trade. Tilting down toward the bay on all sides was a 500-million-year-old shield of bedrock (see map next page). The southern edge of this Canadian Shield followed the St. Lawrence River to near Lake Ontario, then cut across the top of the Great Lakes, briefly dipped south of Lake Superior, then followed a wandering, north-northwesterly route to the Arctic. Nearly all of the major rivers of the Canadian Shield flowed to Hudson Bay. They provided the most efficient routes to market for all furs obtained within an arc extending nearly a thousand miles to both the northeast and the northwest of Lake Superior. In 1713, after two wars spanning twenty-five years, France signed the Treaty of Utrecht and acknowledged British sovereignty over Hudson Bay. The treaty set the stage for the fur trade's entrance into the Rainy Lake watershed.

During the war years, the British had developed an extensive trade with the Crees and Assiniboines who lived northwest of the Rainy Lake watershed near a lake called Oinnipique, or Winnipeg, a remnant of the ancient glacial sea. The natives willingly brought furs all the way to Hudson Bay in exchange for the usual goods — which by now

RAINY LAKE WATERSHED
(SHADED AREA)

LAKE MICHIGAN

LAKE SUPERIOR

LAKE HURON

LAKE ERIE

Figure 2 - Locator map of the Rainy Lake watershed area in relation to the Great Lakes.

included liquor — by traveling down the Nelson River from Lake Winnipeg. Those natives closer to Lake Superior also would go north from that lake by way of the Kaministikwia River. The French could compete with the British only if they could control the waterways near the southern edge of the Canadian Shield. By bringing trade goods to the natives, the French hoped to discourage the long journey to Hudson Bay.

The French established a post at Kaministikwia in 1717. From there, they were able to exploit the watershed that emptied into Lac La Pluie, "Rainy Lake," named for the never-ending mist near the falls at its outlet. Bound for Lake Winnipeg and beyond, the French traders known as "voyageurs" used the region's waterways as highways. They turned the tallest red and white pines into road signs by chopping off the middle limbs, leaving naked trunks and bushy tops that were visible from afar. The Rainy Lake watershed was a place to travel through quickly. The French established a small number of outposts there, but the bulk of the trade goods were whisked across its lakes and lugged over its portages to other destinations.

With the French came the Anishinabe, whose expertise at canoe building and other woodland skills made them an integral part of the trade. They were good friends with the voyageurs; intermarriage was common, and eventually there were whole villages of mixed descendants called *metis*. As the Anishinabes' world changed, so did their world view. Some of them adapted elements of western culture and religion to their wilderness lifestyle; in reaction, others created a mystical religious order based on traditional beliefs. Even their name reflected the passing times; the Anishinabe grew used to being called Saulteurs, and then by a word from their language that referred to the "puckered up" shape of their moccasins. The Human Beings were now Ojibway.

The Dacotah soon also lost their identity. The Ojibway, at war with The Friends, gave them the name Na-dou-esse, or "Snakes in the Grass." The French spelled it Nadouesioux, and eventually it was shortened to Sioux. That the name stuck indicates the power of the

outsiders, both Ojibway and European. The Ojibway dominated the
Rainy Lake watershed within a few decades, and the Sioux retreated
southwest.[12]

It was not just military might that brought victory to the Ojibway.
There actually was little loss of life. The fighting was poorly organized,
and usually involved short raids between villages of not more than a
couple of hundred inhabitants. Some villages would be at peace while
others fought.[13] The Ojibway won, perhaps not so much because of
their warriors as because of favorable environmental conditions.

The Rainy Lake watershed was changing. Beginning about the year
1500, the weather had become cool and moist, a dramatic contrast to
the warm, dry climate that had prevailed for eight hundred years. The
number of wildfires declined, and pine stands that otherwise might
have burned grew to maturity. The consequent loss of browse caused
a decline in moose and caribou populations. The Sioux, dependent on
these animals for food, clothing and shelter, found the increasingly
dense forest much less hospitable than the more open conditions
southwest of the river the Ojibway called Mississippi. Changing
environmental boundaries had made the Sioux outsiders on the Rainy
Lake watershed; it no longer was the home they had known.[14]

The Ojibway, however, were well suited to the region. They ate much
more of fish, berries and wild rice than they did of moose and caribou.
They made dome-shaped, birchbark wigwams instead of hide-covered
tepees; birch was still plentiful. Instead of awkward, heavy dugouts or
fragile, hide-covered boats, they built birchbark canoes and took
advantage of the water trails. Their mobility let them also spread out
their resource base, making depletion much less likely.[15] The Rainy
Lake watershed became *their* home, with a new set of meanings
superimposed upon ancient places.

As occupation of the region shifted from the Sioux to the Ojibway, the
spoils of a distant war put an end to New France; Great Britain now
had sole European claim to the Rainy Lake watershed. The British
arrived at the west end of Lake Superior in about 1768, to take over the

fur trade. They set up a route to Rainy Lake that was more direct than the one the French had used. The route began at the Pigeon River, and went upstream over a series of difficult rapids and portages until North Lake, where it crossed the continental divide and entered the Rainy Lake watershed. This new Voyageur's Highway became the route of the fur trade at its peak. Within a decade, the Grand Portage post at the Pigeon River employed five hundred, and about three hundred voyageurs traveled the lakes and streams that led west toward Rainy Lake. The number using the Voyageur's Highway increased to nearly four hundred by the end of the century; the number of Ojibway living along the route at the time was perhaps under five hundred, and certainly was under one thousand.[16]

The Grand Portage trade was organized, not by the Hudson's Bay Company, but by upstarts, who derisively joked that the initials of their century-old competitor stood for "Here Before Christ." They were Highland Scots, mostly, and in 1787 they rounded up a large number of experienced French and metis voyageurs and formed the Northwest Company. The Nor'westers, with their red knit hats and their blue capotes, their boisterous songs and their feats of endurance, readily became romanticized in the twentieth century, and perhaps had a greater impact on the Rainy Lake watershed as a symbol, invoked by tourist promoters and wilderness preservationists, than they did as actual exploiters. The fur trade contributed to a large short-term decline in the region's beaver, but produced no significant long-term environmental changes; its legacy lay in the minds of those who followed. An early result was a new political boundary.[17]

Great Britain's New World colonies had fought and won their independence, and in 1782 the two sides met to draw the boundary separating Canada from the United States. The British had two main concerns: to keep control over the fur trade, and to have access to the Mississippi River. The United States agreed. The treaty makers drew the boundary down the middle of the lakes and streams of the fur trade, from where the 45th parallel intersected the St. Lawrence River to the west end of Lake Superior and beyond. The two governments used the best source for their boundary-drawing: cartographer John Mitchell's

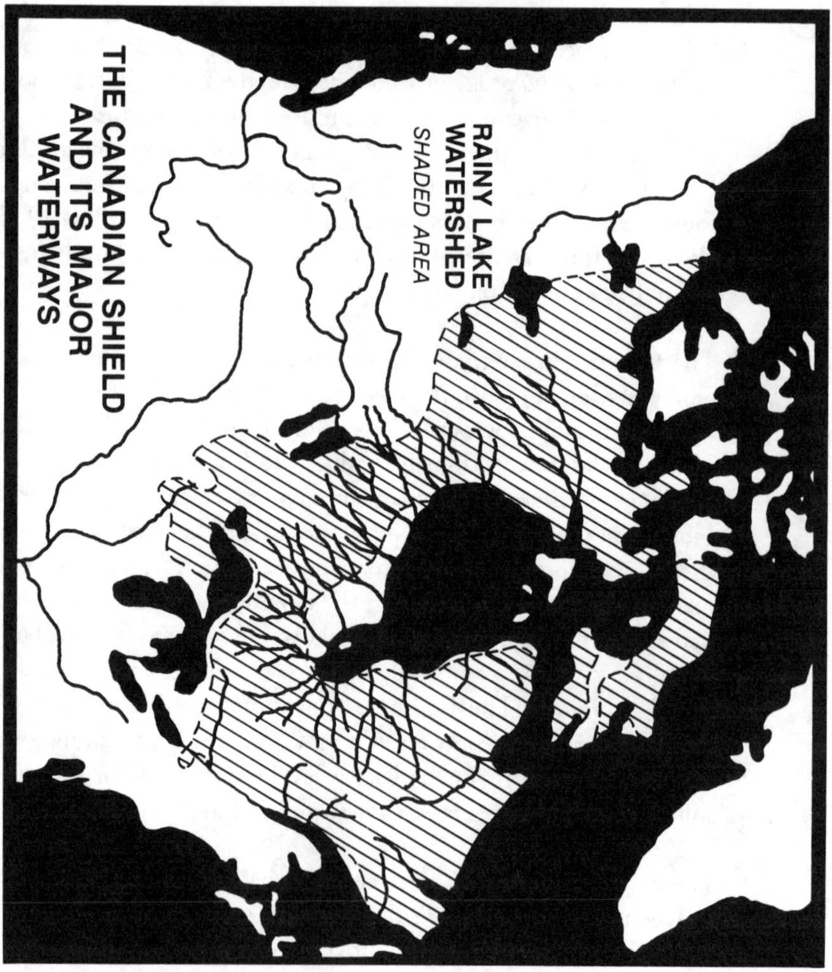

RAINY LAKE
WATERSHED
SHADED AREA

THE CANADIAN SHIELD
AND ITS MAJOR
WATERWAYS

Figure 3 - Major waterways of the Rainy Lake watershed and Canadian shield area.

map of French and British claims in North America, originally published in 1755. But Mitchell's map was seriously flawed in its depiction of the territory west of Lake Superior. And his errors still affect the Rainy Lake watershed.[18]

Mitchell made two major mistakes. First, the map indicated that the source of the Mississippi, while not known, was located somewhere in present Manitoba. Second, it showed Lake of the Woods flowing east to Lake Superior, instead of to Hudson Bay. This encouraged treaty makers to perceive Lake of the Woods as the source for the whole Great Lakes-St. Lawrence River system. The obvious boundary, based on Mitchell's map, would run through the center of the Rainy Lake watershed along the Voyageur's Highway, to the northwest corner of Lake of the Woods, and due west to the Mississippi River. That is what the two countries agreed upon. When the Treaty of Paris was ratified in 1783, the Rainy Lake watershed was split for the first time by a political boundary.

The agreement soon fizzled. The line was protested loudly by the British traders in Grand Portage, which suddenly was part of U.S. territory. And, by the early 1790s, both nations suspected the source of the Mississippi was far south of where Mitchell had indicated. But the British were in a bind, because they had agreed that the boundary should follow the route of the fur trade. Their solution? To claim that the Voyageur's Highway began, not at Grand Portage, but far to the south, near the modern city of Duluth. A boundary drawn from there would put all of the Rainy Lake watershed in Canada. The United States, not to be outdone, claimed that the Voyageur's Highway followed the old Kaministikwia River route. A boundary drawn from there would put most of the watershed in the United States.

Beginning in 1822, representatives of the two nations spent three summers canoeing through the region, to decide which route was the real Voyageur's Highway. The land did not impress them. The U.S. boundary commissioner spoke for both sides when he said the Rainy Lake watershed was "a section of country uninhabited, and I might perhaps add, uninhabitable." But it still was valuable enough to the fur trade that the two countries ended the survey without reaching an agreement.[19]

Jurisdiction of the watershed remained unclear until 1842, when U.S. Secretary of State Daniel Webster met with British special envoy Lord Ashburton to resolve all remaining U.S.-Canada boundary problems. By that time the region no longer was important to the fur trade. The Hudson's Bay Company had absorbed the Northwest Company in 1821; with the southern edge of the Canadian Shield no longer strategically vital to the trade, the more efficient Hudson Bay routes took over the bulk of the traffic. The Voyageur's Highway had become a back road, and neither nation could get worked up about the boundary. Ashburton, who told his superiors "it really appears of little importance to either party how the line be determined," proposed the Grand Portage boundary. Webster agreed.[20]

The Rainy Lake watershed still was undefined, however, save by the one line that split it in two. The watershed was home to the Ojibway, but a wilderness to the average citizen of the nations that claimed it. Wilderness, as applied then, not only often had a negative connotation, but meant an area so large and remote that its boundaries were not completely determined. To most non-natives, therefore, the Rainy Lake watershed still was space, rather than place. It was not widely perceived as a place until civilization encroached, steadily shrinking the size and remoteness of the area's wilderness until it became seen as valuable and acquired labels that expressed a newfound meaning.

Few settled in, or even near, the region until the 1870s. Tucked behind Lake Superior, the Rainy Lake watershed was an eddy in the westward-flowing river of settlement that passed below. Thousands of people drove their covered wagons across the rutted trail that led to Oregon. Thousands more followed the trail of gold as rushes drew them to California in 1849, and to Nevada, Colorado and Washington in the 1850s. It was 1870 before a railroad reached northeastern Minnesota; one had crossed the continent first.

Copper brought the first towns near to the Rainy Lake watershed. Deposits were scattered along the north shore of Lake Superior;

ancestors of the Dacotah had mined them several thousand years earlier. From 1853 to 1857, miners from Michigan's Ontonagon copper district established more than a dozen towns along the Minnesota shore, but the economic panic of 1857 drove nearly everybody out. The interest in copper mining, however, created pressure to open the Ojibway-owned region to Americans.

The Ojibway already had lost all their land to the south and to the east. In 1837 they gave up what is now eastern Minnesota, south of Lake Superior, and northwestern Wisconsin; the lumber industry moved in. In 1842 they lost the rest of what is now northern Wisconsin and Michigan's Upper Peninsula; the iron and copper mining industries moved in. And now, in 1854, they gathered at the Apostle Islands to sign a treaty giving away northeastern Minnesota, including the U.S. portion of the Rainy Lake watershed. They were luckier than many tribes; they at least were assigned reservations in the area. But the reservations were on poor land, and were too small to maintain their traditional hunting, fishing and gathering economy. A few scattered groups managed to eke out a living in the wilderness into the twentieth century, and a number of me'tis, entitled to 80-acre tracts, chose spots along the Voyageur's Highway. But the culture of the Anishinabe was just a memory, and that of the Ojibway had been dealt a mortal blow.

The region first was penetrated by modern civilization in 1865, at its southern edge. A Minnesota government geologist, exploring near Vermilion Lake, discovered veins of quartz containing gold and silver. More than a dozen mining companies soon arrived, cutting an eighty-mile trail through the forest from Duluth to the lake. In 1869, the Vermilion Trail was widened into a twelve-foot roadbed, and became the first Minnesota road to enter the Rainy Lake watershed. But by then there were few to travel it; the gold rush was over.

While workers in Minnesota were widening the Vermilion Trail at the southern edge of the watershed, a militia of fourteen hundred Canadians was building a road through the center, along the old fur trade route that began on the Kaministikwia River. They were hurrying west to stop a rebellion, but used the opportunity to build a trail that would encourage settlement in the Canadian West. Named after the man who had surveyed the route in 1857, the Dawson Trail became as important to Canada as the Oregon Trail was to the United States. Steamboats soon carried settlers across the larger lakes and rivers of the Rainy Lake watershed, and portages were equipped with carts. Lodging was available at a few places along the way.

Opening the northern region to settlement meant, once again, taking territory from the Ojibway. In 1873 the tribe gave up its title to all of the Canadian portion of the region. Farms soon appeared along the northern banks of the Rainy River, just west of the watershed; by 1893 there were six hundred of them. Meanwhile, beginning in 1879, the Canadian Pacific Railway was being laid out to the north of the watershed, creating a large demand for timber for its millions of railroad ties and telegraph poles, and for houses, supply buildings and stations. The western edge of the watershed soon was stripped of trees, which were sent crashing over the falls at Rainy Lake and up the Rainy River to Lake of the Woods. The Hudson's Bay Company and the Northwest Company once had posts on Rainy Lake; now two logging cities sprouted at the falls: Fort Frances, Ontario and International Falls, Minnesota.

The region also was being penetrated from the south. A rapidly industrializing United States demanded iron ore; the Rainy Lake watershed contained it. Millions of years before, the area had been covered by a sea, into which volcanoes spewed iron-rich lava. The iron settled into small pockets, or formations. One band of ore deposits began at Vermilion Lake. It was shaped like a narrow funnel, reaching a point about thirty miles to the northeast. The city of Tower was built at Vermilion Lake in 1884, and the city of Ely was established near the tip of the funnel in 1888. One mine operated at Tower; by the turn of the century, Ely had five. The Duluth and Iron Range Railroad linked them to Lake Superior, where ships took the ore east to feed the industrial revolution.

Although Vermilion Range miners dug more than one million tons of ore nearly every year for six decades, the range paled in comparison to

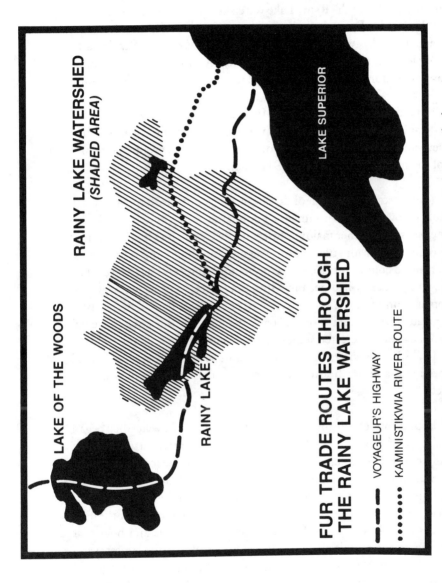

Figure 4 – Location of major fur trade routes through the Rainy Lake watershed area.

its neighbor, the Mesabi. The eastern corner of the Mesabi — an Ojibway word meaning "giant's hills" — was nestled against the southern edge of the Rainy Lake watershed, twelve miles south of Ely at Birch Lake. From there the range zig-zagged southwest in a narrow band, typically two to three miles wide, for a hundred miles. In just a couple of decades twenty cities and nearly twice that many mines appeared along this band of ore, and railroads linked them to Duluth.

Production began in 1892, at Mountain Iron. Three years later the Mesabi became the nation's top iron range, producing more than seventeen percent of America's ore. By 1900 it was producing a third of the nation's total, and by 1916, half.

Mining created a pattern of development in northeastern Minnesota that followed the environmental boundaries of the ore deposits. It also helped spur another major industry in the area — logging. The mines needed timber for studs, floors, wagons, buildings, and railroad ties: The local communities needed timber for homes and businesses. The logging industry had been in Minnesota since 1839, when a sawmill opened on the St. Croix River, northeast of St. Paul. The industry spread development along a path dictated by the environmental boundaries that created stands of white and red pine. By the time the Mesabi Range entered production, most of the state's tall pine had been cut, and northeastern Minnesota contained most of what was left.

The pine forest at the southern edge of the Rainy Lake watershed began falling to the axe early in the 1890s. Section upon section was clearcut and burned. A geologist who had arrived before the loggers couldn't believe the change. "Few areas in the United States have been so completely altered by man," he said. By the end of the decade the pine had been cut almost up to the border. The last big stands were the least accessible, those isolated by the maze of lakes, rivers and bogs that occupied the middle third of the watershed. By far the largest was a swath of pine that extended northeast from Ely and cut across the old Voyageur's Highway, reaching ten miles into Ontario (see map on page 20). Its western limit was the lake called La Croche by the French voyageurs, translated into Crooked Lake by the British. The tall pine extended east for thirty miles to Knife Lake, called Lac des Couteaux by the voyageurs. This swath of land had not had a major forest fire in three hundred years; red pines of up to eighty feet and white pines of up to two hundred feet made up more than 70 percent of the forest, compared to about 40 percent elsewhere in the area.[21]

The best access to the whole stand was by way of Basswood Lake. The international boundary followed the center of the lake's thirty-mile-long, Z-shaped main channel. A dozen bays, each larger than most of the region's lakes, shot off from this channel in every direction. Three of them — Hoist, Jackfish and Pipestone bays — stretched southwest toward Ely, making Basswood Lake a funnel, the broad end of which provided access to all the border lakes to the east and west, and to a vast network of Canadian waters to the north. The voyageurs had called it Lac du Bois Blanc, Lake of White Wood. They likely were referring to the white cedars that lined its shores, but someone along the way thought they meant Basswood, which is light-colored, but not common in the area.

In 1901 the Swallow and Hopkins Lumber Company completed a four-mile railroad portage from Fall Lake into Hoist Bay. The lumber village of Winton was at the other end of Fall Lake, three miles northeast of Ely. Swallow and Hopkins sold the Four Mile Portage to the St. Croix Lumber and Manufacturing Company in 1911, after having hauled across 350 million board feet of pine. St. Croix used the portage for nine more years, then pulled the rails. On the Minnesota side of the border, the swath of pine was gone, clearcut.[22]

Logging also had cleared large sections of the Rainy Lake watershed in Ontario. At the turn of the century, heavy U.S. demand and provincial incentives had encouraged Canadian loggers to move from the Lake Huron area to the forests near Rainy Lake. Minnesota corporations financed giant mills there to turn Ontario's pine and pulpwood into porches and paper. Forest clearings spread eastward as fast as mills and markets allowed. By 1916, the pine began falling in the center of the watershed, north of Lac La Croix and the old Kaministikwia River

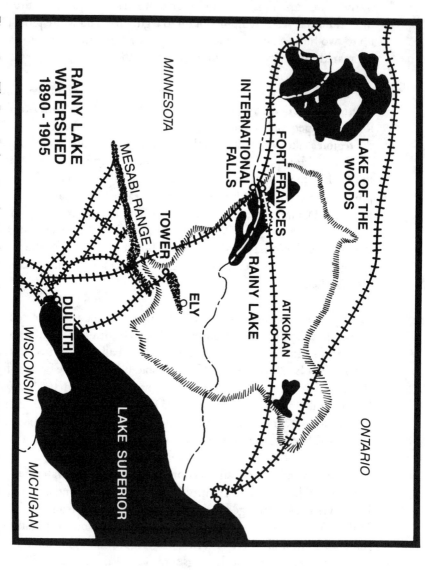

Figure 5 - The Rainy Lake region during the iron boom years of 1890-1905, showing rail routes for ore transportation.

route of the fur trade. The wilderness was rapidly disappearing.[23]

As logging helped to physically transform the wilderness, it also helped psychologically to transform attitudes toward wild land. Wilderness had long meant the unknown, boundless regions beyond the edge of civilization. It was space. But the frontier was gone, and wilderness, surrounded by civilization, had been transformed from a vast space into a series of places; its definition had to change. As a place, wilderness became something to go *to* rather than *through*. And, as people discovered more and more reasons to go to areas of wilderness, they began to pressure governments to manage these areas. In the name of the public interest, the last bits of wilderness would, one by one, be captured and tamed with political boundaries and labels.

In 1902, the year the logging mills in Duluth reached their peak production, Minnesota Forestry Commissioner Christopher C. Andrews convinced the U.S. General Land Office to reserve from sale 500,000 acres of federal property north of Ely. The acreage was of no value to loggers because it had been ravaged by wildfire and contained little pine. Three years later, after a canoe trip along the Voyageur's Highway west from Basswood Lake, the seventy-seven-year-old Andrews persuaded the General Land Office to expand the reserve by 141,000 acres, including the virgin forest along Crooked Lake and Lac La Croix. He also asked the Ontario government to create a forest reserve on its side of these lakes. Andrews thought the area's scenery made it potentially valuable as a "pleasure resort."[24]

The idea gained favor in Ontario during the next several years. The province was concerned about preserving its pine belt from fire, and also about protecting the region's dwindling moose herd. Logging companies had hired professional hunters to supply food for their camps, some of which used a hundred moose in a season. American trophy hunters also had killed many moose, taking the antlers and leaving the meat to rot. Alarmed by the slaughter, Ontario citizens supported the idea of a forest reserve. When U.S. President Theodore Roosevelt established Superior National Forest on February 13, 1909, Ontario quickly followed suit. On April 1, it created the adjoining

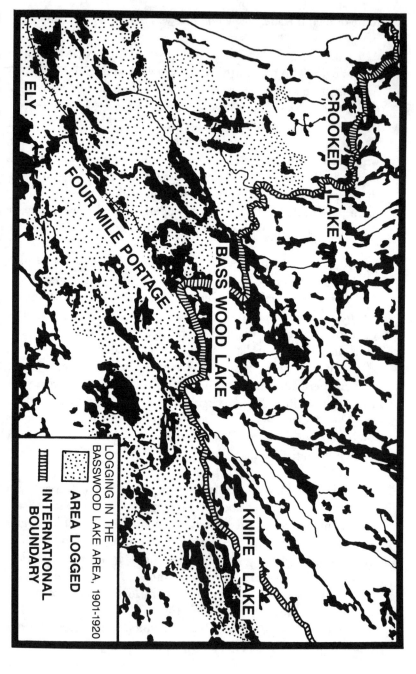

Figure 6 – Map showing area logged in the Basswood Lake region between 1901 and 1920.

Quetico Provincial Reserve (see map next page). Superior National Forest consisted of three units — including the land withdrawn at Andrew's request — totalling 1,400,000 acres. Quetico Provincial Reserve was one block of 1,120,000 acres. About a fifth of the Rainy Lake watershed had become officially protected from uncontrolled exploitation. In 1913, as a measure to better protect its wildlife, Ontario designated the Quetico a provincial park.[25]

North of the Canadian National Railroad, the old-fashioned wilderness still existed, stretching all the way to Hudson Bay. But amidst the moldering dams of the Dawson Trail, denuded of its tall pine on the southern side of the Voyageur's Highway, there arose a new kind of wilderness. Bound by the limits of the mind and the lines on the map, the new wilderness was no longer space, but place. It was the Quetico-Superior. What kind of place was it? The answers — and there were many — stirred numerous conflicts in the decades ahead.

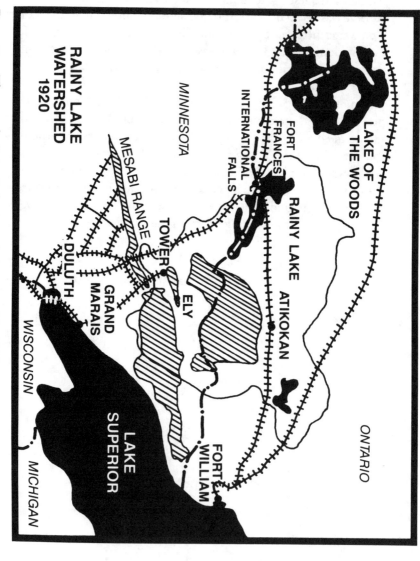

Figure 7 - The way the Rainy Lake watershed appeared by 1920.

CHAPTER 2
SAGANAGA LAKE

...time is always time
And place is always and only place
And what is actual is actual only for one time
And only for one place

— T.S. Eliot (1930) [1]

When President Theodore Roosevelt created the Superior National Forest in 1909, he was acting in the name of "conservation." The first use of the term in its modern sense has been attributed to George Bird Grinnell in 1875, but it was made popular in the early 1900s by Roosevelt and others in his administration, notably Gifford Pinchot, the first chief of the U.S. Forest Service. The conservation movement arose from Roosevelt's efforts to design policies for efficient development of forests and Western water supplies. [2]

As historian Samuel P. Hays has shown, the movement at this time was a "scientific movement" led by professionals in such fields as forestry, geology and hydrology. These professionals shared with big business a hatred of unrestricted competition and an undirected economy. "Both groups," says Hays, "placed a premium on large-scale capital organization, technology, and industry-wide cooperation and planning to abolish the uncertainties and waste of competitive resource use." [3]

Nineteenth-century logging practices had destroyed whole forests; by the end of the century only 20 percent of the nation's original forest cover remained. Land prices were low in the last half of the century and many Americans entered the industry. The heavy competition encouraged waste; many loggers cut only the most valuable trees, then abandoned the land and started over in new locations. As late as the

1890s, when the industry entered the Quetico-Superior, most lumber company executives believed conservation's emphasis on sustained-yield management was out of touch with economic reality. But in the early 1900s, as loggers began to find it impossible to move to virgin land after clearing their holdings, they began adopting scientific methods of conservation, and supported the American Forestry Association (a private conservation group) and the U.S. Forest Service. In 1909, for example, logging companies helped buy the equipment for the agency's Forest Products Laboratory in Madison, Wisconsin. The Forest Service cooperated by pushing research to develop new manufacturing processes and forest products. The agency also supported higher lumber prices and large-scale logging operations, which could increase efficiency and make sustained-yield management more economical.[4]

By 1901, when Theodore Roosevelt became president, roughly forty million acres of forest reserves had been set aside by earlier administrations. Not until after 1897, when the Forest Management Act was passed, had logging been allowed in the reserves. That Act gave much regulatory discretion to the managing agency, and when the newly created Forest Service got control of the reserves in 1905, Pinchot used his power to create a broad multiple-use program. He worked with the livestock industry to allow grazing in the national forests, and with the irrigation and water power industries to ensure efficient management of national forest water supplies. Areas within national forests were classified according to their "highest use," with commodity uses taking precedence over recreation.[5]

The Roosevelt administration's goal of rational, scientific resource management was perhaps most politically controversial in the area of water development. It was evident to conservation leaders that maximum development required careful planning, with the entire river basin in mind. Careless development could lower the number of potential uses. Because rivers crossed state lines and local investment was unstable, the administration pressed for federal funding of waterway development, with all projects to be under the direction of a commission of river experts. Congress and the Army Corps of Engineers fought against any loss of their authority, and by 1913 the federal waterways program was at a standstill that lasted seven years.[6]

In 1908, as Roosevelt's waterway conservation policies began to run into opposition, the administration turned to the general public for support of a comprehensive conservation policy for all natural resources. Many organizations that promoted efficiency allied themselves with Roosevelt. The four leading engineering societies, for example, were in close contact with the administration, and promoted hydro-electric development, more efficent mining methods, and scientific management in factories. The editor of one engineering journal wrote: "When humanity shall have learned to apply the common sense and scientific rules of efficiency to the care of body and mind and the labors of body and mind, then indeed will we be nearing the condition of perfect."[7]

This goal of wise use, of efficiency, of *conservation*, was part of the overall progressive ideal that directed change toward centralization. Progressive conservationists believed that resource problems were technical and so should be handled by experts rather than by politicians. They saw no place for emotion-based decisions. Federal agencies of disinterested experts would use the newest scientific knowledge to reorganize a wasteful, unprepared America into a centrally planned, efficient, technical, forwardlooking society. Conservation, so defined, enjoyed great support from the timber industry, irrigation and water power companies, livestock associations, oil companies and mineral interests.

But something happened when the Roosevelt administration tried to turn conservation into a national crusade to generate public support for its policies. The term lost its original definition; as Hays says, "its meaning expanded to include almost every movement of the day."[8] The term became appropriated by different groups of people whose perceptual boundaries enclosed differing world views. Congress talked about "the conservation of human life."[9] Private organizations spoke of the conservation of beauty, the conservation of morals, and the conservation of international peace and friendship.

More than anything else, utilitarian conservation became redefined and absorbed into a larger "back to nature" spirit that was sweeping the country. One of its focal points was the Quetico-Superior. The appeal of the simple life brought people and conflict to the border lakes in the 1920s. Events during that decade, in turn, set the stage for the increasingly intense conflicts of the following fifty years. To understand what people saw of value in the Quetico-Superior, to know why they went there and why they used the area in the ways that they did, to understand the environmental, social and political changes that occurred in the area in the 1920s and after, it is helpful to examine the period's cultural climate, and to show how it interacted with people's perceptual boundaries and made wilderness attractive to millions of Americans. In large measure, the history of this area during these years reflected varying responses to what Nietzsche had called a "weightless" society, characterized by loss of purpose and autonomy, the weakening of moral standards, and a sense that modern civilization was somehow "unreal."[10]

The sense of weightlessness arose in large measure from an unreconciled, and often suppressed, conflict between the values of a nation symbolized by rural life and the frontier, and the ideal of technological progress that was destroying both. The former cluster of values is sometimes called agrarianism, but Leo Marx better identifies it as pastoralism. The main difference is the value each term places on economic factors. Marx argues that, contrary to popular belief, Thomas Jefferson was not an agrarian. The true agrarians of his time had already shown the efficiency of large-scale agriculture, but Jefferson remained committed to the ideal of small, family farms, because he mostly wanted to preserve rural values.

> "Unlike the fully committed agrarians," says Marx, he admits that an agricultural economy may be economically disadvantageous. But that does not trouble him, because he rejects productivity and, for that matter, material living standards, as tests of a good society. The loss of what nowadays would be called "national income," he [Jefferson] explains, "will be made up in

happiness and permanence of government."[11]

This sentimental form of pastoralism is what most eighteenth-century Americans believed in when they praised the dream of an agricultural society. But it was a naive vision. It advocated eliminating wilderness and praised economic progress, so long as it was kept within certain limits. Nobody, however, could clearly define the point where material progress became more bad than good. Marx says that this sentimental expression of the pastoral ideal therefore became, in the nineteenth century,

> a rhetorical formula rather than a conception of society, and an increasingly transparent and jejune expression of the national preference for having it both ways....It enabled the nation to continue defining its purpose as the pursuit of rural happiness while devoting itself to productivity, wealth, and power.[12]

The destruction of pastoral America played a major role in the creation of a weightless society. It was accomplished by the combined effects of urbanization, technological growth, and the change to a corporate economy.

In 1870, three out of four Americans lived in rural areas. In 1890 the rural proportion of the population numbered two out of three, and was increasingly declining, to just over one out of two in 1910, and to one out of three in 1930. Urbanization separated more and more people from rural life and nature, and the creeping growth of the built world belied the pastoral rhetoric. Technological progress further separated Americans from rural life and nature, and chipped away at individual autonomy. Americans no longer needed to raise and slaughter cattle; they could go to the grocery store and buy a roast, cut and packaged by others. They no longer needed to fell their own trees for fuel; they had oil furnaces that were supplied and repaired by others. They no longer needed to haul water; they could turn on a faucet and let others do the pumping. There were always others, and here perhaps was the greatest hidden cost of technological progress: in return for the

29

physical comfort it promised, Americans gave up their ability to provide for their needs themselves.

This loss of autonomy was further promoted by the shift from segmented, regional economic markets to a national, corporate economy. Corporations began to dominate the economy late in the nineteenth century. By 1930, they produced more than 90 percent of all products manufactured in the United States, and 100 of these corporations controlled nearly half of the nation's manufacturing assets.[13] The corporate-based economy added to feelings of weightlessness in two key ways: through its obsession with efficiency, and through its bureaucratic structure.

Because of the corporation's obsession with efficiency and need for central control, jobs became ever-more specialized and rationalized. Frederick W. Taylor epitomized the goals of big business in his early twentieth-century crusade to promote scientific management. "In the past," he argued, "the man has been first; in the future the system must be first."[14] Using Taylor's methods, industry specialists broke down factory jobs into their components, timed each one, and then designed the most efficient method for each step. Scientific management, says historian Daniel Boorstin, "made the worker himself into an interchangeable part."[15]

Nor were business people immune from the corporation's assault on individuality. To achieve success in business, it had once been enough to have ambition, dedication, talent, and, preferably, to follow a rigid moral code. In the bureaucracy of the corporate world, success depended upon one's ability to deal with people of similar and higher rank, and the surest way was to mask one's individuality. By the early twentieth century, advice articles and books were telling business people how to project good images. The way to advancement, as historian T.J. Jackson Lears puts it, was to become "as an empty vessel to be filled and refilled according to the expectations of others and the needs of the moment."[16]

The central control required in a national corporate economy also meant that the individual's livelihood became increasingly tied to decisions made far away. The Horatio Alger story of self-made success faded into mythology as the economy became ever more complex. "Instead of opening doors into a magical kingdom," says historian Robert Wiebe, "almost every small enterprise bound its sponsor into a bewildering complex of business relationships which seemed to restrict rather than extend his freedom."[17]

Wage-earners felt the effects of the changing economy more than almost anyone else. Distant corporations temporarily or permanently closed local factories with seemingly little regard for the laborers. New technology constantly claimed jobs, and the increasingly-specialized workplace stripped workers of their individuality. "Rapidly losing control over their working lives," says Wiebe, "they knew only that decisions made somewhere else pushed them about like so many cattle."[18]

The old pastoral vision of America was grounded in a fervent belief in the individual, in self-sufficiency, and in conservative moral standards. Its fatal flaw was self-deception, a refusal to acknowledge that powerful forces were sweeping the nation and undermining the ideals symbolized by rural life and the frontier. Urbanization, technology and the corporate economy eroded Americans' perceptual boundaries, exposing holes in their self-identities and in their world views. To many, life made less sense, seemed less real.

Their dilemma often was intensified by a weakening faith in Christianity. Urbanization and technological advances in transportation and communication had made it inevitable that Americans of all backgrounds eventually would come into contact with secular beliefs. By the 1920s, magazines and best-selling fiction regularly popularized the faith-destabling beliefs of leading scientists. Psychologists argued that there was no such thing as a soul or free choice, that instincts and habits dominated human behavior. Anthropologists had traced the development of culture and concluded that God was created in man's image, a product of human needs. Physicists, geologists and biologists challenged the historicity of the Old Testament. Harvard's Percy Bridgeman, reacting to the fundamental changes in the scientific world view, told readers of **Harper's** that "the world is not intrinsically reasonable or understandable."[19]

That there was no meaning, no sacred purpose to life, not even a free will — these were ideas that shattered the faith of many and cast varying levels of doubt upon the faith of countless others. Nietzsche had predicted that secularization would make it "seem for a time as though all things had become weightless."[20] The effect upon Americans of the revelations of Darwin, James, Einstein, Freud, and others bore out the prediction. Rational thought had become Christianity's crown of thorns: it was impossible to ignore, impossible to stop, and faith trickled out of its wounds.

Longing for some kind of experiential substance to their lives, many Americans reacted to this sense of weightlessness by turning to nature. Beginning at the turn of the century, there was a great increase in natural history museums, landscaped parks, and zoos. There was a new movement to the suburbs. Frank Lloyd Wright created a stir with his "organic" architecture. Liberty Hyde Bailey of Cornell University led back-to-the-land and country life campaigns. The Boy Scouts, founded as a way to hand down frontier knowledge and values, grew in membership from 245,000 in 1917 to a million in 1929. National Park visitation grew from 69,000 in 1908 to 200,000 in 1910, to 1 million in 1920 and 2.5 million in 1928. In the national forests, where total visitation increased from 4.7 million in 1924 to 7.1 million in 1929, wilderness areas showed a visitor gain that was nearly 20 percent greater than that in developed areas.[21]

Americans also turned to nature in their popular literature. The wilderness was a symbol of faith, hope and freedom; the city and the machine were symbols of depravity, conformity, and despair. The seven top-selling novels between 1900 and 1930 all featured a wilderness setting.[22] Millions of Americans withdrew for a time from the complexities of modern life by exploring the primitive with Edgar Rice Burroughs, and by returning to the frontier with Zane Grey. Popular wilderness fiction romantically portrayed larger-than-life heroes overcoming adversity in the grandeur of a wild, virgin land. The wilderness novel was an almost desperate glorification of the old pastoral vision, the last battleground where rural values could emerge victorious. To emphasize the anti-modernist message, authors dwelled on the purity of the wild landscape, and the ugliness of civilization. In **When a Man's a Man,** Harold Bell Wright, whose first twelve novels sold an average of 750,000 copies, called wilderness "a land of far-arched and unstained skies, where the wind sweeps free and untainted and the atmosphere is the atmosphere of those places that remain as God made them."[23] James Oliver Curwood, who between 1908 and 1926 wrote twenty-six novels of wilderness adventure, called civilization "a hell of big cities, of strife, of blood-letting, of wickedness."[24]

In many popular novels, wilderness took on a religious aura. Gene Stratton Porter, who wrote the top four-selling books of 1900-1930, portrayed wilderness as a source of spiritual truth, a link to God. Such a theme is as old as mankind, but early in the twentieth century it underwent a popular revival, and by the mid-twenties the religion of the outdoors was widely publicized. "This religion of the fields is not a mere Pantheism," said **Good Housekeeping,** "though it has much to do with natural phenomena. It is essentially Christian — a pastoral Christianity."[25]

Many Americans who grew to idealize nature also began identifying themselves as conservationists, and joined such groups as the Sierra Club, the National Audubon Society, the National Wildlife Federation and the Izaak Walton League. But the newcomers to conservation tended to be quite different from the progressive conservationists. As Hays says,

> they were prone to look upon all commercial development as mere materialism, and upon conservation as an attempt to save resources from use rather than to use them wisely. The problem, to them, was moral rather than economic. An exclusively hardheaded economic proposition, therefore, became tinged with the enthusiasm of a religious crusade to save America from its materialistic enemies.[26]

CANOE COUNTRY

By the 1920s, wilderness had become an abstract symbol with a powerful emotional appeal to Americans from all walks of life. But the complexity of the forces that led to its appeal ensured that the responses to wilderness were equally complex. Wilderness did not mean the same thing to progressive conservationists and the new breed, and even within each group there were many disagreements. When turning from the abstract symbol to a specific location such as the Quetico-Superior, then, the differences could spark conflicts.

A case in point is a 1921 incident involving two men who played important roles in Quetico-Superior history. One of them was Sigurd Ferdinand Olson, a twenty-two-year-old who had just completed his first year of teaching at a high school in Nashwauk, Minnesota, a city on the Mesabi Iron Range. Over the next half century Olson, in his writing, helped create the dominant image of the border lakes region.

Olson and three companions took their first canoe trip in the area late that June. Beginning just north of Ely in Winton, by then an almost-abandoned logging village, the men paddled east along the international boundary. For at least twenty miles the border separated the virgin Ontario wilderness from the logged and burned shoreline of Minnesota. Somewhere on Knife Lake the canoeists passed beyond the cutover, and continued east.

Meanwhile, to their south, another young man was traveling the lakes and streams within the Superior National Forest, taking notes and photographs. His name was Arthur Hawthorne Carhart, and he was a landscape architect employed by the U.S. Forest Service. The agency, responding to competition from the recently established National Park Service and to widespread public interest in outdoor recreation, had hired Carhart to visit forests and recommend recreation plans. This was his second trip to the Superior; he had made a brief trip in 1919, and was now spending several weeks in the back country before writing his final report.

Carhart was quietly paddling along the forested shores of Saganaga

Lake, east of the border cutover, when he heard gunshots. He investigated, and soon came to a campsite occupied by four young men, one of whom was target-shooting with a pistol. It was Sigurd Olson. Years later, Olson recalled that Carhart angrily approached the campsite and demanded to know "what in the hell was going on."[27]

The two men were standing on the same campsite, and viewing the same scenery, but they did not perceive the same place. To Olson, the Quetico-Superior was a refuge from civilization, a place to rekindle a sense of autonomy and reality. Olson, the middle son of a Baptist minister, was among those who were most affected by the forces described above. A couple of years earlier, while attending the University of Wisconsin at Madison, Olson had nearly pledged his life to the foreign missions. He had become the leader of the local chapter of American Protestantism's most important missionary organization, the Student Volunteers. Formed in the late 1880s, the Student Volunteer Movement had vowed to complete the "evangelization of the world in one generation." But the university also had exposed Olson to the modern scientific world view, and he became increasingly troubled with what he felt was an overly narrow Baptist faith. When it came time to publicly declare his intent to become a missionary, Olson instead resigned. He spent the next forty years forming a spiritual philosophy to fill the gap created by rational thought.[28]

Lears argues that, as Christianity declined into "sentimental religiosity," such people as Olson felt their personal identity weakening. The "iron cage of a bureaucratic market economy" aggravated this feeling. "A weightless culture of material comfort and spiritual blandness was breeding weightless persons who longed for some intense experience to give some definition, some distinct outline and substance to their vaporous lives," Lears says.[29] This sense of longing was evident in Olson's first published article, an account of the 1921 canoe trip that appeared in the *Milwaukee Journal* a month later:

> Life is good to those who know how to live. I do not ever
> hope to accumulate great funds of worldly wealth, but I
> shall accumulate something far more valuable, a store of

wonderful memories. When I reach the twilight of life I shall look back and say I'm glad I lived as I did, life has been good to me. I will not be afraid of death because I will have drunk to the full the cup of happiness and contentment that only close communion with nature can give. Most of us do not live. Convention looks down on modern man and says "There is my product, a creature bridled by custom and tradition." He is not natural, even his emotions are superficial. He is happy in a sense, a misguided sense, living and dying without knowing the joy of one natural breath.[30]

Olson's air of bravado about not fearing death rings false. He had not yet had time to build "a store of wonderful memories," and comes across as a man who wants to believe — but is not yet sure — he will live a meaningful life. The Quetico-Superior eventually provided Olson with the spiritual experiences he sought, but this first trip was largely one of escaping from the weightlessness of modern life through intense physical effort:

This struggle for existence and the fearless battle with the elements is what makes the manhood of the north big and clean and strong. The north asks for strong men, not weaklings, for her manhood is tested down to the core. To those whom she selects she reveals all her riches and if she does not give them riches in gold she gives them riches far more worthwhile that mean happiness and contentment.[31]

No wonder Carhart found Olson shooting a pistol!

It also is not surprising that Carhart was upset by the sound of a gun. The previous December the twenty-eight-year-old Forest Service employee had published an article in **American Forestry** in which he expressed his disgust with people who took potshots at chipmunks and squirrels and other small animals. "In their place," he wrote, "the timber squirrel and water ouzel are as important landscape values as a whole herd of deer." He also indicated disapproval of big game hunting, saying that "a live buck seen a dozen times a season" by many people has a "greater total value in the nation than a mounted head with dead eyes staring over a den full of skins, weapons and other mounted heads."[32]

Like Olson, however, Carhart was worried about the effects of modern civilization on the individual. In his final report for the Superior National Forest, submitted the following spring, he said his recreation plan was "dedicated to the ideal of human service and to the purpose of making Americans of greater mind, body and soul, and through them preserve our national life from disintegration because of its oppressing association with man-made, artificial life."[33] He argued that wilderness preservation was a necessary antidote:

> If we are to have broad-thinking men and women of high
> mentality; of good physique, and with a true perspective
> on life we must allow our populace a communion with
> nature in areas of more or less wilderness conditions.[34]

Carhart's appreciation of the Quetico-Superior, however, had little to do with the physical exhilaration that seemed to dominate Olson's thought at the time, but with its aesthetic values. Carhart had graduated from Iowa State College in 1916 with a bachelor's degree in horticulture, focusing on landscape architecture. He believed in preserving wilderness because of its scenery:

> These areas can never be restored to the original condi-
> tion after man has invaded them, and the great value lying
> as it does in natural scenic beauty should be available, not
> for the small group, but for the greatest population. Time
> will come when these scenic spots, where nature has been
> allowed to remain unmarred, will be some of the most
> highly prized scenic features of the country.[35]

To Carhart, wild scenery was a sufficient condition for a wilderness experience. To Olson, wild scenery was necessary but not sufficient.

His wilderness experience needed to be more than aesthetic; it needed to be visceral. In their brief meeting in June, 1921, their difference seemed to be merely over the use of a pistol. Actually, as time would show, they disagreed on fundamental issues of wilderness preservation.

Olson and Carhart were raised in a cultural milieu in which great numbers of people responded to a perceived weightlessness of modern life by idealizing wilderness. Like millions of others, the two sought out the wild, and, each in his own way, found what he wanted. Also, like Stewart Edward White, Zane Grey and James Oliver Curwood, both men tried to capture on printed page the essence of the wilderness as they knew it. The novelists wrote mostly of a bygone era. But Olson, Carhart and many others, who often were raised on such novels, wrote about wilderness that still existed. They were guides, pointing out the trailheads to would-be pioneers. Such writers as White, Grey and Curwood helped crystallize the public longing for wild places; others, including Olson and Carhart, showed people where to find such places, and what to expect when they got there.

CHAPTER 3
CANOE COUNTRY

*It was a scene of such beauty that we sat back in the canoes
in silence, already anticipating the aching regret with which
we must bid those vistas farewell a brief ten days hence.*

— *V.K. Brown (1926)* [1]

During the 1920s, when the Quetico-Superior was just beginning to receive publicity, it acquired a descriptive label. In
feature stories, advertisements, and brochures, the Quetico-
Superior was called "the greatest canoe country in the world."[2] Such
a label implies that the area was environmentally well suited for canoe
travel, and also may imply that canoeists dominated the area's recreational use. Both interpretations were correct until at least the late
1920s, a function largely of environmental boundaries upon human
use, and partly of mass communication, which created several kinds of
value-based images that exaggerated the area's wildness.

That the Quetico-Superior was well suited for canoe travel requires
little more proof than a glance at a map. There were at least five
thousand lakes and interconnecting rivers in an area less than half the
size of New Jersey. The lakes were mostly small, and the larger ones had
irregular shorelines and were dotted with islands, so canoeists were not
often windbound. Most portages were under a quarter-of-a-mile long.
No place else on the continent could match all these features.

In fact, traveling the Quetico-Superior *required* a canoe. Boats were
usable mostly at the periphery of the region, where roads and railways
provided access. The rapids and portages that joined the lakes acted as
environmental boundaries that blocked large craft from most of the
interior. Even on the periphery the canoe dominated, because outboard motors had yet to gain wide acceptance. They were slow, loud,
heavy, and expensive.

Also, in the 1920s the Quetico-Superior was suited for little else than recreation. The end of tall pine logging was at hand, and there were not any known mineral deposits important enough to warrant detailed exploration. The Quetico-Superior was *de facto* canoe country.

There were four ways tourists could get to the region: from the north, along the Canadian National Railway; from the west, through Crane Lake, Minnesota; from the southeast, by way of Grand Marais, Minnesota; or from the south, through Ely, Minnesota, and its neighbor, the nearly deserted logging community of Winton (see map next page). None of the first three could compete with Ely. There was no incentive for Americans to travel to Fort Frances or Port Arthur, Ontario, and take the long ride north on the Canadian National Railway. This northern entry to the region did open to a wide choice of canoe routes into Quetico Park, but the northern rim of the Quetico was being intensively logged, and canoeists faced a couple of days' paddle through the cutover. Since very few Canadians visited the Quetico-Superior, nearly everybody entered from Minnesota.[3]

Crane Lake, located at the northwestern edge of Superior National Forest, provided access through cutover pineland to Lac La Croix, one of the largest and most beautiful lakes in the Quetico-Superior. The virgin pine that covered the American shore was part of the 141,000 acres preserved by the General Land Office in 1905 at the request of Christopher C. Andrews, Minnesota's forestry commissioner. But there was just one practical way from Crane Lake to Lac La Croix, and canoeists had to paddle twenty-five miles or more before having a choice of routes.

Grand Marais, on the shore of Lake Superior at the southeastern edge of Superior National Forest, was the starting point of the Gunflint Trail, a rugged road that twisted for nearly fifty miles to Gunflint Lake on the international border. Gunflint Lake gave access to Quetico Park by way of Saganaga Lake, and the Gunflint Trail provided access to canoe routes over the hundreds of tiny to medium-sized lakes and streams that filled the eastern portion of Superior National Forest. But the road was so rough that few used it. In the early 1920s, even getting

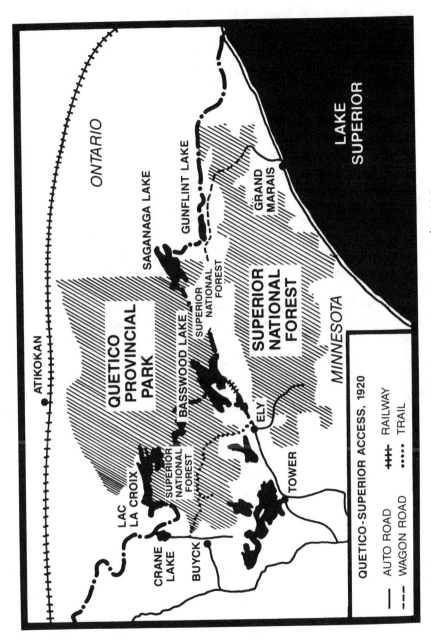

Figure 8 - Travel access routes existing in the Quetico-Superior region by 1920.

41

to Grand Marais by car was cause for celebration.[4]

Ely, on the other hand, because of its longtime importance in the iron mining industry, was easily accessible by road and by rail, and offered an unsurpassed choice of canoe routes. These facts did not escape the attention of tourist promoters and outdoor writers. Ely soon became popularly established as, in the words of its commercial club, "the Gateway to the Borderland."[5]

A city that promotes itself as a gateway acknowledges that the destination beyond, not the city itself, is the real attraction.[6] What was the drawing power of the Quetico-Superior? To those who promoted tourism, the answer was wilderness, and they built their advertisements and brochures around images of the canoe country that exaggerated its wildness by downplaying — in fact most often ignoring — the scarred landscape left behind by the logging industry.

The Quetico-Superior certainly was not the wilderness that the Sioux had known, nor was it the wilderness that the Ojibway and the voyageurs had known. Every canoe route leading from the Ely area began on waterways that had been logged to the shoreline, and it took a day of paddling, sometimes more, to get beyond the cutover. Dozens of small dams altered water levels, leaving stretches of drowned trees and sometimes flooding out portages. Here and there were abandoned tools, machinery, tote roads, railroad spur lines, even entire logging camps.[7]

These were not the sorts of scenes one found favorably described in the wilderness novels of Harold Bell Wright, or depicted on postcards or on the covers of magazines. Americans expected wilderness to appear wild, and that is exactly how the Quetico-Superior was presented to them. Ely, according to its commercial club, was "where the wilderness begins....Starting at its very doorstep are several million acres of unspoiled wilderness."[8] A county business group promoted the area as "totally untouched by the hand of man."[9] Even the U.S. Forest Service joined the chorus. Superior National Forest, claimed the agency, was "a northern wilderness, untouched by civilization, where the silence of the woods is broken only by the laugh of the loon, the splash of muskalonge or trout, or the bellow of the moose."[10]

It wasn't just local tourist promoters who exaggerated the area's wildness. Those who had no financial stake in the canoe country did the same thing. Sigurd Olson spent at least two days during his 1921 trip paddling along the American cutover, and later that same trip he ran into heavy logging operations at the northern edge of Quetico Park, but he mentioned neither in his *Milwaukee Journal* feature published a month later.[11] Donald Hough, a writer who had worked for the Forest Service in the Superior National Forest, told readers of *Outdoor Life* that the region consisted of "6,000,000 acres of virgin pine forest."[12] Another article in this leading outdoor magazine claimed, "No vestige or sign of human progress can be found out there among the pines. It is America as the Indians found it — wild, beautiful and vast."[13]

Some writers, in fact, cautioned prospective visitors that the Quetico-Superior might be too wild for their enjoyment. Arthur Carhart told readers of *American Forestry:*

> But remember in picking on this forest as a place to spend a vacation that it is a country best suited to real outdoor lovers and that there is a good lot of hard hiking to do over portages and some steady pulling on canoe paddle if you want to get anywhere.[14]

An *Outdoor Life* writer was more foreboding:

> ...do not go unless you can be absolutely out of touch with the outside world. No one will hear from you and you will not know if your business has gone to smash and your wife and children are dead.[15]

These negative references were exceptions, however. Writers rarely mentioned the potential dangers of canoe trips, and purged from their accounts the black flies and mosquitoes. Time and again, those who wrote about the area during the 1920s, whether they were tourist promoters or freelance writers, highlighted the attractiveness of the Quetico-Superior wilderness. And, by going beyond simply using such labels as "virgin wilderness" and "canoe country," they created particular, value-based images that defined the area's meaning for the readers. They did this by combining three kinds of information: by providing a physical description of the Quetico-Superior, often with accompanying photographs, both of which helped readers build a mental picture of the landscape and its wildlife; by providing an abstract description that gave readers a sense of what it was like to travel in the canoe country, and the values of such a trip; and by providing information that showed readers what to do in the Quetico-Superior.

Physical descriptions emphasized the area's scenic beauty and wildlife, and so lent weight to the sweeping statements about the area's wildness. "Special charm is lent to a canoe trip through the Superior National Forest by the fact that the country one passes through is truly a wilderness," wrote the Forest Service in 1919.

> In its beaver-dammed streams one may catch an abundance of fish in a half hour's trolling. Often one meets a deer, which gazes at the intruder in startled wonderment, or the canoe may glide silently upon a giant moose, feeding on the grasses along the shore, which watches the intruder's coming with sullen surprise before crashing out of sight through the brush. Rounding the point of a winding stream, one catches sight of the bank beaver as it dives under the water, or a glimpse of a mink or fisher gliding to cover. On the portage a porcupine waddles hastily across the path ahead, and with much scratching and wheezing climbs the nearest tree for safety. All about the voyager is the ever-moving wild life of forest, lake, and stream.[16]

This generic kind of description was most common in promotional literature. Feature stories in newspapers and magazines during the 1920s often were about the writers' particular experiences, and so gave readers a sense of what the Quetico-Superior looked like by providing descriptions of specific parts of the canoe country:

> Lac La Croix, most charming of all lakes in that north country, spread its hundreds of pine-crested islands before our delighted gaze; the Minnesota shores in the distance rose high and green above it all. I shall never forget the joys of that day's paddle as we wound among the islands; nor of the next, when we first saw Curtain Falls, pride of the boundary; nor shall I forget the next, when we saw seven moose at one time in Crooked Lake and raced one old bull to shore.[17]

Those who learned of the Quetico-Superior from mass communication during the 1920s would hardly have guessed that it was being intensively logged along its northern rim, or that, on the American side, three hundred thousand acres that had once contained red and white pine were now full of stumps and aspen saplings. Less than 10 percent of the original tall pine remained. The new environmental conditions meant that the few red pine remaining could produce new stands only with great difficulty. Such reproduction requires a vast source of seeds, bare soil, and little competition. The loggers had removed the seed source, and post- logging fires left ash on the soil, which not only in itself inhibited red pine seed reproduction, but also encouraged the growth of competing vegetation. The white pine, on the other hand, was well adapted to post-logging conditions; under normal circumstances it would have been able to reproduce stands. But another environmental boundary had been introduced: white pine blister rust, a disease brought from Europe to the eastern United States in the 1890s, had reached the canoe country wilderness in about 1919. During the next decade-and-a-half the disease established itself in the border lakes ecosystem, and from that time on killed most white pine saplings in the area before they reached the age of thirty. Only recently, with the successful development of rust-resistant white pine, have scientists begun to see hope for a new tall pine forest in the canoe country.[18]

The descriptions of the area's wildlife also presented a more pristine image than reality warranted. The white-tailed deer mentioned in the Forest Service pamphlet quoted above were actually newcomers to the canoe country, following the heels of the loggers. Deer were first seen in Ely in 1891, and soon dominated the cutover. Caribou had become nearly extinct in the Quetico-Superior by the 1920s, and the number of moose were rapidly declining. The fisher, the otter, the marten and the bald eagle nearly were gone, victims of trapping and habitat change. The fox, beaver, lynx, coyote and timber wolf were declining in numbers for the same reasons.[19]

But most of these environmental changes were not noticeable to average canoeists. Only the visual effects of logging were obvious. After one or two days of paddling, however, canoeists could leave the cutover and travel for days without encountering such obvious signs of civilization. This was the part of their canoe trip that they most fondly remembered. This was the part that brought them back time and again, gave them what they were looking for. Those who wrote feature stories about the area wrote about the highlights of their experiences, and those who developed promotional brochures and advertisements likewise focused on the major attractions of the canoe country. In doing so, they not only created a dominant media image of the Quetico-Superior as a wild landscape, they also encouraged readers to superimpose upon this landscape the cluster of values that they attached to wilderness, values shaped by individual experience and the cultural milieu.

Seeking to bring as many tourists to Ely as possible, the city's Commercial Club published an annual brochure that, throughout the 1920s, focused on the canoe country's ability to relieve the weightlessness of modern life. After describing the area's scenic beauty, its abundance of fish and wildlife, the brochure said:

> Imagine all of this, you city-bound people, as you swelter
> among the tall buildings and breathe smoke and gasses,
> and who never feel the breezes of the open places, breathe
> the pure air of the pines, nor hear the murmur of the
> sparkling waves against the rocks — never hear the soft

symphony of the wind through the pine tops.

Imagine all of this, if you can —

And think of Ely.

> In an hour's travel by canoe you can lose your business
> cares in the swirl of your paddle; throw away your worries
> in the strike of a big fish; swap an artificial social existence
> for the primitive joys of the camp fire — cough the last
> traces of soot out of your lungs, inhale the sweet, moist
> ozone of the pines, and for a few weeks at least place your
> mind, spirit, and body in the hands of Nature.[20]

This pamphlet touched upon each of the three images of the canoe
country that dominated in the mass media during the following
decades: the images of the Quetico-Superior as a fishing paradise, as a
sanctuary from civilization, and as a sacred place. These images, along
with a less-publicized fourth image — that of the canoe country as a
resource bank — provided the emotional force behind the major
conflicts over the area's management.

The image of the Quetico-Superior as a fishing paradise emphasized
the excitement of fishing in a beautiful, pristine environment, where
remoteness guaranteed a big catch. It became well-established in the
1920s. The canoe country, said an article in *Parks and Recreation,*
"is a fisherman's paradise, its waters are stocked with the gamest of
American fresh water game fishes."[21] Readers of *Outdoor Life* were
told that the Quetico-Superior was "the world's best fishing country,"
and those who read *Outdoor America* were promised that they could
"wear out many a fishing tackle there and still find plenty more fish."[22]

Those who saw the Quetico-Superior as a fishing paradise wanted to
experience the freedom and zest of the American frontier as they
imagined it, but without experiencing too much of frontier discom-
fort. They welcomed any form of modern technology, such as motorboats and seaplanes, that could transport them from comfortable

resorts to the "virgin lakes" and back again quickly and with ease.

The image of the canoe country as a sanctuary dominated media coverage during the early to mid 1920s, but then fell behind fishing paradise imagery until after World War II. A key theme in sanctuary imagery was a sense of permanence and autonomy. The Quetico-Superior was a place where the world had not changed; here was, as the Ely Commercial Club put it, "that ever entrancing Old."[23] Entering the canoe country was like going back in time to a period of stability, to a time of faith, not doubt, to a time of individual self-sufficiency.

To those who saw the canoe country as a sanctuary, these intangible values were more important than fishing, and too many modern conveniences could destroy the experience. "A few strokes of the paddle and all the encumbrances of civilization are exchanged for the freedom of the wilderness," promised a promotional pamphlet.[24] Paul Riis, who in the early 1920s played a key role in the first conflict over the canoe country, told readers of **Parks and Recreation** that they could "paddle anywhere that fancy dictates, time and ambition alone determine the boundaries."[25] Sigurd Olson, who began selling his first magazine feature stories in the mid-1920s, wrote in **Field and Stream** that modern civilization forced people to live "like millions of other human machines." The canoe country, on the other hand, gave the individual an outlet for "the God-given right to exercise his own free will."[26]

Readers of canoe country literature were told that by exercising this freedom in the primitive surroundings of the Quetico-Superior, they would restore both physical and mental health. Physical restoration came through paddling, portaging, and simply being out in the fresh air. Mental restoration was more complex. To Olson, the physical exertion could in itself bring a kind of peace. He wrote that it led an individual to feel "really alive," and that "there is no joy quite so complete or content, quite so blissful as that which comes at the end of a killing portage, when he can flop down to rest, half dead of exhaustion."[27] But writers more often portrayed the mind-healing qualities of a canoe country vacation as a subtle compilation of the trip's experiences:

By the time we had washed the pots and pans, darkness began to settle about us. Already a full moon had risen; one by one stars began to peep from the heavens. The fire was rekindled to a big blaze. Bill took his cigarettes, and I got my pipe and tobacco. We smoked and played cards, all the while feeling like a million dollars. Our stomachs were full, our cares and worries forgotten, so why shouldn't we be contented?[28]

The image of the Quetico-Superior as a sacred place focused on the canoe country's opportunities for people to experience ultimate reality, to feel a transcendent power that was manifest in nature. Those who perceived the area as a sacred place sought spiritual sustenance, a feeling that easily could be shattered not only by the presence of outboard motors and seaplanes, but even by too many other canoeists. The image became politically powerful after World War II, but received little media attention in the 1920s. Perhaps its most explicit expression was in the Ely Commercial Club's tourist guide:

Here the Philosopher can find his mystery, the Young Man his vision, and the Old Man his dream. Here, the soul of the silent spaces still hallows the legends of a past people whose camp fires glowed along the shore.

These are the things that make the primitive. Clean, virile and entrancing threads lure you back, again and again, to this Garden Spot of Deity. Here is the religion of the Great Out-of-Doors, which makes you feel the exultation of living. Here is the Mighty Vacuum of the Primitive, pulling you away from petty opinion and dwarfed estimates of things.[29]

Another image of the Quetico-Superior received little attention in the media except during times of conflict over the area's management. This was the image of the canoe country as a resource bank, a supplier of timber, minerals, furs, or hydropower. A key element in resource bank imagery was its focus on the economic value of natural resources.

Trees, for example, as the 1929 Ely Commercial Club tourist guide shows, were depicted not solely in terms of beauty, but as a crop:

> Logging and lumbering, wisely conducted and scientifi-cally managed, is encouraged. A timber crop is not different from any other crop. Unless it is harvested when ripe, decay sets in and there follows a loss to the nation and locality just as surely as loss follows failure to harvest any crop.[30]

The resource bank image granted importance to aesthetic values so long as they did not interfere with the bottom line:

> The forester is carefully trained to so mark his timber that the best will be retained and to so remove the cut that natural beauty and wealth may remain undisturbed con-sistent, of course, with sensible economy.[31]

These four basic images of the canoe country — as a fishing paradise, as a sanctuary, as a sacred place, and as a resource bank — are not mutually exclusive. People could perceive the canoe country in a way that encompassed parts of several, perhaps all, of these images. Each one is composed of a cluster of beliefs, some of which also can be found in other images. The belief that the canoe country has beautiful scenery, for example, is compatible with all four basic images. The kind of place that the canoe country became for people, however — the overall meaning of the area to them — depended on their perceptual boundaries, which determined the weight that they gave to the various beliefs that make up each of these four images. And, in forming this overall image of place, they determined the kinds of exploitation they felt were appropriate there, and the kinds that were "out of place."

CHAPTER 4
INSIDERS AND OUTSIDERS: WHEN IMAGES COLLIDE

One last place where manhood's spirit
Finds escape from man-made things,
Where no sound of traffic reaches,
No insistent buzzer rings.
Let us earn the thanks of manhood:
Save the ever-luring North!
Voyageurs of many nations,
Duty calls your spirit forth.

— Julius M. Nolte (1928) [1]

They came in greatest numbers from Finland, bearing such names as Laitala, Ojala, Saari and Koski. Close behind were those who came from Yugoslavia and nearby countries, and called themselves Zupancich, Smrekar, Grahek and Kapsch. They were outsiders, pushed from their homelands, and brought by circumstance and opportunity to the land northwest of Lake Superior. Between 1880 and 1920 they came, and carved new communities out of the wilderness.

It was an old story, at least two hundred years old. A similar fate had befallen the Anishinabe, whose subsequent search for freedom and the good life had likewise brought them to this rugged country. The land had belonged to the Dacotah, but time had favored the outsiders.

So it was again. The Anishinabe were now called Ojibway, and the Ojibway had been dispossessed and moved to reservations so that outsiders could come to level the forest and dig the earth.

The Finns and Slavs were misfits even among the outsiders. When they

51

arrived in America they found themselves viewed with hostility by the native-born and by such earlier groups of immigrants as the Irish and the Germans. Most did not stay in the urban East, but pushed west, creating ethnic enclaves in the Great Lakes region.

Northeastern Minnesota was a place for outsiders. Those who were well established in the mainstream of American life, who worked for good wages and enjoyed access to modern comforts, had little incentive to move to the frontier communities near the Quetico-Superior. No corporation wanted to set its headquarters hundreds of miles from the nearest major American city, in a land with long, bitterly cold winters. But there was timber for the taking and, more important, unexcelled reserves of iron ore. The timber and steel industries legally bought more than a million acres of the available wilderness, illegally acquired perhaps another million, and offered a fresh start to those left out of the mythical melting pot of urban America.[2]

Northeastern Minnesota was a place where the Finns and the Slavs once again could be insiders, free to control their individual destinies and those of the communities they formed. Or so perhaps they thought. It was true that they again became insiders, but these immigrants who had fled political control soon found themselves under economic control. Nearly all of them worked for companies owned by people who lived elsewhere, companies that had no stake in the region beyond what could be extracted from it.

The iron and steel industry was by far the biggest employer. In 1919 the Iron Range mines employed more than sixteen thousand; that same year just over fourteen thousand worked for the logging industry in the entire state. The steel industry also drew the most anger. Mine expansion had forced local citizens from their homes, and encircled cities with huge open pits and dumps of over-burden. In the village of Hibbing, mine blasting damaged homes and led to numerous lawsuits, until the industry bought a third of the townsite and relocated residents and businesses at a cost of $16 million. The rest of the village, however, was left at the edge of the world's largest open-pit iron mine, with deflated property values and poor business.[3] Technological innovation also hurt local residents. Changing from hand shovels and mule-drawn dump cars to steam shovels and trains, and from these to electric shovels and locomotives had nearly tripled the individual miner's output, but eliminated many jobs. When ore supply outstripped demand, this led to long periods of unemployment for the rest.[4]

Northeastern Minnesotans, even more than most Americans, grew to understand how the national corporate economy had tied their livelihood to decisions made far away. Local politicians struck back by encouraging hatred of "Eastern capitalists" and the "Steel Trust," thereby building support for heavy mining taxes and high property taxes. By the early 1900s steel companies commonly paid 80 percent or more of local taxes, and iron range cities became lavish spenders. In 1925, the per capita debt in iron range municipalities was $234.51. This was more than three times the U.S. average of $75.06, and nearly four times the $65.33 average per capita debt of other Minnesota communities. "They could have paved the streets out of silver dollars here for all the money they have grafted," commented one mining company official. A range city firefighter gave the common response: "Why shouldn't these towns have everything they want? If we don't get it, it will go down to New York to buy cigars for the damn capitalists down there. All we'll have left anyway is big holes in the ground out there."[5]

The region's ethnic makeup not only contributed to the distrust of outsiders, it fostered local conflict. In 1907 more than 80 percent of the twelve thousand Oliver Mining Company employees working on the Mesabi and Vermilion ranges were foreign-born. Half of them had been in the United States less than two years. They identified strongly with their native cultures; even two decades later many children entered grade school unable to speak English. Language and cultural barriers made it easy for members of one local ethnic group to see members of other ethnic groups as outsiders. The steel industry increased this prejudice during a bitter strike in 1907. More than ten thousand miners — as many as three-fourths of them Finns — refused to work after Oliver Mining Company laid off two hundred employees who had attempted to unionize. The company broke the strike by bringing in thousands of immigrant Slavs and other southern Europeans as replacements. The resulting distrust between these ethnic groups enlivened community politics for decades, often taking the form of religious competition. The predominantly Catholic southern Europeans fought for municipal control with the predominantly Protestant northern Europeans. "Whichever denomination placed the most members of a school board, controlled the denomination of the teachers, principals, and superintendents," wrote one minister. "Local political offices have been filled, not according to the qualifications of the office seeker, but according to his religious persuasion."[6]

In short, ethnic loyalties created a divisive insider-outsider ethos within iron range cities. Local leaders best succeeded at achieving their goals by playing up these conflicts or by trying to bring the community together by focusing on a mutual outside enemy.

The widely publicized spending habits of the range cities soon attracted the Minnesota state legislature's attention. Angry at what it called a waste of mineral wealth, and arguing the state should rightfully have a share, the legislature in 1921 claimed a portion of local mineral taxes. At the same time, the state increased its own taxes on the industry and, over the outraged cries of iron range politicians, reduced local power to tax the mining companies. The resulting lower revenues plungeed range cities into debt when long-term loans became due in the late 1920s. By 1931 Hibbing, the biggest spender, was $3 million in debt. Range citizens ranked downstate politicians with the steel industry as despised outsiders.[7]

In the early 1920s, then, with lower mining revenues imminent and the logging industry pulling out, northeastern Minnesotans turned increasingly to the two industries over which *they* could exert some control: agriculture and tourism. The number of farms in Cook, Lake and St. Louis counties — which contained the Superior National Forest — increased from 4,420 in 1920 to 5,297 in 1930. Dairy farms were the most numerous, accounting for 36 percent of the 1930 total. For those who lived near the canoe country, however, commercial agriculture was a poor source of economic development. Most of the national forest was located in Lake and Cook counties, where poor soil was such an environmental boundary that just 425 farms operated there in 1930, covering less than two percent of the land area. One quarter of these farms consumed most of what they produced; they were engaged in a modern version of the subsistence lifestyle practiced for centuries on the same land by tribal cultures. In St. Louis County, which was nearly twice the size of the other two combined, farms occupied just 11 percent of the land in 1930. This was the fifth-lowest percentage in the state. Nearly all of the land suitable for farming was in several small belts in the southern half of the county. For those who lived near the canoe country, then, the only potentially important source of locally controlled economic development was tourism. They built an industry out of attracting outsiders to the local wilderness.[8]

In 1924, chambers of commerce representatives from cities across northeastern Minnesota gathered in Duluth to form a new organization that would attempt to turn the region into a nationally recognized vacation area. They called the group the Northeastern Minnesota Civic and Commerce Association, but soon decided the name was unwieldy and colorless. Seeking a title not only for the organization but for the region it served, the group sponsored a highly publicized contest offering $500 to the person who submitted the best name. More than thirty thousand entries arrived from all over the United States, as well as from Canada, the Philippines, Mexico and Europe. The winner was Odin MacCrickart of Pittsburgh, who suggested calling the region The Arrowhead. Thanks to a political boundary, the international border, it took only a little imagination to see that the northeastern corner of Minnesota resembled an arrowhead. The label also nicely emphasized the primitive qualities that would attract tourists. MacCrickart had even canoed along the border lakes once, and wrote that he would "never forget the beautiful views of island-dotted lakes that passed before my eyes as I traveled through the Arrowhead Country." And so, on July 13, 1925, the name suggested by an outsider became the local tourist industry's label for the region, and the Minnesota Arrowhead Association began promoting the area's attractions, with the canoe country as the centerpiece.[9]

Not many tourists traveled through the canoe country in the early 1920s. While roughly twenty thousand visitors passed through Superior National Forest each summer, it is likely that fewer than a thousand a year ventured into the wilderness. Tourist promoters believed a well-developed road system would increase business. Together with Forest Service, county and state officials, they planned a series of roads that would provide greater access to the national forest and the major canoe routes. (See map next page.) In 1922, construction began on the first major road, a highway through Superior National Forest connecting Ely with Finland on the north shore of Lake Superior. Three other routes were on the drawing board. One road would extend the Gunflint Trail to Seagull Lake. Another would start at Ely, head eastward just above the forest's northern boundary along the Kawishiwi River, then continue east through national forest land and join the extended Gunflint Trail. The third route would extend northwestward from Ely to the village of Buyck. Spurs would connect this road with Lac La Croix and Loon Lake on the international boundary, and with Trout Lake to the south.[10]

This locally conceived plan to attract outsiders to northeastern Minnesota soon ran into opposition from those outsiders who wanted to keep the Quetico-Superior wild. The conflict was stirred by Arthur Carhart, who had his own plan for the area.

Carhart first visited the Superior National Forest in 1919, when, at the Forest Service's request, he made a preliminary investigation of the area's recreational possibilities. After a second trip in 1921 — during which he met the 'pistol-shooting' Sigurd Olson — Carhart wrote the final draft of the nation's first large-scale wilderness recreation management plan. This has earned him a place in history books as a leader of the wilderness preservation movement, or even the "Father of the Wilderness Concept," as Donald Baldwin argued in his influential work *The Quiet Revolution.*[11] But Carhart's views about wilderness were somewhat closer to those of northeastern Minnesota tourist promoters than they were to those held by the leading wilderness proponents. Consistent with his training as a landscape architect, Carhart's idea of wilderness focused on scenery. A large area domi-

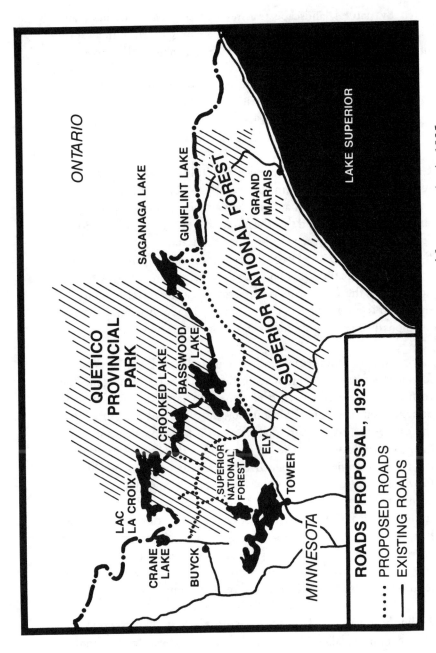

Figure 9 – Existing Quetico-Superior area roads and those proposed for construction in 1925.

nated by natural landscape features was *de facto* wilderness, and Carhart saw it as a federal obligation to help preserve the human spirit in a complex world by making such areas available to the masses:

> These areas can never be restored to the original condition after man has invaded them, and the great value lying as it does in natural scenic beauty should be available, not for the small group, but for the greatest population.[12]

Carhart, hired by the Forest Service primarily in response to outdoor recreation competition from the recently established National Park Service, was well aware that national park visitation had quadrupled since 1914. He predicted that the number of Superior National Forest recreationists might reach one hundred thousand by 1927, more than five times the 1919 use. His goal was to bring as many of these people as possible into the Quetico- Superior, while preserving what he believed was the area's primary attraction — water travel along scenic shores. "It is purely a boat or canoe forest and it is only making the best of all possible existing values when this is done," he wrote.[13]

Environmental boundaries, rather than political boundaries, were foremost in Carhart's mind when he wrote his recreational plan. The cornerstone focused on cutover American land that was outside Superior National Forest. Most importantly, Carhart recognized that the canoe country's future depended to a large extent upon what happened to Basswood Lake. Its geologically determined position as the tip of a funnel that opened to the uncut portions of Quetico Provincial Park made Basswood as valuable to the tourist trade as it had been to the logging industry. Just as good roads made Ely, Minnesota the best city from which to enter the Quetico-Superior, geology made Basswood Lake the best jump- off place to the virgin wilderness on the other side of the border. Sigurd Olson and his companions passed this way in 1921; nearly everyone who visited the Quetico-Superior followed in Olson's wake for many years to come.

As did the voyageurs of a century before, Carhart saw Basswood and the other border lakes to its east and west as a highway, and he argued that it should be developed as such, with dams strategically placed to make travel more convenient. "Such improvement of highways on water routes in the Superior," he wrote, "is as important as the improvements of auto highways in other sections and it is highly proper to look upon these as part of our regular highway system and allot highway funds to their proper development."[14]

Carhart planned to use this natural highway as a "motorboat trunk line." Outfitters in Ely and Winton would tow vacationers up Fall Lake, haul them over the two short portages to Basswood Lake's Pipestone Bay, and tow them north to the border. There the travelers could pick up tows going east as far as Saganaga Lake, or west to Lac La Croix. In Carhart's opinion, this was the best way to distribute quickly the immense tourist traffic he was sure would soon descend upon the region. He did not suggest any limits on outboard motor sizes. At the time, the fastest outboards were only three horsepower; it wasn't until 1926 that Johnson Motor Company produced a faster one, its six-horsepower Big Twin Outboard.[15]

But the large numbers of people would require more than motorboat highways; they would need hotels. He proposed eight of them, evenly spaced along the border from La Croix to Saganaga. Half of them would be within Superior National Forest boundaries, half of them outside in the cutover. They would not be large, holding a maximum of a hundred people each. Carhart envisioned the developments not as city hotels, but "as extensions of the camp ideal." They would be large log cabins, with concrete floors that could be "made more pleasing through being painted with deck paint." At each development, the key point was this: "The whole place should be kept as near wilderness as possible, the wilderness feature being developed rather than any urban conditions."[16]

The motorboat highway-hotel system would serve two purposes, Carhart wrote. First, it would give those people who were "unable to stand the rigors of a canoe trip" a chance to see a number of the "best scenic displays" of the region. Second, it would establish a series of base camps "from which short canoe trips into the back country may be

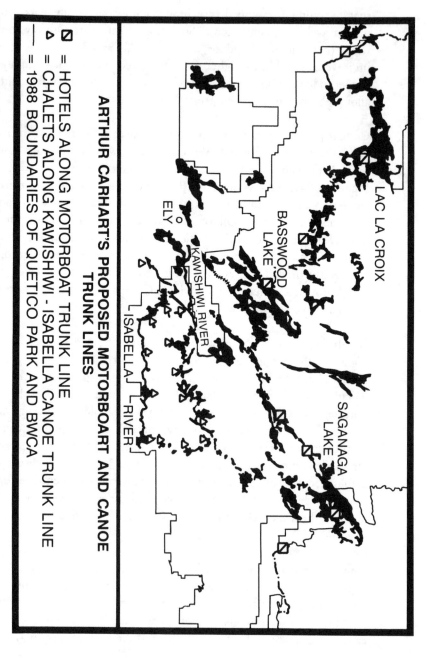

ARTHUR CARHART'S PROPOSED MOTORBOART AND CANOE TRUNK LINES

◪ = HOTELS ALONG MOTORBOAT TRUNK LINE
▷ = CHALETS ALONG KAWISHIWI - ISABELLA CANOE TRUNK LINE
— = 1988 BOUNDARIES OF QUETICO PARK AND BWCA

Figure 10 - Developments proposed by Arthur Carhart to cultivate tourism in the boundary waters area.

taken." In other words, Carhart's plan would develop the Minnesota side of the border partly to exploit the Ontario wilderness.[17]

Carhart also proposed extensive development along "canoe trunk lines" on the major routes completely within Superior National Forest. The government would mark the waterways to make it "impossible for a reasoning person to become lost.? He proposed building a series of fourteen chalets along the Kawishiwi-Isabella rivers route, and an unspecified number along the route joining the Kawishiwi River with Saganaga Lake. He added that, "with some improvement," the chalet system also could be added to the Dahlgren River route that led to the southeastern corner of Lac La Croix. Chalets would contain beds and everything needed for cooking, including such basic supplies as flour and salt. "Such an arrangement will eliminate the necessity for people going into this territory carrying a tent, cooking utensils, tools, etc.," Carhart wrote.

> The company owning such places could merely give the traveler a key and route him out over the line of travel either alone or in company with a guide....Such an arrangement will make a canoe trip into this section more pleasant than at the present time and still there will be a large element of genuine wilderness vacation in such a trip.[18]

Carhart did not ignore the small sections of Superior National Forest not included in the hotel or chalet systems. He wrote that campsites in these areas should include latrines, native-rock-and-cement fireplaces, and water pumps.[19]

Carhart used the word "wilderness," but this does not mean that the kind of wilderness he espoused was the kind typically envisioned by other proponents at the time. Aldo Leopold, with whom Carhart is often compared, makes a good case in point. While Carhart was writing his final report for the Superior National Forest, Leopold, also a Forest Service employee, wrote what became the seminal article about wilderness preservation in the national forests. Published in the

November 1921 *Journal of Forestry,* Leopold's article defined wilderness as "a continuous stretch of country preserved in its natural state, open to lawful hunting and fishing, big enough to absorb a two weeks' pack trip, and kept devoid of roads, artificial trails, cottages, or other works of man."[20]

In 1924 Leopold convinced a district ranger in Arizona's Gila National Forest to set aside 574,000 acres as the nation's first wilderness area. That same year he took a two-week canoe trip through the Quetico-Superior, traveling, as did Olson, by way of cutover Basswood Lake. In 1925 he returned for a nine-day trip, and, after recording in his journal the news that a Minneapolis man was about to build cottages on Basswood's islands, wrote this epitaph: "so that's the end of the wilderness south of the boundary." Two months later, in *American Forests* magazine, Leopold showed how his idea of wilderness conflicted with Carhart's view:

> Driving a pack train across or along a graded highway is distinctly not a pack trip — it is merely exercise, with about the same flavor as lifting dumbells. Neither is canoeing in the wake of a motor launch or down a lane of summer cottages a canoe trip. That is paddling — and the supply is unlimited....I had better explain that motor roads, cottages, and launches do not necessarily destroy hunting and fishing, but they destroy the wilderness, which to certain tastes is quite as important.[21]

Carhart's wilderness was a beautiful, relatively natural landscape where one could withdraw from civilization's complexity without having to sacrifice too much of civilization's comforts. This was the guiding idea behind national park administration, where roads and concessionaires provided easy access and comfortable accommodations to the masses. The success of the national parks had led to Carhart's hiring; the Forest Service had begun paying attention to recreation largely because it was afraid of losing some of its land to the Park Service. Throughout the 1920s and 1930s many national forest areas were proposed for national park status, including the Superior. Olympic National Park of Washington and Kings Canyon National Park of California both were carved out of Forest Service land. Carhart — who unsuccessfully had applied to the Park Service — knew it was his job to tell Superior National Forest officials how to establish a competitive recreational program that would help them keep jurisdiction of the area. This meant balancing wilderness preservation with the goal of attracting large numbers of tourists.

To many activists, it was enough to simply bound a wild area with lines on a map, designate it a wilderness, and leave it alone as much as possible. Few gave much thought to the question of how a political boundary could preserve natural processes in the face of a steadily encroaching civilization, and few considered visitor access and distribution an important issue. Carhart's Superior National Forest report indicates a belief that wilderness preservation requires intensive management rather than a hands-off approach. In particular, and far more than Leopold or any of the other wilderness promoters of the time, Carhart recognized the problems inherent in attracting crowds of recreationists to wilderness areas. His motorboat trunk lines and rustic hotels were meant not only to bring non- paddlers into the wilderness, but to spread out the visitors so as to preserve a sense of getting away from it all. Forty years later, and on this very piece of land, the Forest Service caught up to Carhart on this latter idea and established its first visitor permit system to distribute use. By that time, the canoe country was crowded and strewn with litter.

Carhart placed more importance on catching fish in a scenic, relatively wild setting than on an authentic experience of primitive living. In 1964, when Sigurd Olson and others called for complete wilderness protection for the Boundary Waters Canoe Area, Carhart called the idea "extremist," and said, "I have not too much patience with the far-out wilderness group now rushing in to shout about making this a wilderness area without the sound of an axe or outboard motor...."[22] This gave him something in common with northeastern Minnesota tourist promoters, who were spreading the image of the Quetico-Superior as a fishing paradise. But Carhart's 1922 proposal showed he disagreed strongly with local entrepreneurs in one major aspect: his management plan barred all roads from the canoe country.

Local business leaders were as enthusiastic as Carhart about the region's potential as a tourist mecca, but they did not want to restrict the growth of their only promising, insider-controlled industry. The *Ely Miner* editorialized: "We feel that with more advertising and more roads, we will have more tourists and more tourists means more money, more business, better roads and a better distribution of our incomparable climate, game and scenic wonders."[23]

Superior National Forest officials also wanted roads. They sympathized with Carhart's idea of keeping the canoe as the only form of transportation within the current forest boundaries, but argued that this was not practical. Preventing and suppressing wildfires — the single most important concern of forest officials at the time — was extremely difficult when rangers had to haul the equipment by canoe. Ely foresters had to paddle and portage twenty miles to reach the nearest fire tower. The seven foresters in the Grand Marais district had almost a thousand square miles to patrol by canoe. Forest supervisor Calvin Dahlgren argued that the planned roads were necessary for proper administration.[24]

Sensing that the Forest Service had no intention of carrying out his plans, Carhart resigned from his position as recreational engineer at the end of 1922. Meanwhile, however, he inspired a friend to begin the first outside opposition to Superior National Forest management policies. Paul Riis, an Illinois landscape architect, wilderness enthusiast, and an officer of the American Institute of Park Executives, soon began attacking the road proposal through articles in his organization's magazine, *Parks and Recreation.* The newly formed Izaak Walton League of America also took up the fight and gave the issue national exposure among outdoor enthusiasts.

Riis set the tone of debate in a March 1923 article in *Parks and Recreation.* In a theme that preservationists often used in the decades ahead, he played upon the romantic image of the voyageur:

Shades of Radisson, du Lhut, Hennepin, Verendrye and brave companies of rovers, have you blazed, battered and bled that others may follow your arduous trail in the somber forest in luxurious ease, by no effort of their own, fouling the sweet fragrance of the woodland, hushing the sacred strains of its cathedrals with screaming claxon and discord, piecemeal tearing asunder and destroying the elements of wilderness beauty.[25]

The Izaak Walton League echoed a similar theme in the pages of its magazine, **Outdoor America.** While the league did not oppose the increasingly popular fad of auto camping, and devoted a section of its magazine to the hobby, it strongly opposed opening the canoe country:

The Superior National Forest is perhaps the last place where a person may spend a little time away from the stink of gasoline and the roar of civilization....As it now stands it is necessary to paddle or hike to the points of beauty and interest, and it must be obvious to all, that those who are too blooming lazy to hike it, or paddle it, would not appreciate these beauties upon arrival, and as a result would indifferently destroy everything worthwhile.[26]

The controversy over building roads into the canoe country set the pattern for all future Quetico-Superior conflicts. Participants fortified their perceptual boundaries, closing off access to other viewpoints, and joined the battle for public opinion. They attempted to make their image of the Quetico-Superior socially and politically dominant. The rhetoric often was polarizing, presenting the issues in stark black and white, as in the **Outdoor America** editorial that warned its readers about the "greedy hand of commercialism...reaching for the throat" of the canoe country, led by a "small ring of ambitious promoters visualizing the vast financial possibilities of this great virgin wilderness."[27] Such language not only added to the exaggerated image of the canoe country as an untouched wilderness, but struck a raw nerve in northeastern Minnesota, where the tax base had just been dealt a severe blow by the steel industry and downstate politicians. Wilderness preservationists became the new group of outsiders on which to focus local frustration; the *Ely Miner* warned its readers that the Izaak Walton League's position was "foreign to the principles of Democracy and striking at the very root of Americanism."[28]

Contrary to what the mass media rhetoric implied, there was room for compromise. From the very beginning, Carhart had assumed there was no chance to stop the Ely-Buyck road, and his goal in opposing it was to stop the spurs from being built to the international border. In 1926, after several years of deadlock, the Forest Service also was ready to budge. On May 8, Superior National Forest released a statement that endorsed the wilderness idea. "Practically every resort keeper and summer cottage owner would like to have an automobile road to his front door and a wilderness canoe area at his back door," the statement said. However, it continued, in what must have been a slap at Carhart's version of wilderness, "the majority of the canoeists do not wish to encounter summer cottages, resorts, motorboats, automobile roads or other forms of recreation on the canoe trails." The agency supported a development-free canoe area within the national forest, and was willing to give up the main portion of the Ely-Gunflint road, settling instead for a twenty-mile, dead end road to the Fernberg fire tower on the Kawishiwi River. It also was willing to give up the spurs from the Ely-Buyck road to Lac La Croix, Loon Lake and Trout Lake.[29]

Several months later, the Izaak Walton League's leaders accepted the Forest Service plan. Because of the conflict's intensity, U.S. Secretary of Agriculture William M. Jardine issued the final policy statement; from that time on, all Superior National Forest management plans required the current secretary's approval. Jardine created three wilderness areas, named the Caribou Lake, the Little Indian Sioux and the Superior. "Not less than 1,000 square miles containing the best of the lakes and waterways will be kept as wilderness recreation areas," he promised. The agency could improve portages and build latrines and fire grates if needed, but would not build roads or other recreational developments. Jardine also committed the government to consolidating the national forest and eliminating private land within the wilder-

ness areas. The new political boundaries — mere lines on the map —
would not adequately protect the wilderness, he warned, until the
federal government controlled all of the land within. Achieving
Jardine's goal sparked furious insider-outsider battles after World War
II.[30]

Historians have portrayed the road compromise as a preservationist
victory, but it was a mixed blessing at best. By 1928 the Ely-Buyck road
— called the Echo Trail — was half built, bisecting the canoe routes
between the Little Indian Sioux and Superior wilderness areas, making
the former essentially useless to many canoeists. Those who sought to
escape civilization did not want to cross a road in the middle of their
journey, and the Little Indian Sioux Wilderness Area was too small to
satisfy ardent canoeists. It also was too demanding for casual users,
requiring several one-mile-or-longer portages to reach its beautiful
lakes. Few people visited this isolated corner of the canoe country. The
road from Ely to the Fernberg ranger cabin also was completed in
1928. It cut across canoe routes leading from the Kawishiwi River area
north to Canada. The Kawishiwi-Isabella rivers route never became as
popular as the larger roadless section to the north. Most important,
these two roads — the Echo Trail and the Fernberg — broke the
environmental boundaries that had prevented resort development in
the canoe country, and in the 1930s were partly responsible for a
changing mass media image of the Quetico-Superior.[31]

Before the road conflict ended another battle began, one that gave
much more widespread publicity to the border lakes. The publicity, in
turn, worked in harmony with the new roads to advance the goals of
those whose perceptual boundaries led them to see the canoe country
as a fishing paradise. The battle was over a waterpower development
plan proposed for the region by Edward W. Backus, a lumberman with
political clout in both Minnesota and Ontario. He sought nothing less
than control over the water and timber resources of the entire Rainy
Lake watershed.

Backus had begun operating in the area in 1904. Already well-known as
a highly successful lumberman, the forty-four-year-old entrepreneur

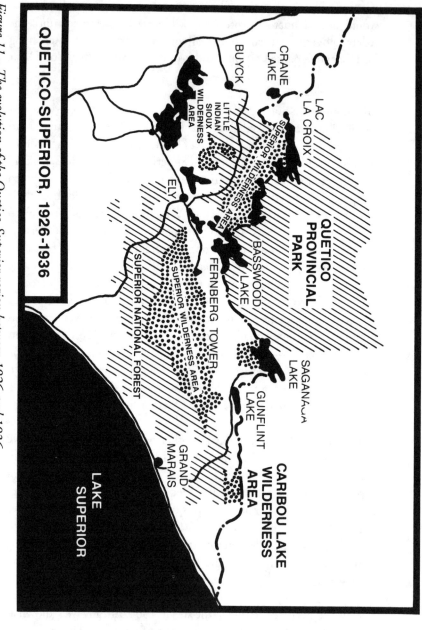

Figure 11 - The evolution of the Quetico-Superior region between 1926 and 1936.

bought or leased most of the potential dam sites along the international border in the Rainy Lake watershed. The most important of these was at Koochiching Falls on the Rainy River. The entire watershed emptied here, and in 1908 Backus completed a dam to control the flow. Six years later a dam at Kettle Falls gave him control over Namakan and Kabetogama lakes. Meanwhile, he spent $4 million extending the Minnesota and International Railway from Brainerd to International Falls, bought a sawmill at Kenora, Ontario, and built a pulp mill in Fort Frances, Ontario. By 1920 Backus was the continent's fourth-largest newsprint manufacturer, and was largely responsible for the development of International Falls and Fort Frances.[32]

In 1925 Backus succeeded in getting his waterpower plans on the agenda of the International Joint Commission. A 1909 treaty between Canada and the United States had created the commission to study and resolve questions over the use of international waters. Backus proposed building nine storage dams, eight of them in the heart of the canoe country. The storage dams would generate an additional twenty thousand horsepower for the power dams between Rainy Lake and Lake Winnipeg. He suggested that the costs be apportioned among all power users as well as the two governments.[33]

At least a dozen lakes would have been submerged under Backus' plan. Lac La Croix, set aside by the federal government in 1905 because of its great beauty, would have been raised sixteen feet, destroying the virgin pine along its shores and submerging nearly all of its three hundred islands. The dams would have raised Saganaga and Crooked lakes by fifteen feet, Loon Lake by thirty-three feet, and Little Vermilion Lake by eighty feet. Basswood Falls, Curtain Falls, Rebecca and Birch falls would have disappeared. The Voyageur's Highway would have become a reservoir.[34]

The plan was that of a man whose perceptual boundaries led him to view the Quetico-Superior as a resource bank, valuable primarily for its supply of timber and hydropower. This image had dominated the use of the region since the dawn of the fur trade. But when the International Joint Commission began hearings on September 28,

1925, at International Falls, Backus was the only one of forty-five witnesses supporting the plan.[35]

It might seem surprising that he did not receive local support, considering all the money he had poured into International Falls and Fort Frances, but Backus was not an insider. Area citizens considered him dishonest and ruthless. His dam at Koochiching Falls had flooded settlers' farms and homes. He had illegally blocked another local company from driving its logs into the Rainy River, and he often took small claims cases as far as the Minnesota Supreme Court. He even attempted to cheat a widow with ten children out of her river-front property that he leased. One of her children had died, and she asked for advance rent of $62.50 to pay for the funeral. Backus gave her the money, but the receipt that she thought she was signing actually was a document giving the company the right to use her property from that time forward without paying rent. The woman sued, and Backus lost after an appeal.[36]

Fort Frances officials told the commission they opposed the project because they feared the changing water levels would wreck the city's sewage system, destroy its park, and damage tourism. The Minnesota Arrowhead Association and Lake County commissioners also spoke against Backus, saying his plan would destroy the scenic beauty of the canoe country without adding a cent to the local tax base. The Ely Commercial Club announced it was "very energetically opposed to any proposition that will mean the ruination of the vast International wilderness areas to which it is the Gateway." The other power companies along the Winnipeg River, which would have had to absorb much of the cost of the project, said there was no need for additional waterpower.[37] Even so, it took the commission nine years to reach a decision, and the pressure that lead to the proposal's rejection came not from local groups, but from outsiders. Conservationists and the mass media brought the issue to millions of Americans, and rallied to support yet another plan for the region, proposed by another outsider, a Harvard University graduate.

Ernest C. Oberholtzer, born in Davenport, Iowa in 1884, first saw the

Quetico-Superior during a canoe trip in 1908, just after graduating from Harvard. He enjoyed the area so much he moved to an island on Rainy Lake and soon, despite a heart condition, took long journeys into the Canadian North, exploring regions no white man had seen in 150 years. He enjoyed studying native cultures, especially the Ojibway of the Quetico. He lived with them during the summers, and learned to speak their language. Because of his intense interest in their stories of the old way of life, the Ojibway called him "Atisokan," which means "legend."[38]

Oberholtzer, like Arthur Carhart, was a landscape architect. He earned his degree under the field's leading scholar, Frederick Law Olmsted. Believing that the only way to defeat Backus was to propose an alternative plan, Oberholtzer in 1927 developed a proposal for an international land management program far beyond anything either the United States or Canada had previously tried.

The plan divided the entire Rainy Lake Watershed into three zones. Arguing that the public wanted to preserve as much of the watershed as possible, he designated most of the region as wilderness, "with no roads and no sign of human activities except such as pertain to the present normal life of native Indians." This inner zone would be surrounded by a buffer area, accessible but not highly developed, where the two governments would lease land to private camps. The remainder of the watershed would contain the cities and highways, businesses and homes.[39]

Oberholtzer proposed that Canada and the United States sign a treaty accepting the zoning plan, as well as four specific principles. First, the governments should protect from logging as much of every shoreline as was visible from the middle of lakes and streams. Second, they should allow "practical forestry for economic purposes" on other forested lands within the watershed. Third, the governments should increase fish and game to "maximum productivity." Fourth, a joint commission should direct management under the treaty.[40]

The proposal placed Oberholtzer on the cutting edge of one of the leading intellectual movements of the time — regional planning. His educational background was similar to that of other planners and social theorists who recently had formed the Regional Planning Association of America. Benton MacKaye, a founder of the group and the designer of the Appalachian Trail, became a good friend of Oberholtzer. In 1935 the two joined Aldo Leopold, Robert Marshall and several others in forming the nucleus of the Wilderness Society.

Oberholtzer's plan was similar to that of Arthur Carhart. Both called for preserving the shorelines and permitting logging everywhere else. Both encouraged increasing fish and game productivity. Both allowed cottages and hotels on some large, partly settled lakes. But Oberholtzer's plan emphasized preserving the status quo on uninhabited lakes and rivers in an area far greater than the present Quetico Park-Boundary Waters Canoe Area, while Carhart's proposal advocated developing an extensive system of chalets and hotels within the modern BWCA.

When Oberholtzer sent his proposal to the Forest Service and the secretary of agriculture at the end of 1927, he did not know about Carhart's plan — it had never gotten off the shelf at Superior National Forest headquarters. And, early in 1928, when Carhart threatened to go public with his plan unless the national forest acted on it, he knew nothing about Oberholtzer's proposal. Earl W. Tinker, his former boss, apparently did not have the heart to tell Carhart the truth. "Contrary to your impression," he wrote to his former employee,

> "the recreation plan you conceived for the Superior has not been allowed to accumulate dust but rather has been a very live document and as time has gone by has formed the basis for the preparation of the controlling plan governing recreation and other activities within that Forest. While the wording in that plan may not be identical with that used by you, yet the fundamental policies are the same, which I presume will be the source of some satisfaction to you."[41]

To the current Superior National Forest supervisor, however, Tinker wrote differently, "Carhart's idea of hotel chains within wilderness areas and of artificial developments is not in accord with the fundamental idea in back of wilderness use." Tinker hoped Carhart would act on his threat and make his plan public, because "we would be placed in the enviable position of defending the wilderness ourselves, and all I can say is, 'More power to him.'" Another forest official agreed, saying that if Carhart's chalet system had been built, "the finest wilderness canoe route of the forest might have been ruined....

> The real, red-blooded, he-men and women canoe campers have stated in no uncertain terms on the outdoor pages of the newspapers, in prominent periodicals, and right here on the ground in person that they want their wilderness pretty wild, that they do not come up here to go out in a canoe and stop at a hotel. That they want bough beds or air mattresses, not hair mattresses. That they want to pitch their tents or sleep under the stars. That they do not want to be coddled and that they are nauseated by the smell of gasoline. One man even objected to meeting parties too lazy to do their own packing on portages. I sincerely agree with these canoeists.[42]

The conflict over roads, which Carhart had precipitated, had played a major role in convincing the Forest Service there was strong support for wilderness preservation. Nearly a year before Oberholtzer sent the agency his proposal, Chief Forester William B. Greeley had ordered all forest supervisors to study the lands they managed for possible wilderness areas. In the Superior National Forest, Oberholtzer's ideas dominated for the next forty years.

Oberholtzer's vision of wilderness, which allowed logging so long as it was kept out of sight, was well-suited to the Forest Service. It was more restrictive than the fishing paradise image supported by local tourist promoters, less restrictive than the anti-logging, anti-motorboat sacred space image that Sigurd Olson eventually promoted. Oberholtzer saw the canoe country wilderness as a refuge from civilization — a sanctuary. All three images had spiritual connotations that drew widespread support from Americans who were searching for meaning to bolster or replace their eroding religious beliefs; through mass communication, all three played key roles in shaping the cultural and environmental future of the Quetico- Superior.

Carhart, apparently satisfied by Tinker's letter, did not campaign for his recreation plan. Oberholtzer, with the support of the Forest Service, the secretary of agriculture and the Izaak Walton League, began the campaign against Backus. In January, 1928, he organized the Quetico-Superior Council, associated with the Izaak Walton League. Oberholtzer became its president. Carhart joined its advisory committee, along with such prominent Americans as Jane Addams, William Beebe and Karl Compton, and such leading conservationists as Aldo Leopold, Robert Sterling Yard, Ovid Butler, William Greeley and Harold Ickes. Oberholtzer's proposal became known as the Quetico-Superior program, and the Council took it to the mass media.[43]

Twenty years earlier Backus might have been unbeatable. But times were changing, and so were perceptual boundaries. The once domi- nant image of wilderness as a resource bank, there for the taking, was losing ground in a culture that demanded virgin wilderness in its novels, in its movies, and, increasingly, in its national parks and forests. The *New York Times,* the *New Republic,* and the top three outdoor magazines — *Sports Afield, Field and Stream,* and *Outdoor Life* — were among the national media opposing Backus. They portrayed him as an elderly rogue, one of the last of a dying but still dangerous breed of exploiters that had, as one writer put it? "reaped forests with Paul Bunyan's scythe...worked skin games on the animals until a hideless brute was more common than one with its original covering...traded thin dimes for mighty acres that are now spoken of in terms of dollars and square inches."[44]

An article in *Outdoor America* best captured this sense that Ameri- cans were in the process of crossing the boundary from one era into another. Speaking of the days of tall pine logging, Donald Hough wrote, "The thing to do was to turn the outdoors into money, because there was just too much outdoors and not enough money, and that is just what was done." Now, however, he continued, "there is too much money and not enough outdoors." The old viewpoint still was politically powerful, because it used the language of power — economics. It spoke of board feet and kilowatts, things that were easily measured and converted into dollar figures. The new perspective emphasized the intangible values of outdoor recreation, and Hough wrote that those who believed in these values had their work cut out. "It is a pretty tough assignment to try to explain something that you can't take hold of and feel, or look at and see," he wrote. "Electricity, which is similarly invisible, is measured by the words 'watt' and 'volt,' but outdoor recreation can be measured only in terms of long speeches, and who likes long speeches?"[45]

Nevertheless, those writing in the mass media did their best to frame the debate in *their* terms. And the best way to attack the political power of money was to wield one of the most popular cultural symbols of the times — the religion of the outdoors. "Are not some spiritual assets as important to our growth and our well-being as material ones?" asked the editor of **Outdoor America.** "Yes," he answered:

> It must not be forgotten that the man who at home enjoys the benefits of water power productions has a right absolutely as necessary to his spiritual well-being, to go forth into the wilderness away from man-made comforts and *find there* the God-made consolations of *primitive and unspoiled beauty.*[46]

Outdoor Life called the Quetico-Superior "one of the few remaining Eden spots of our continent," and preached:

> Red-blooded men know that there are things in this world more valuable than money. Fishing and hunting, growing healthy in body and wholesome in mind in the enjoyment of God's great outdoors, are some of these things. No paunchy, fat-jowled, chair-warming capitalist shall be allowed to spoil our forests, pollute our streams, destroy our

remaining fish and game at will without a fight.[47]

Minnesota Senator Thomas D. Schall, a Republican and a Minneapolis lawyer, received national publicity for a statement in which he labeled Backus "the De-Creator," and intoned, "It gives us pause to consider the colossal selfishness that would lay barren God's work, the wilderness."[48]

Although the national media, the Quetico-Superior Council and the Izaak Walton League were on the same side as local groups in the fight against Backus, this does not mean they had become viewed by the locals as insiders. Conservationists found this out the hard way in 1928, when they decided to try an end run around Backus. They hoped to convince the U.S. Congress to pass a bill that would forbid altering water levels and would ban shoreline logging on federal land in the area, as well as withdraw all the public land from entry. Most local politicians opposed the bill, introduced in the House by Republican Walter H. Newton of Minneapolis and in the Senate by Henrik Shipstead, a Farmer-Laborite. Representative William A. Pittenger of Duluth said he did not trust "outsiders bearing gifts," and labeled the proposal "the Minneapolis bill." Pittenger, a Republican, introduced an alternative bill that he said would not make northeastern Minnesotans depend upon "the whims and uncertainties of Congressional relief any time they desired to do any development in the country."[49]

After lengthy debate the two sides reached a compromise, and on July 10, 1930, the Shipstead-Nolan Act[50] was signed by President Herbert Hoover, a former national officer of the Izaak Walton League and its honorary president. It was the first time Congress had passed a law to preserve wilderness.

The International Joint Commission did not give wilderness supporters such a clear victory. In 1934, after nine years of studying the arguments for and against the Backus and Oberholtzer plans, the commission decided to do nothing. While this angered conservationists, who had hoped for a strong statement of support, it also meant the defeat of E.W. Backus, for he could not achieve his goal without a favorable decision. A series of business errors and legal troubles had recently thrown him into bankruptcy, and shortly after the commission's ruling Backus died of a heart attack. The image of the Quetico-Superior as a resource bank had fallen from power.[51]

That same year (1934), President Franklin D. Roosevelt, by executive order, established the President's Quetico-Superior Committee, made up of three presidential appointees and one representative each from the interior and agriculture departments. Its purpose was to work with the U.S. and Canadian governments toward achieving the Quetico-Superior program. Oberholtzer, Charles S. Kelly and Sewell T. Tyng — the latter two lawyers who served on the Quetico-Superior Council — were members, with Tyng as chairman. Earl Tinker, Carhart's former supervisor, represented the Department of Agriculture, and Robert Marshall, who would enlist Oberholtzer as a founder of the Wilderness Society, represented the Department of the Interior. Oberholtzer's image of the canoe country as a sanctuary had become the official U.S. government position.[52]

But the sanctuary image still was a long way from achieving political dominance in Canada. The vast majority of the land that Oberholtzer hoped to preserve as wilderness belonged to Ontario, and as yet received almost no tourists. The only significant wilderness tourism was in Quetico Provincial Park, which, because of lack of Canadian access, was used almost exclusively by Americans. Ontario citizens, surrounded by wilderness, saw no need to establish special regulations to preserve it. Businessmen already were upset about seeing their tax dollars go toward keeping the Quetico wild for the benefit of outsiders — the Minnesota tourist promoters. By the 1940s they would insist that their government not preserve one more acre than that preserved on the American side of the boundary, and would threaten to open the Quetico to resorts. Responding to these pressures, the Ontario government in 1946 would prepare to lease cabin sites in the Quetico for $10 an acre, and would solicit pilots to fly in fishing parties. Only a firm promise and subsequent follow-through by U.S. government officials and conservationists to buy out wilderness area resorts and ban airplanes would convince Ontario to keep the Quetico wild.[53]

These political difficulties also would prevent Oberholtzer's plan for the entire watershed from becoming a reality. Instead, the Quetico-Superior — which in Oberholtzer's eyes consisted of 15,000 square miles — would, to the mass media, the public and government officials, come to mean the 3,200 square miles within Quetico Provincial Park and the Superior National Forest Wilderness Areas.

What would have happened had the U.S. Forest Service approved Carhart's plan for the Superior National Forest? The political problems that damaged Oberholtzer's plans likely would have made it impossible to achieve Carhart's vision of an easily accessible American wilderness that opened to a more rugged and pristine Canadian wilderness. Had the U.S. government established hotel and chalet chains in the area that has become the Boundary Waters Canoe Area, Ontario most likely would have followed suit and similarly developed the Quetico. It is impossible to say with certainty how the Forest Service — or Carhart, for that matter — would have reacted to such development. Perhaps the agency would have abandoned the hotel chains idea in hopes of a similar ban in Ontario. If not, the wilderness character of the major canoe routes would have disappeared long before public sentiment had grown strong enough to convince both the province and the U.S. Congress to set aside Quetico Park and the BWCA as official wildernesses. This is not necessarily to state that the area would be less popular today, but that it would be quite different from what Carhart envisioned. However, the political complexities inherent in managing this international wilderness seem to indicate that Carhart was right in at least one fundamental idea: Wilderness management cannot be purely "natural," but must instead consist of a set of political and environmental compromises.

The form of such compromises, of course, depends to a large extent upon the mixture of values in the culture at large. And, while the image of the canoe country as a sanctuary was endorsed by the U.S. government in the early 1930s, it still was far from dominating the media coverage of the area. The publicity from the conflict over waterpower, as well as from the earlier one over roads, had generated many feature stories about the Quetico-Superior. *Outdoor Life,* for example, which from 1920 through 1926 published just one article that dealt exclusively with the canoe country, published ten such features between 1927 and 1932. Although the national media often referred to intangible values, such as remoteness and solitude, as well as to spiritual values in their articles opposing Backus, this does not mean that they strongly promoted either the sanctuary or the sacred space image of the Quetico-Superior. Most articles emphasized something very tangible — fishing. The overall effect was to create an image of the Quetico-Superior in which intangible and spiritual values were sometimes associated with, but subservient to, a specific form of recreation. It was the image of a fishing paradise, just what tourist operators on both sides of the border promoted. The outsiders had the U.S. President's backing, but the insiders dominated the turn of events in the Quetico- Superior for the next twenty years.

CHAPTER 5
FISHING PARADISE

And Buck cussed; because the sun was shining, the waters dancing, and his own heart was glad with the joy of living.

— Arthur Carhart (1932)[1]

After 1926, new roads and new technology increased the accessibility of the Quetico-Superior. Dozens of resorts were built during the next two decades. Motorboats became wide spread, houseboats appeared on several lakes, and seaplanes began carrying tourists deep into the wilderness. All this, ironically, became possible because of an implicitly antimodern ethos that pervaded American culture. The timing, however, was determined by a shift in the economy that dramatically altered Americans' perceptual boundaries and allowed the business world to capitalize on antimodernism.

A decline in the rate of capitalistic expansion, begun before World War I, had by the 1920s created a surplus of capital. At the same time, technological advances, a national system of marketing and distribution, and more efficient management practices had increased productivity and lowered prices. Corporate and political leaders worried that the economy would collapse unless Americans made the change from a production-oriented society, dominated by the self-denying Protestant work ethic, to a society focused on consumption.

To promote spending, businesses increased wages and shortened working hours; the eight-hour day and annual vacation were established in the 1920s. Installment buying became widely available. And public relations experts, business leaders and politicians used the mass media to barrage Americans with the command to buy, buy, buy. "People may ruin themselves by saving instead of spending," said an economist. A newspaper editorialized that an American's "first importance to his country is no longer that of citizen but that of consumer. Consumption is a new necessity." Material possessions became the measuring stick of success; President Calvin Coolidge went so far as to claim that "wealth is the chief end of man."[2]

It was not difficult to create a consumer culture in an increasingly pluralistic society. The rational, secular world view of science and industry was spreading from the elites to the masses, aided by urbanization and by technological advances in transportation and communication. Barraged by numerous conflicting political, social and religious beliefs, Americans had begun journeying down the slippery slope of relativism; what once were seen as absolute truths were becoming mere matters of personal opinion. Historian T.J. Jackson Lears argues that the "crucial moral change" that allowed the consumer culture to emerge was "a shift from a Protestant ethos of salvation through self-denial toward a therapeutic ethos stressing self-realization in this world - an ethos characterized by an almost obsessive concern with psychic and physical health defined in sweeping terms."[3]

A central theme underlying the therapeutic ethos was a nostalgic attachment to nature. And of all the outdoor activities that became increasingly popular in the emerging consumer culture, fishing had the most impact on the Quetico-Superior. President Hoover had called it "good for the soul of man," and the leading outdoor magazines praised its therapeutic values. "There are bigger fish in fishing than the fish we catch," editorialized *Sports Afield:*

> They are...health and happiness. Health and happiness yield
> confidence, enthusiasm, serenity and appreciation....In days
> like these, when many of us are assailed by doubts...beset by
> worries...suspicious that the world is tottering...we need to
> go fishing.[4]

Outdoor Life called the angler "the thirteenth disciple," and, in an editorial describing a typical fisherman, the magazine showed its readers how fishing promoted self-realization:

> ...all day long he waded and whipped the stream, working
> riffles, drifts, logs, piers and stumps; not catching many
> fish, but evening found him with soothed nerves and, tho
> tired, a rested feeling had entered his system.

> At peace with nature, the world and men, he drove home
> possessing the greatest of all to be desired-peace with
> himself, and after all there seems only one conclusion that
> satisfies,... 'Go Fishin.'[5]

The implicitly antimodern sentiment behind the popularity of fishing
was readily co-opted by the modern consumer culture. Manufacturers
created new products designed to make fishing a more satisfying
experience. They made lightweight rods and reels, a dazzling array of
colorful lures, and more effective clothing for cold and wet weather. Of
all the new products, however, the most important was the Big Twin
outboard, unveiled in 1926 by Johnson Motor Company of South
Bend, Indiana. The motor weighed eighty-five pounds and reached a
speed of thirty miles per hour, nearly twice that of its competitors.[6]

Outboards had begun making their way into general use shortly after
the turn of the century. Cameron B. Waterman of Detroit began
selling his "Waterman Porto" in 1906; by 1916 he had sold more than
thirty thousand. Ole Evinrude tried out his first handmade outboard
on Milwaukee's Kinnickinnic River in 1909, and quickly became the
leading producer. By 1919, almost one hundred thousand Evinrudes
were in use.[7]

These earlier models, however, were crude, noisy machines snubbed
by many as "coffee grinders" and accused of scaring away fish. They
often were difficult to start, and their heavy weight - at least sixty
pounds - was hardly justified by the mere two or three horsepower
generated. Motorboats labored across lakes, with most of their force
spent plowing the hull through the water.[8]

All this began to change after 1921, when Lou, Harry and Clarence
Johnson, and Warren Conover formed the Johnson Motor Company.

In 1922 they introduced their first outboard motor, the Johnson Light Twin, still low in horsepower but weighing just thirty-five pounds. The company sold three thousand that year and seven thousand in 1923, an industry record. But boaters wanted speed even more than they wanted light motors. When Johnson produced its heavy but fast Big Twin, which planed the hull over instead of through the water, consumer demand skyrocketed. By 1929 the company was the leading manufacturer of outboard motors, and sold more than thirty-one thousand. Sales declined during the early years of the Great Depression, but returned to the 1929 level in 1937. Two years later the company broke the forty thousand mark, and in 1949 sold nearly ninety thousand. By that time nearly two million outboard motors were in use in the United States.[9]

Advertisers identified the outboard motor with the therapeutic ethos. They presented the machine as a necessary part of the simple life, the best way to escape from civilization to the freedom of the wilderness:

> To those who own outboard motors and boats, thousands of untrammeled highways lie open where there are no white street lines, no red stop lights and no hurry and bustle of straight pavements. Every bay and river invites the water tourist to rest, to explore, or hunt or fish without bother.[10]

The outboard motor was especially popular with fishing enthusiasts. No longer did anglers need to spend most of the day rowing or paddling to and from the best fishing spots, until their arms and backs ached and their hands blistered. Now they could spend the bulk of their time fishing, and could try out new locations that previously had been too far away. The motorboat became, in a sense, a modern version of the covered wagon, opening to everyone wilderness waterways that previously had been accessible only to the hardiest. And one of the places it opened was the Quetico-Superior.

Henry Chosa, who ran the Four Mile Portage between Fall and Basswood lakes, was probably the first local businessman to use outboards routinely. By the early 1920s he began picking up canoe parties at Winton, towing them across Fall Lake, hauling them over the Four Mile Portage, and towing them up Basswood Lake to the Canadian border. The tow service saved up to two days of paddling, and was standard practice among all of the outfitters by the early 1930s.[11]

Motors soon spread beyond Basswood Lake. While the more powerful outboards were too heavy to lug across portages, the newest two and three horsepower versions were not, and fishermen began carrying these small motors and gasoline cans along with their canoes, deep into the wilderness. Resourceful entrepreneurs hauled larger craft and motors to isolated lakes during the winter, so summertime fishermen could leave their boat at one end of a portage, carry their gear across, and hop into another boat at the other end of the portage. By the mid-1940s, motorboats were commonplace on all of the lakes along the international border, and Ely, Minnesota businessmen had cached boats across the border in such Quetico Park lakes as Robinson, Argo, Sara, Elk, Brent and others north of Basswood.[12]

The 1926 wilderness compromise that allowed construction of the Fernberg Road and the Echo Trail from Ely helped motorboats move into other parts of the country south of the boundary. Soon boats were on such Fernberg Road waters as the Kawishiwi River, and Snowbank, Moose and Wood lakes, and on such Echo Trail lakes as Fenske, Big, Everett and Jeannette.

The motorboats and roads (and, in the 1940s, the seaplane) broke through the environmental boundaries that had earlier discouraged development. And resorts began spreading into the newly opened wilderness. By 1936 at least sixteen resorts were operating in the Ely area. By 1950 the number had grown to sixty-five; thirty-three of these depended on the two roads, motors, or both for access. Twelve of them were along the Fernberg Road extension, seven were along the Echo Trail, and another fourteen could be reached either by a combination of using these roads and motorboats, or by flying in.[13]

The resort buildup depended on a steadily increasing number of visitors to the area. By 1940 Forest Service officials estimated the number of hotel and resort guests visiting Superior National Forest to be nearly sixty-one thousand. Summer home residents and guests accounted for another forty-five hundred, and campers for about eighteen thousand.[14]

No reliable American figures exist showing how many people used the lakes and streams of the U.S. portion of the Quetico-Superior wilderness during the 1930s. Most use centered on the area from Basswood to Knife lakes, which did not become part of the national forest until late in the decade and so was ignored in Forest Service visitor use calculations. Quetico Park, however, kept fairly accurate statistics. In 1929 the park sold twelve hundred fishing licenses to Americans. In 1932, the worst year of the Depression, the number dropped to a low of two hundred. In 1937 Americans returned to Quetico Park in pre-Depression numbers; about a thousand bought fishing licenses. By 1941 the number doubled to two thousand.[15]

The numbers may be a bit low. They do not include, for example, those Americans who entered the park but did not buy fishing licenses, and they do not include Canadians. But there were few of either group. Fishing was so taken for granted that in 1927 Ontario officials had to *order* Quetico Park superintendent John Jamieson to not force visitors to buy fishing licenses. And few Canadians entered the park. In fact, park records show no Canadian visitors in 1941 and 1942. "Very few Canadians know anything about the Park and the kind that do are mostly poachers," Jamieson once wrote.[16]

American statistics are a little more reliable for the 1940s, and show a five-fold increase in the use of the wilderness areas (which by then included Basswood and adjacent lakes), from thirty-eight thousand visitor days in 1942 to well over two hundred thousand in 1950. The increase forced Canada to expand its number of ranger stations along the Quetico Park border from two to five.[17]

The tourist boom depended upon publicity as much as it did upon roads and outboard motors, for people had to know about the Quetico Superior before they would travel there. Some of the publicity undoubtedly was by word of mouth, but local promoters, led by the Minnesota Arrowhead Association, intensified their efforts in the 1930s. The Arrowhead Association published a map brochure that briefly described the region and gave the addresses of local chambers of commerce. The organization distributed thirty thousand copies in 1931; a third of these were given away at Chicago's Outdoor Life Exposition in May, and the balance were sent to two hundred information bureaus across the country, placed in automobile service stations, and mailed to individuals who requested information about the area. From March to August, the association also advertised in such regional newspapers as the *Chicago Daily News,* the *Omaha World Herald,* the *Des Moines Register and Leader,* the *St. Louis Post Dispatch,* the *Kansas City Star,* the *Minneapolis Tribune* and the *Milwaukee Journal.* By 1933 the organization began distributing a larger booklet that included information about each tourist city in the region and contained advertisements placed by local resorts and outfitters.[18]

Individual chambers of commerce worked in concert with the Arrowhead Association, publishing annual tourist guides that enthusiastically described the local communities and recreational possibilities, and contained advertisements placed by resorts and outfitters. The Arrowhead Association helped distribute these guides at its information booth in the Duluth City Hall, and helped fund chamber display booths at the Chicago Exposition. Chamber representatives distributed copies of their guides as well as brochures published by a number of individual resorts and outfitters.[19]

The Quetico-Superior enjoyed one key advantage over other nearby regions competing for tourism: lots of free publicity, particularly in the national outdoor magazines. This was crucial to the area, because the other regions often had much more money for promotion. In 1931, for example, Michigan's Upper Peninsula spent $42,000 on publicity, nearly six times the $7,400 spent by the Arrowhead Association. But the three leading outdoor publications *Sports Afield, Outdoor Life,* and *Field and Stream* published forty-eight nonfiction feature stories about the canoe country during the decade. The coverage in these and other magazines, combined with newspaper articles and local promotional efforts, drew the attention that built the area's tourist trade. At the same time, the coverage firmly established the Quetico's image as a fishing paradise.[20]

It was a romantic and nostalgic image, based on a fervent desire to believe that the American frontier and traditional values still existed, unaffected by economic and social change. A paradise is a place set apart from the everyday world. Its spiritual connotation implies beauty, purity, vitality. In paradise, living is easy and rewarding. Food is abundant, ready for the taking. Activities performed with little thought in everyday life take on a new luster: the chore of grocery shopping is replaced by the enjoyable sport of fishing; the boredom of mealtime preparation is supplanted by the excitement of campfire cooking. Even sleep, whether under the stars or in a log cabin, assumes a new character.

Tourist promoters and writers reflected this desire for a paradise by continually exaggerating the wildness of the Quetico-Superior, ignoring the devastation from tall pine logging and, eventually, the increasing numbers of resorts and outboard motors. After all, there were many other places in the country with good fishing; one of the most publicized was nearby Lake of the Woods, famous for its muskellunge. But Lake of the Woods lacked one thing that the canoe country had in abundance — a remoteness from civilization that allowed people to imagine they were the first ones there. Sigurd Olson explained the attraction in a *Field and Stream* article that described how he and another man spent a day blazing a trail north from Bart Lake to one that had no name:

> Those who have never found new bass water cannot understand the feelings that were ours as we pushed our canoe into the sunset that evening. Here we were, all alone - perhaps the only white men who had ever been on these waters, and surely the only bass fishermen. And to know that here was country entirely primitive was enough

to make us more than happy.[21]

These "virgin lakes," as they came to be promoted, provided a sense of adventure, freedom and independence that seemed to be slipping away from modern society. To many, these feelings were more valuable than the solitude and quietness also found in wilderness. And there was no better way to establish a link to the nostalgic past than to harvest nature's bounty. Most of the tourists wanted fish, lots of fish, and the image of "virgin lakes" implied a piscatory abundance of which hard-bitten fishermen dreamed. Advertisers tantalized prospective tourists with big claims: "The waters are alive with salmon, trout, pike, pickerel and bass"; "Thrill to battles to the finish with fighting landlocked salmon, explosive great northern pike, scrappy bass, wonderful eating wall-eyed pike"; "We throw them back under ten pounds."[22]

These claims were backed by the feature stories in the outdoor magazines. **Sports Afield** published such articles as "Quetico Bass (The Villains)" and "Where Big Ones Lurk." **Outdoor Life** features included "The Warriors of Wind Bay" and "Wilderness Walleyes"; **Field and Stream** ran such pieces as "Lucius the Mighty" and "We Wanted Bass."[23] The authors of these and other features made it clear that the Quetico-Superior was indeed a fishing paradise. As Arthur Carhart put it:

> Nowhere - not even in Yellowstone - is there such a game sanctuary....In numerous rapids and sandy shallows pike, walleyes, perch, lake trout, bass and many other game and food fish spawn literally by the millions. It is one of the greatest fresh-water gamefish areas in existence....The unscarred lakes are scenic landscapes of unmatched beauty. In all our great National Parks system there is no scene that will surpass their aesthetic values.[24]

It was the frontier all over again - even better, because hardship was unnecessary in a paradise - and there was biological gold in the lakes and rivers of the Quetico-Superior. Those who saw the region as a fishing paradise greatly appreciated the area's rugged beauty, but categorized lakes by the species of fish they contained, and ranked highest those places where the fish were large and plentiful. This came across loud and clear in the outdoor magazines, and perhaps was best expressed in the feature stories written by Emil "Ogima" Anderson.

Nobody in the 1930s wrote as many fishing stories about the Quetico-Superior as did Anderson, a young, curly haired Ely guide who smoked a Calabash pipe and had a quick sense of humor. He wrote ten features for the Minneapolis-based *Sports Afield*, which by 1939 was the leading outdoor magazine, with a circulation of 250,000. Each of his articles was about Quetico Park, and Anderson made it clear that fishing was the primary attraction. "There is virgin fishing in Quetico Provincial Park to this day," he wrote in 1933, and took his readers on tour:

> Let's go east along the International Boundary. Here's Carp Lake trout and bass, and Emerald [Lake] trout....And here's Knife Lake - more trout, and walleyes, and Great Northerns - and bass, too!...
>
> Out of Bayley Bay of Basswood - there it is - Burke Lake for trout and walleyes, then Sunday Lake....And look at Lake Agnes - 4, 6, 8 - gosh, 15 miles of scenic grandeur, trout and walleyes....
>
> Now let's go down Basswood River to Crooked Lake. Just look at all those little lakes to the North! This is bass country. Over here is Robinson [Lake], trout, walleyes and *blasé* bass. Two Grandpa lunkers in a certain bay swim out to meet every canoe and look the visitors over. Bass Lakes all about, here. A little east lies [Lake] Sarah, trout, walleyes and abundant beauty. North of Crooked there is also Argo, an outstanding trout lake.[25]

Basswood Lake gained the most publicity. Not only did it become known as the best gateway to the canoe country and serve as the starting point for the vast majority of canoe trips (in fact, Americans venturing into Quetico Park via Ely *had* to stop at Basswood to check in at customs), it became widely publicized as a top-notch fishing spot. This was especially true after 1929, when a Chicago tourist caught a world-record, 45 lb., 12 oz. northern pike in Wind Bay. "Ye gods and little fishes! What a pike!" exclaimed Seth Briggs in *Field and Stream*, as he awarded the angler first prize in the magazine's annual fishing contest. When *Sports Afield* referred to the pike just four months later, the fish had gained nearly two pounds.[26]

The record-breaker was caught on a lure, rod and line all made by the South Bend Bait Company of Indiana, which wasted no time in playing up the catch in its advertising. Basswood resorts were quick to follow suit. "Where the world's largest northern pike are caught," exclaimed Peterson's Fishing Camp. "In all the world, no fishing like ours," bragged Wegen's Wilderness Camp. "Come where they are," urged Pinecliff Lodge. "The fishing can't be beat!" claimed Pipestone Falls Lodge. Northern pike from Basswood Lake were *Field and Stream* prize winners again in 1933 and 1934. The lake's great fishing-not only for northerns, but for walleyes and bass - prompted *Outdoor Life* magazine in 1964 to call it one of the nation's "25 top fishing holes."[27]

Such publicity was an important factor in determining which parts of the canoe country received the heaviest use. Anderson, who had played a key role in identifying the best fishing lakes to a national audience, wrote in 1936 that heavy publicity given to Quetico Park's Bart Lake had led to such an increase in fishing that "today it is only mediocre." A year later he wrote that Quetico canoe parties were heading straight for the best-known lakes, and ignoring the excellent fishing in lakes and streams along the way. As one of his examples he mentioned Grey Lake, which contained an abundance of largemouth bass, but was usually passed over because canoeists were anxious to reach Kashipiwi, which "has a reputation."[28]

Such concentrated angling was hard on the area; environmental boundaries made it relatively easy to over-fish Quetico-Superior lakes. Gouged by glaciers into Precambrian Shield bedrock, the lakes had fewer dissolved salts than did lakes south of the Shield, and were much lower in biological productivity. Despite the heavy publicity to the contrary, few species of fish inhabited the area, and populations were relatively low. As early as 1924, Superior National Forest Supervisor Calvin Dahlgren noted that the lakes and streams next to Ely were "practically fished out." The ever-increasing numbers of fishing enthusiasts, lured to the area by an image of abundance, were essentially mining the canoe country. Clearly, Fishing Paradise would not be an eternal one without human intervention. Large numbers of fish needed to be raised and released to keep the anglers satisfied.[29]

As early as 1909, residents of northern Lake and St. Louis counties submitted applications to the Minnesota Game and Fish Department to release state hatcher-raised fry and fingerlings into the lakes and rivers of the canoe country. When the state approved such a request, it would deliver the fish at no cost to the applicant. But, except for on Burntside Lake just north of Ely, little stocking was done in the area before 1930.[30]

During the 1930s and 1940s, as the tourist industry began rapidly growing, widespread stocking commenced in earnest. All the major canoe route lakes were regularly stocked. Basswood Lake, for example, was stocked seventeen times with state-reared fish between 1930 and 1945, most often with lake trout and largemouth bass, but also with walleye and,beginning in 1941, with smallmouth bass. The walleye stockings, while not as frequent, were the largest, with sometimes more than a million fingerlings released in a day.[31]

Resort owners were among those who applied for fish, seeking to build up their lakes' angling potential. Canadian Border Lodge and Hibbard's Lodge released walleye into Moose Lake; Deer Trail Lodge stocked largemouth bass and lake trout in Twin Lake; Burntside Lodge planted walleye and lake trout in Burntside Lake. Others did the same on different lakes; the state provided to all who asked.[32]

Nobody asked more often than the Ely Commercial Club. The club's Ray Hoeffler released walleye, lake trout and largemouth bass into dozens of Lakes and rivers, and stocked rainbow and brook trout in streams and small lakes. Hoeffler arranged nine of the seventeen Basswood Lake releases, planting twelve thousand lake trout, sixteen thousand largemouth bass, and seven hundred thousand walleye. This last species was a favorite with anglers, and Hoeffler stocked it liberally in lakes along the major canoe routes. By 1945 he had released more than four million walleye into Snowbank Lake, nearly three million into Fall Lake, well over two million into Ensign Lake, and more than a million into both Moose and Big lakes.[33]

Hoeffler also frequently stocked many lakes outside the wilderness areas. A number of these were popular resort lakes such as Burntside, Shagawa, and White Iron, but some were small, obscure lakes known only to local fishermen, such as seventy-acre Dunnigan Lake, where by 1945, he had released nearly seven hundred thousand walleye and a couple of hundred largemouth bass. Fishing Paradise wasn't just for outsiders.[34]

Stocking did not depend solely on local citizens. The Minnesota Game and Fish Department also stocked the border lakes. So did the federal Fish and Wildlife Service and, until some time after World War II, the U.S. Forest Service raised and released fish in the canoe country. While records estimating the total annual number of state and federal-raised fish released in Superior National Forest have not been compiled, forest officials estimated the 1936 total to be nearly twenty million.[35]

The canoe country's image as a fishing paradise depended upon the myth of natural abundance. Maintaining fish populations, or even increasing them, was essential to the image's success. But the myth of abundance was part of a greater paradox. The fishing paradise image was based on the same sentimental pastoral dream long dominant in the United States, which praised rural life and the frontier as the source of virtue and happiness, and yet allowed to go unchecked the nation's material progress that was transforming the land and traditional values. Nostalgic for the simple life, but committed to modern amenities, those who believed in the old pastoral dream naively hoped they could have the best of both worlds without sacrifice.

This paradox behind the fishing paradise image was perhaps best evident in the writing of Bob Lincoln. One of the United States' best-known outdoor writers, Lincoln was a leading promoter of the Quetico-Superior during the 1930s, writing eight feature stories for **Sports Afield.** He wrote sentimental, exhuberant prose about the primitive, but advocated the use of modern conveniences. Lincoln called Superior National Forest's wilderness areas "the exclusive haven of the canoeist, the Area Primeval!"[36] Yet he rigged his canoe with an outboard motor for most of his trips through the canoe country, and enthusiastically wrote an elegy for the paddle:

> The outboard motor has eliminated the romance of the spruce blade, but it has likewise laughed at the miles and with its canvas covered charge has gone gallivanting over the waves with a light-hearted put-put that spells conquest of time and distance. Gone are the bark craft of the voyageurs and fur traders with the time-honored "H.B.C." painted at the bow for all men to see and give heed to. Modern inventiveness has transportation that is unrivalled.[37]

Lincoln detested the "dollar-minded lumberman," and happily (also incorrectly) reported in 1937 that in the Superior National Forest's wilderness areas "no resorts are permitted and aside from the trails and portages from lake to lake there is little evidence of civilization and its devastating effect on the wild domain."[38] Yet his writing about the outboard motor implies a perspective that *appreciates* the conquest of nature, so long as the objective is catching fish. He wrote about how he "penetrated" the virgin lakes of the Quetico, where he and his companions found fish "that hit our lures with all the viciousness of finny ones that had never witnessed the presence of those glittering frauds on which they so often commit suicide."[39]

To those who saw the Quetico-Superior as a fishing paradise, as did Lincoln, the excitement of catching fish while in a scenic setting was ultimately more important than an authentic experience of wilderness living. They wanted to experience the freedom and vitality of pioneer life, but not the hard work. The simple life that they sought was a modern version, not a pre-industrial one, and was tailor-made for the consumer culture. Fishing Paradise required large and fast outboard motors for the more accessible lakes, small and lightweight ones for the interior. It required resorts with rustic log cabins that had warm beds and well-stocked fireplaces, and with main lodges that provided "good home cooking." It required guides who could take people to the best fishing spots, haul gear over portages, set up comfortable base camps, clean and cook the fish. One guide told a *Field and Stream* writer of his disdain for the lack of hardiness among the new tourists:

> Some of 'em are reg'lar babes in the woods. They can't do a darn thing an' expect us guides to be a sort of French chef, redcap, bell-boy, outboard motor an' pack mule all combined. It's our fault if it rains or if the fish don't bite. You would think we was to blame for the mosquitoes an' black flies, for the rocks bein' hard an' sharp; and we're expected to shrink the portage trails up to a couple of jumps an' then pave that. We have to do everything but tuck 'em into bed an' kiss em good night.[40]

Resort owners were careful to advertise their "electrically lighted" cabins, their showers, saunas, linen, dining rooms and sand beaches. They pointed out the good roads leading to their lodges. But they did not neglect the key attraction: the surrounding frontier conditions that linked people to simpler times and guaranteed a big catch of fish. "New country has been made accessible for the first time and we are among the pioneers," said a brochure for Canadian Border Lodge, 20 miles northeast of Ely on Moose Lake:

> Since the Fernberg Road, tapping the boundary lake wilderness, was only recently completed, the fishing done thus far has made no impression on the vast supply in the unlimited waters available. This region is one vast network of open water teeming with fighting fish....Many of our parties last year caught the limit of walleyed pike in an hour.[41]

The desirability of locating at the edge of the wilderness directed the resort boom of the 1930s and 1940s. With much of the American side of the canoe country logged over, a number of entrepreneurs advertised the proximity of their resorts to the international boundary. "Farthest north lodge on Moose Lake," claimed the Winton Trading Lodge. "Close to Canada," advertised Pipestone Falls Lodge. "Near Canadian Border," said the ad for Evergreen Lodge. "Within a stone's throw of the Canadian Border," promised Johnson Bros. Fishing Camp.[42]

These last three resorts were located on Basswood Lake. Much of its American shore was still an eyesore at the end of the 1920s, although a thick second growth of aspen and fir was well on its way. But glorious virgin stands of red and white pine lined the northern side of the lake, standing sentinel over the Canadian wilderness. They were there because a political boundary had set them off-limits to American loggers, and because environmental boundaries had so far kept Canadian loggers away. They served as a major attraction to those whose perceptual boundaries led them to seek wild places, including those who came to catch Basswood's increasingly famous northern pike. Despite its lack of road access, Basswood became the most popular resort lake of the canoe country. In 1928 there were two resorts; fourteen years later there were fourteen more. In 1944, the Ely Commercial Club boasted, "The total guest capacity of all the resorts is well over a thousand people." By then there were houseboats on the lake, and daily mail service. A dozen private homes also occupied Basswood's shores, several of them the year-round homes of local Ojibway, the rest summer cottages.[43]

Born of a vague nostalgia for the contentment associated with a younger, wilder America, and bred to a strong faith in modern technology, Fishing Paradise had emerged from the minds of men and become incarnate in the Quetico-Superior. Basswood Lake, its center-piece, was the meeting ground of the past and the present, which were nicely separated by the international boundary. And it was here, along the thin line that divided nations and minds, that Fishing Paradise ultimately made its final stand. Beginning in the late 1950s, the owners of each resort and private cabin sold to the federal government. They did it one by one, unwillingly, under the threat of condemnation.

CHAPTER 6
SANCTUARY

The airplane by its noise destroys for the man in the canoe the intangible, almost indescribable quality of the wilderness, a quality compounded of silence and solitude and a brooding sense of peace that sinks into the spirit.

— Harold Martin (1948) [1]

As the resorts began to appear along the popular canoe routes on the American side of the Quetico-Superior, physically confirming its reputation as a fishing paradise, the Forest Service and such groups as the President's Quetico-Superior Committee and the Izaak Walton League continued their work to maintain primitive conditions. Their goal was to convince the United States and Canada to sign a treaty creating an international wilderness area. To succeed, they first had to gain control over commercial development. They made little progress until after World War II, when the rapidly increasing use of hydroplanes would force into the open a long-simmering conflict over the meaning of wilderness. Treaty supporters chose Sigurd F. Olson to rally international support for their cause. The ensuing battle set important precedents for wilderness preservation, and put on the defensive those who supported the canoe country as a fishing paradise.

Olson's history is valuable for a complete understanding of Quetico-Superior events, because he personified the tensions between wilderness preservation and commercial exploitation. Although he is best known today for his books about wilderness and for his role in preserving the Quetico-Superior, for more than twenty years Olson also played a significant part in the area's commercial development. The story of his early career yields important insights about the ease with which the fishing paradise image became established, and the difficulty many had in recognizing its naivete. It was quite natural for those who loved the wilderness to seek a career that allowed them to spend time in it, but it often was hard for them to perceive the subtle ways in which they contributed to the declining wildness of the land they loved.

After his first canoe trip through the Quetico-Superior in 1921, during which he encountered Arthur Carhart on Saganaga Lake, Olson knew he wanted to live as close by as possible. He returned to the University of Wisconsin in Madison, where he had received a bachelor's degree in agriculture, hoping that a master's degree in geology would land him a job in one of the mining communities at the edge of the canoe country. Before Olson completed his program, however, the new junior college in Ely offered him a position as head of its biology department. Along with his wife, Elizabeth, who was expecting their first child, Olson moved to Ely in February, 1923. Four months later he got involved for the first time with the tourist trade, becoming a guide for Wilderness Outfitters.

Olson didn't become a guide so that he could *exploit* the wilderness; he became a guide so that he could *explore* the wilderness. "I did not realize what it would mean beyond satisfying the urge to see new country," he later recalled. He also wanted to associate with the old-time guides, to gain insights into the land and wilderness living: "I felt that only by knowing the men who made their living there could I ever really understand and catch the full flavor and meaning of the land itself."[2] And yet in doing so Olson began participating in the commercialization of the Quetico-Superior.

His role in the tourist trade was not particularly important until 1929, when, along with Mervin W. Peterson and Walter A. Hanson, he founded the Border Lakes Outfitting Company and became its manager. Peterson owned Peterson's Fishing Camp, one of the first two or three resorts on Basswood Lake, located on Hoist Bay near the Four Mile Portage. The Border Lakes Outfitting Company was situated in Winton, at the edge of Fall Lake. This combination, right on the route used by most tourists who entered the Quetico-Superior, bode well for both businesses. Many canoeists outfitted by Border

Lakes got towed up Fall Lake by motorboat, rode the truck over the Four Mile Portage, spent the night at Peterson's resort, and got towed up to the international border the next morning. After their trip, they were picked up at the border and towed back to Peterson's.

In almost no time Border Lakes rivalled Wilderness Outfitters, the oldest such business in Ely, as the area's leader. The competition undoubtedly played a large role in Wilderness Outfitters' decision to open a resort of its own on Basswood Lake in 1930. That company's Basswood Lodge, built in a rare stand of virgin pine, became one of the region's most popular resorts, and one of the largest, with more than twenty buildings.

Nobody called Olson a wilderness destroyer for his role in developing Basswood Lake. The loggers had destroyed the wilderness there; an aesthetically inferior forest of aspen and fir was only beginning to cover the scars when the Border Lakes Outfitting Company and Peterson's Resort began operating. Several families of *metis* (French-Ojibway ancestry) had settled on Basswood, and miles of its American shoreline were privately owned. It was not within the boundaries of Superior National Forest in 1929 (although the forest did touch the lake at its outlet), and the federal government had no plans to extend those boundaries. Basswood Lake was considered the jumping off place to the wilderness, not the wilderness itself.

Furthermore, Olson already was known locally as a staunch preservationist. He had participated in the fights to keep roads and hydropower developments out of the canoe country, and founded a local chapter of the Izaak Walton League. By the late 1930s local opponents of wilderness preservation threatened to use their influence to have him removed as dean of the Ely Junior College unless he toned down his activism. But Olson was not one to retreat under fire. Writing for a charter membership to the Wilderness Society in 1935, he asked to be included as one "who has never learned to compromise when the question of wilderness has come up."[3]

In subtle ways, however, Olson *did* compromise the wilderness. The evidence appears in his advertising and in his personal papers, and shows that Olson helped promote the image of the canoe country as a fishing paradise.

Olson's Border Lakes Outfitters was the only Ely business to regularly advertise in all three leading outdoor magazines. Most tourist operators, if they advertised nationally at all, did so only in **Sports Afield,** not only because it was the leader, but because it was published in Minneapolis and gave much more coverage to the canoe country than did the other magazines. Olson's ad beckoned readers to "make this vacation different: take a wilderness canoe trip," and continued:

> Follow with pack and canoe the travel lanes of Indian and Voyageur through the SUPERIOR NATIONAL FOREST and QUETICO PROVINCIAL PARK of Ontario, Canada. Thousands of lakes and rivers where you can cruise and camp undisturbed for weeks or months, fish in virgin waters, photograph big game, explore new country. The greatest wilderness canoe area on the continent.[4]

Olson's ad emphasized adventure and retreat more than it did fishing, and so did not promote the image of a fishing paradise nearly as much as did the ads of most other resorts and outfitters. But Border Lakes *was* a business, and the way to increase business was to attract a variety of tourists. The company's mail-out brochure, written by Olson, showed an ambivalence that allowed the fishing paradise image to gain a foothold in the canoe country.

"For those who seek solitude and escape from the usual resort atmosphere, the wilderness is waiting," Olson wrote in his brochure:

> If you want the maximum in strenuous physical adventure, you will want to cruise, and for you there are countless lakes and rivers to explore, portages to cut and virgin fishing territory to open...

On the other hand, though you may want this sort of trip,
you feel that it is a little too strenuous to be entirely
enjoyable. Then take a guide or packer or both to do all
of the routine work, leaving all of your time for fishing,
exploring, taking photographs, or whatever you like best
to do.

Perhaps, you do not want to travel at all, but have come
up primarily for rest and relaxation. Then let us establish
a permanent tent camp for you somewhere along the
border wilderness, where you can read, swim, fish and
loaf to your heart's content.[5]

By trying to attract the business of those who did not want to paddle
and portage canoes, Olson unintentionally helped promote Fishing
Paradise. He advertised a comfortable wilderness, as did resort owners
and outboard motor manufacturers. The Border Lakes pamphlet also
made it clear that fishing was a key attraction:

The finest fresh water game fishing is to be found in these
border lakes. Here are waiting for your lure, the mighty
lake trout, great northern and walleyed pike and the
fighting largemouth bass. In hundreds of these lakes you
will find the kind of fishing that heretofore you have only
read about.[6]

But Olson did more than publicize Quetico-Superior fishing; he
altered its character and redefined the region's environmental boundaries in the process. He introduced a new species to the ecosystem, the
smallmouth bass.

It was not a far-fetched idea. The smallmouth was a Minnesota native,
naturally occurring throughout the Mississippi River drainage basin to
the south of the Quetico-Superior. In the early 1900s, loggers had
successfully introduced the species to the Lake of the Woods region,
just west of the canoe country. At least until 1940, however, there were
none in the Quetico-Superior.[7]

In September 1939, Olson wrote to Ken Reid, the executive director of the Izaak Walton League. Olson said he had completed applications to stock smallmouth bass in Burntside and Basswood lakes, and also hoped to put them in Knife Lake. "I agree with you that this little experiment might really mean something to this country in the future," Olson wrote.

> If they take here the way they did in the Lake of the Woods country, we will really have something to be proud of.
>
> From Basswood and Knife the bass will spread to all of the border lakes, both American and Canadian and it might be that eventually the entire Quetico-Superior will be stocked. That is something worth working toward.[8]

Olson brought the first shipments to Basswood and Knife lakes in 1940, and repeated the stocking for several years. The Fish and Wildlife Service, the Forest Service, and the Minnesota Fish and Game Departments all participated in the program started by Olson and Reid, stocking smallmouth in such lakes as Basswood, Knife, and nearby Newfound and Moose. Olson's last stocking apparently took place late in October, 1944, when he and Superior National Forest ranger Bill Trygg planted smallmouth in Sarah and Robinson lakes, both of which are across the international border in Quetico Provincial Park.[9]

By the end of 1943 Olson knew the bass were taking hold. In a letter to *Outdoor America,* he enclosed what he called "the final proof" — a picture of him holding a two-and-a-half-pound smallmouth from Basswood Lake. Ken Reid predicted he and Olson would receive "the heart-felt thanks" of thousands of anglers who thought of the small-mouth bass as "a king amongst fresh water game fish."[10]

The smallmouth bass spread throughout the border lakes as Olson had predicted, with two results: the bass changed environmental boundary conditions and added to the image of the area as a fishing paradise. Gillnet records showed increasing concentrations of smallmouth between 1950 and the early 1970s, and decreasing concentrations of walleye, leading a number of people to conclude that the bass outcompeted walleye for the yellow perch that both species eat. This circumstantial evidence, however, does not seem to reflect accurately what happened. The only in-depth study of Quetico-Superior lakes concluded that competition for food "was probably not the principal factor" in the walleye decline. The researchers found that, contrary to common belief, both walleye and smallmouth bass eat a variety of food; perch accounted for just one percent of the smallmouth's summer diet.[11]

Research in Wisconsin has shown that long-term climatic changes likely are the most important factor in smallmouth bass and walleye interactions. Smallmouth prefer warmer temperatures than do walleye; at the northern edge of their range, such as in the Quetico-Superior, they will grow and reproduce best during warmer-than-average summers. That was the condition occurring throughout the 1940s and 1950s, particularly during the early stocking years when the bass were just becoming established. In the 1960s and 1970s, summer temperatures dropped below normal, and gillnet records showed a declining number of smallmouth bass in the canoe country.[12]

The above-normal temperatures of the 1940s and 1950s did not necessarily stress the walleye population. Walleyes prefer cooler temperatures, but seem to be very adaptable. The Wisconsin research suggests that predation may have been a factor in the walleye decline. Adult smallmouth and walleye will eat each other's young; when climatic trends favor the smallmouth, the greater numbers of adult bass may eat greater numbers of walleye fry, suppressing the walleye population. When cooler trends favor walleye, the reverse may occur. Complicating an accurate understanding of the process, however, is the unknown effect of the continuous stocking of both species. But at the very least, bringing smallmouth bass into the Quetico-Superior added a new environmental boundary that limits walleye populations when the climate is warmer than average.[13]

Nobody at the time, of course, knew what effect the smallmouth might have on other fish populations. Olson conceivably could have had some reservations, given his educational background. He had earned a master's degree in animal ecology in 1930 from the University of Illinois, studying under Victor Shelford, the field's leading scholar. But, while ecologists might have become concerned about introducing an exotic species from another part of the world, few, if any, would have thought twice about transplanting a fish to an adjacent watershed. Olson apparently expressed no doubts at the time.

The introduction of smallmouth bass also had an impact upon perceptual boundaries, however, substantially increasing the area's reputation as a fishing paradise. By the late 1950s, articles began to highlight the "blue-ribbon smallmouth water" of the Quetico-Superior.[14] A canoe country smallmouth won *Field and Stream* magazine's national contest in 1965. *Outdoor Life* listed Basswood and Saganaga lakes among the nation's best for bass fishing. It especially praised Basswood:

> This lake holds more lunker smallmouth bass than many lakes now enjoying international fame as bass spots....Here's what one of the top guides at Basswood writes: "A party of four New York doctors landed 1,682 smallmouth bass in eight days during July 1957, releasing all but 12 kept for frying."[15]

By initiating the smallmouth bass stocking program, and through his work with the Border Lakes Outfitters, Sigurd Olson helped promote the image of the Quetico-Superior as a fishing paradise. Certainly the prime motive for introducing the smallmouth was to promote tourism. It is in this sense, rather than in the environmental effects of the bass program, that he unintentionally compromised the wilderness, for the publicity helped attract hundreds, perhaps thousands, of anglers who saw the area in a way that differed from Olson's perspective. They wanted to stay at rustic resorts, travel by motorboats or seaplanes into the wilderness, catch lots of big fish, and get back to the lodge in time for drinks and dinner. During the same period in which Olson added to the area's reputation as a fishing paradise, however, he developed and publicly committed himself to a philosophy that put him at odds with some of the commercial activities he inadvertently had helped promote.

When Olson moved to Ely in 1923, he saw wilderness as a place where he could escape from the weightlessness of modern life through intense physical recreation. He also sought in wilderness a sense of spiritual fulfillment to replace his no-longer-satisfactory Baptist faith. His desire for escape made him see the Quetico-Superior as a refuge from civilization, a sanctuary. His desire for spiritual experiences led him to see the canoe country as a sacred place, where he could *feel* a sense of oneness with nature. Olson dreamed of becoming a successful freelance writer. He wanted to be an essayist, emphasizing the intangible and spiritual benefits of wilderness. He found, however, that outside of the small-circulation, conservation group magazines it was hard to get such material published. Editors wanted adventure, not philosophy. In rejecting one feature, **Outdoor Life** called it "too pastoral for our audience," and added, "It fails to convey the thrills and excitement of traveling and fishing that roadless wilderness."[16] Another critic advised, "If you really want to sell stories, Mr. Olson, you simply must accelerate the action....In addition, we'd suggest that you try some new themes, instead of keeping to the north country entirely, since there just isn't a market for this type of thing. With action, and plenty of it, yes, but not in the presentation you've given us."[17]

The demand of outdoor magazine editors for action amounted to <u>de facto</u> support for the fishing paradise image, because writers could most easily provide action by focusing on fishing. Olson, seeking to become an established writer, wrote such articles as "Fishin' Jewelry," "Cruising in the Arrowhead," "Spring Fever" and "The Immortals of Argo," all of which played up the fishing paradise image.[18]

Still, with persistence, Olson managed to get bits and pieces of his wilderness philosophy into articles, and occasionally published an entire essay. He considered the article "Search for the Wild" his first breakthrough. In the article, published in the May 1932 **Sports Afield,** Olson professed his belief that deep within each human being is an instinctive desire for the primitive lifestyle our species led for millions of years. It would take hundreds or thousands of years of adapting to urban civilization, he wrote, before this "racial memory" noticeably fades. Meanwhile, this need for experiencing the primitive conditions of wilderness is "a deeply rooted cancer gnawing forever at the illusion of contentment with things as they are." Denying the call leads to "frayed nerves, loss of enthusiasm and appetite for present modes of existence."[19]

Despite what a man may say, Olson wrote in "Search for the Wild," it isn't for the fishing or hunting that he goes into the wilderness, but to satisfy this subconscious need to maintain close ties to his primitive heritage. The real goal "is that intangible something he calls 'the Wild.'" He gets pleasure from sun and clouds, finding rare flowers, watching a beaver, or "listening to the whistle of wings over a marsh."[20]

It became increasingly evident to Olson that strict limits on economic exploitation were necessary to protect these intangible values. An essay he wrote in January, 1941 indicates he had come to understand the naivete of the typical American preference for both rural values and unlimited technological development. The essay was about a late afternoon walk he had recently taken along the Moose Lake Road northeast of Ely. For more than an hour he had been forced into the deep snow on the shoulder of the road while logging trucks roared by, and he was afraid he'd never find a moment of peace to enjoy the forest around him. But then the trucks stopped coming, and Olson stepped back onto the hard road and walked softly, listening. Soon he stopped:

> I had not long to wait, for over the darkening hills came the note of a great horned owl, hoo - hoooo - hoo - hoooooooo — and an answering note much deeper and more resonant than the first - hoo - hooooo - hoo - hooooooooooo - . Back and forth went the booming, haunting calls of Bufo virginianus and with them went the fear of death to the cowering snowshoes [hares] in the alder swamps, to the budding partridge in the groves of aspen, to countless waiting birds and animals for miles

around. That call was the most feared hunting call in the wild. It came again and again and for the moment, I was far from the road and trucks and civilization itself were forgotten. As I listened, a swift vision came to me of big timber and miles of wilderness, lonely valleys bathed in moonlight, rivers and lake shores where there were still no sounds but those of the wild.

Then I was conscious of a sound as of a great wind coming out of the north, as though a storm was breaking over the country that might tear every tree from its roots and at that moment, the calling of the horned owls stopped. The sound of storm increased until it seemed as though it would engulf me and every living thing on earth. Blinding lights burst over the hill behind me and a hurricane of shrieking metal roared out of the night. Desperately, I sprang for the side of the road as an empty truck sped by. The interval was over.[21]

Olson's imagery shows that he was not simply a sentimentalist praising the peace and harmony he found in nature. He was deeply aware that the values long attached by Americans to a wild or rural landscape were being annihilated by the force of another long-held American value: technological progress. Olson's description of the logging truck, that "hurricane of shrieking metal," is an image that has been used by a number of the best American writers since Hawthorne. Historian Leo Marx, who labels this "the machine in the garden" image, says, "It is remarkable how evocative the simple device is, especially when we consider that at bottom it consists of nothing more complicated than noise clashing through harmony....[But] Like the focal point of a complicated visual pattern, this elemental, irreducible dissonance contains the whole in small." The roar of progress' symbol, the machine, replaces nature's peace with anxiety and a sense of dislocation.[22]

Among those who have engaged in this sophisticated kind of romantic pastoralism were Thoreau, Melville, Twain and Henry Adams, each of whom understood that the symbol of an ideal rural landscape lost its meaning in the face of technology's domination. Each one took a more deterministic view than the one before. Adams closed his book, *The Education of Henry Adams,* with a picture of civilization out of control. None of these writers could conceive of a new vision that could take over the role of the rural ideal and also serve as a check on technology. At best they could realize an individual satisfaction, as did Thoreau, who decided that meaning and value could not be found in the physical world, but only in the world of mind.

The conflict between rural values and economic progress was not an easy thing for most Americans to recognize. The pastoral dream had achieved such mythic stature that they wanted to believe in its reality, despite all evidence that they had let it slip away. Americans had come to depend upon its static view of history, its romanticism, its nostalgia, and its simple answers as a crutch to use in an increasingly complex world. And yet they were the ones who were making the world complex, for they wanted all the new things that the consumer culture had to offer. Americans were enticed by the prospect of an ever-rising standard of living, but nostalgic for simpler times and traditional values, and did not want to make an explicit choice.

It was this ambivalent attitude toward modern society that led to the resort buildup in the American half of the Quetico-Superior. Thousands of tourists wanted to experience the simple life associated with the wilderness, but did not want to forego the comforts of civilization. The resort owners met this demand, as well as the demand to provide lots of fishing action, and so the canoe country became widely viewed as a fishing paradise.

Those — such as Olson — who provided comforts to tourists, who helped build up the area's image as a fishing paradise, were not anti-wilderness. They depended on the wilderness for their livelihood, and often as not had themselves spent a number of summers traveling and fishing the border lakes before deciding to start a business there. They loved the canoe country, and if they failed to see that unrestricted tourism would destroy the wilderness, it likely was because they entertained the same ambivalent feelings as did most Americans. As

Olson's career shows, it was very easy to misunderstand the naivete of the pastoral dream, and therefore to advance the image of the Quetico-Superior as a fishing paradise.

The arrival of a new machine in the garden, however, shattered the complacent ignorance of many, and forced a bitter conflict that set national precedents for wilderness preservation. The seaplane, much more than the outboard motor, threw the primitive wide open to modernity.

Sportsmen began flying seaplanes not long after World War I, but the machines were dangerously unreliable. The planes became safer during the 1930s, and outdoor magazines began giving them favorable coverage. In October, 1930, **Sports Afield** became the first of the leading outdoor magazines to establish a monthly aviation column, telling its readers that airplanes would "improve the fishing" by spreading it out over a wider number of lakes.[23] In his first column, Charles W. "Speed" Holman, a noted stunt flier, told about flying over the Quetico-Superior region:

> At any place in the northern wilderness country, at an altitude of 10,000 feet, as many as fifty to one hundred lakes can be seen, and nearly every one of them is an ideal landing field....Below you are lakes not even on the regular canoe routes — virgin fishing lakes.

> If you are on a fishing trip and using a plane for transportation, it doesn't make much difference which direction you take, just so you get to some real fishing grounds. If you are traveling by canoe, you give quite some study to the map, lingering cautiously over the spots marked, "Portage." Your route usually is determined by the number and length of the portages.[24]

Holman made it clear that the seaplane broke through the environmental boundaries of portages, which had limited the number of people traveling into the wilderness. The longer or more difficult the portages to reach a given spot, the fewer the people who went there. These boundaries had also limited the advance of the outboard motor. The seaplane, however, was bound only by the size of its landing field, and all but the smallest lakes qualified.

The ease with which the seaplane could break through environmental boundaries gave a new significance to the area's political boundaries. The roughly one million acres within Superior National Forest's three wilderness areas (which by 1939 were reclassified as "roadless areas") contained 113,000 acres of state land and 135,000 acres of private land. The latter were open to commercial development, and entrepreneurs saw a golden opportunity to build fly-in fishing resorts. Surrounded by federally protected wilderness, with air travel the only easy access, they had built-in monopolies on their private preserves.

The first two fly-in resorts were built in 1940 within a hundred yards of the international border on Crooked Lake, one of the favorites of canoeists. By 1944, nine Ely-area resorts advertised fly-in fishing trips. But the real explosion occurred after World War II. *Outdoor Life* predicted what would happen as thousands of pilots returned home and aircraft industries geared excess factory machinery for the consumer culture: "In the next ten years they will cause the most rapid expansion of outdoor sports since the popularization of the auto."[25] In 1945, as the war came to a close, construction began on 17 new resorts in the roadless areas, and fly-in fishing received national promotion from such magazines as *Outdoor Life*, which published features titled "Plane Talk for Sportsmen," "Fly Your Own Plane in 1946," and "I Went By Plane — So Can You!"[26]

Many of those who flew enjoyed an aesthetic experience dominated by a sense of pure freedom — not unlike what many canoeists felt. But the key difference was the way in which they found that freedom. Canoeists found it by yielding to the forces of nature. Fliers, however, found it by gaining power over nature:

> Have you ever flown cross-country at night with the blackness all around you, the song of your engine the only

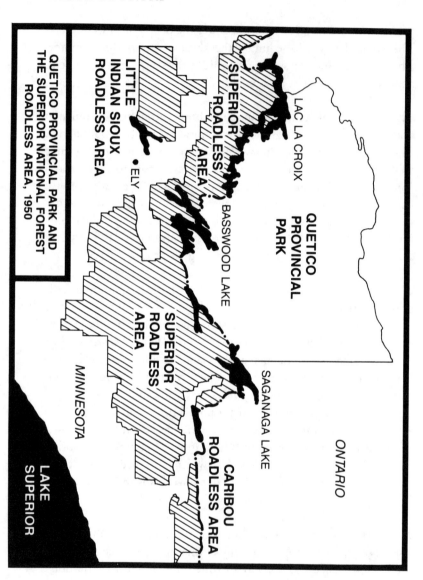

Figure 12 - The way the boundary waters area appeared following WWII

sound in the stillness, seen the stars overhead and the lights of cities and farms below — and felt that tearing, choking feeling of absolute supremacy and power that is almost overwhelming in its immensity?

There is a power and a limitless breadth to flying that is like nothing you have ever felt before. It sends the blood singing through your veins — an exaltation flooding through your very soul.[27]

This sense of power, however, may not have been felt by the passengers being flown in to wilderness lakes. Geographer Yi-Fu Tuan argues that merely riding in a plane diminishes the sense of power: "Passengers have no control over the machine and cannot feel it as an extension of their organic powers. Passengers are luxury crates — safely belted in their seats — being transported passively from point to point."[28]

To the passengers, then, flying was not an end in itself, but a means to an end — the abundant fishing, wild scenery, and comfortable accommodations of Fishing Paradise. The advertisement for Curtain Falls Fishing Camp, a fly-in resort on Crooked Lake, best summed up the advantages of a private business located in the middle of a government- protected wilderness. After describing the available species of fish and the resort's modern comforts, the ad said: "I pray to the Good Lord daily that my camp remain Roadless. Doubtless you are aware of what auto highways mean to Good Fishing. — Amen."[29]

To many of those who saw the Quetico-Superior as a fishing paradise, the seaplane was a godsend. They could fly out of Ely, be at a secluded wilderness lake in twenty minutes, catch more fish than they could legally keep, and be back in town by suppertime. Or they could fly to an interior resort, such as the one at Curtain Falls, and have guides take them out on day trips by motorboat. Physical durability no longer was necessary to reach even the most remote lakes. The wilderness was open to all.

Not everyone who saw the canoe country as a fishing paradise, however, was joyful about the seaplane. In particular, the owners of Basswood Lake resorts could not have been too happy, because the seaplane took away their great geographical advantage. Any resort owner could now easily transport guests to any lake. The Basswood Lake resorts not only lost their geographical advantage, but were forced to go to the expense of hiring pilots so that they could compete with the outlying resorts and the new fly-in resorts.

But the airplane also allowed people to fly in to the Quetico-Superior without stopping in *any* bordering communities. By 1947 pilots from Duluth, Minneapolis, Chicago, Cleveland and St. Louis advertised weekend fly-in trips, and one pilot supposedly advertised a non-stop flight from Florida to Crooked Lake.[30] Even the local canoe outfitters eventually were forced by competition to fly in fishing-minded parties.

Most unhappy with the seaplanes were those to whom catching fish was less important than escaping from civilization. To them the Quetico- Superior was a sanctuary — to some of them a sacred place — and hearing or seeing an airplane greatly upset them. They had been able to get away from nearly all of the motorboats by going a few portages into the wilderness, but they could not get away from the planes. By 1948 Ely was the largest freshwater seaplane base on the continent. Nearly seventy planes were each making up to twenty round trips a day into the wilderness, sometimes landing alongside canoe parties to offer rides at $2.50 per person. Pilots cached motor-boats on remote lakes in both the Superior Roadless Area and Quetico Provincial Park, and set up permanent camps on a number of the best sites. Canoeists sometimes paddled until late in the day, searching for an open spot.[31]

Those who saw the canoe country as a sanctuary reacted by staging a two-part national campaign: first, to get the U.S. Congress to pass a bill authorizing the Forest Service to buy private land within the roadless areas; and second, to ban private planes from flying into the roadless areas.[32] The campaign was especially urgent because Ontario was ready to open the Quetico to roads and lease resort sites if the Americans failed to preserve their side of the canoe country. Such development would ruin any chance of a United States-Canada treaty establishing an international wilderness, but Ontario businessmen were tired of seeing Quetico Park provide economic benefits to only Minnesota resort owners and outfitters.[33]

The President's Quetico-Superior Committee, led by Chicago lawyer Charles S. Kelly, worked on the anti-airplane campaign. Committee member Ernest Oberholtzer, who had led the earlier fight against E.W. Backus and proposed the international wilderness, again played an active role. Other key campaign planners included Frank B. Hubachek, Kelly's law partner and part-owner of Wilderness Outfitters and Basswood Lodge, the largest resort on that lake; Ken Reid, the executive director of the Izaak Walton League; and Jay Price, the Forest Service official in charge of the region that included Superior National Forest.

These men had good connections in the legislative and executive branches of the U.S. government, but few ties to Canada, so they hired Ralph P. Wentworth, a New York publicist who had many Canadian contacts from his wartime work with a clothing drive. His first assignments were to meet supporters of the program in both countries, to raise funds, and to organize a Canadian group similar to the President's Committee.[34]

While Wentworth knew a lot about publicity, he knew little about wilderness or the Quetico-Superior program. Kelly and his associates needed someone who could arouse public opinion against airplanes and fly-in resorts, someone who knew the wilderness intimately and had friends on both sides of the border. Late in 1947 they turned to Sigurd Olson, who recently had resigned from the Ely Junior College to devote full time to his writing.[35] The request for help gave Olson an opportunity to firmly establish his writing career and to promote a cause in which he strongly believed. He accepted. During the next two years Olson crisscrossed the country giving speeches, wrote articles for a number of U.S. and Canadian magazines, and created a documentary film. He spread the image of the canoe country as a sanctuary, and portrayed the seaplane as the evil in the garden. An article titled

"Wings Over the Wilderness" was typical.[36] Olson wrote about the history of the effort to preserve the canoe country, and wove that into an experiential narrative:

> It was our third day out. We had come down the international boundary chain of lakes through Basswood, Birch and Knife and were heading to the south to find a spot we had been dreaming about for months. It was a small lake we were going to, but it was full of trout. It was quiet and secluded and off the beaten routes of travel to the north.
>
> Very few knew of this little lake, only some trappers and cruisers like ourselves. It wasn't important enough to attract great numbers of people. No resort would ever want to start there. No one had ever given it a name. It was as virgin and unsung as any bit of wilderness in the whole Quetico-Superior country.

After reaching the lake, the two caught some trout, and found the peace and solitude of which they had dreamed. But at dusk their serenity dissolved as they heard an airplane to the south. Soon it appeared:

> We prayed it would go on, head for one of the larger lakes beyond, but to our dismay it began to circle, widely at first, then in closer and closer spirals, its roar and vibration engulfing the entire valley beneath. Perhaps the pilot was looking for a landmark. Surely no one would charter a flight into this tiny isolated body of water with so many greater lakes to choose from. No one knew of the trout, just a few of the guides and a trapper or two and they all felt exactly as we. This was one spot we'd sworn to keep to ourselves, one last sanctuary of the wilderness we used to know.

Dashing their hopes, the plane landed. Olson described how the number of fly-ins had mushroomed, and how the interior resorts took advantage of the roadless area designation:

> The two resorts on Crooked Lake and the one on Lady Boot Bay were typical. Completely surrounded by federal lands, they were actually private preserves seemingly created by the government for their own personal exploitation. Guaranteed immunity from competition by federal decree, the owners blessed the foresight of the Forest Service, lauded the roadless area plan that had given them such profitable sanctuary.

After explaining the urgency of banning airplanes from the Superior National Forest roadless areas, Olson said such measures would have to be taken elsewhere as well, because "wings were casting the shadow of gloom over all of the primitive regions of the continent, a shadow that might mean the end of all wilderness experience in America." He ended the article with a return to the narrative:

> As though to echo my thoughts, a loon called long and mournfully out on the open lake. Bill stirred restlessly in his sleeping bag, sat up suddenly and rubbed his eyes.

> "Daylight?" he asked, "Let's get going. There's a little lake about a day's travel from here. Trout in there, too."

> "Still dark," I said, "better go back to sleep."

> He groaned, burrowed down deeply in his bag. In the morning we'd start traveling again, find some place where the shadow of wings was still unknown.

By using the machine-in-the-garden technique, Olson highlighted the clash between the fishing paradise and sanctuary images of the canoe country. For nearly thirty years the media had portrayed the Quetico-Superior as virgin wilderness. Olson's depiction of the airplane was meant to crash against the perceptual boundaries of those who believed the area would be wild forever. He wanted to shock readers into action.

Olson articles promoting an airplane ban in the canoe country appeared in such other American publications as *The Christian Science Monitor, Sports Afield, Nature Magazine, Living Wilderness, National Parks Magazine* and *Outdoor America*, and in Canada's *National Home Monthly* and *Forest and Outdoors*.[37] To put pressure on Congress, Charles Kelly ordered that copies of one Olson article be sent to all newspapers in Minnesota, Wisconsin, Michigan, Illinois, Indiana, Missouri and Ohio. Olson, a member of the Outdoor Writers Association of America, sent another 960 copies to that group and also reached members through its newsletter.[38]

Favorable editorials soon began appearing. By the time the airplane conflict was over, the image of the canoe country as a sanctuary received support in such newspapers as the *New York Times, Washington Post, Chicago Sun-Times, Milwaukee Journal,* and newspapers across Minnesota.[39] The campaign also generated favorable coverage in the leading outdoor magazines and in the *Saturday Evening Post,* in addition to conservation group publications.[40]

Olson's thirty-minute, color documentary film, "Wilderness Canoe Country," played a key role in the campaign. Produced by the President's Quetico-Superior Committee and narrated by Paul Harvey, the film dramatically captured the machine in the garden image.[41] In one scene, Olson and his son Bob paddled past such historic sites as Basswood Falls, where French voyageurs had lost their lives, and a set of Ojibway pictographs at the eastern end of Crooked Lake. As the pair rounded a point and caught the full sweep of Crooked, a seaplane droned in the distance. The plane approached, engine roaring, and landed nearby, water spraying wildly. Harvey, in his trademark staccato, exclaimed, "Twenty minutes from town? With no portaging, no paddling, no fighting the wind, no overnight camps. Crooked Lake — a place to catch a limit of fish...just a colored panorama from the air."

Later, the father and son reached Curtain Falls, one of the canoe country's most famous scenic attractions. Next to the falls was a fly-in resort. "There at last was the proof!" declared Harvey. "Where once a timbered shore, now boathouses, docks and cabins, even a plane moored alongside? It was out of place, almost unreal in that setting."

The father and son turned their canoe and headed north for the Quetico, where they knew they could still find some wilderness. They soon passed a lone canoe. "Canoes are a part of the legend of wilderness travel," Harvey reminded, "part of the silence and the ancient scene. A hundred canoes could have been on the lakes nearby and we wouldn't have known they were there, but one plane and the feeling of isolation is destroyed." If conservationists lost the battle against airplanes, Harvey said at the end of the film, if an international wilderness wasn't soon set aside, "the wilderness canoe country will live only in our memories."

The Quetico-Superior Committee held a special showing in Chicago for the news media. Those present included outdoor writers from the Chicago newspapers and from the leading outdoor magazines; and reporters from the *Christian Science Monitor*, Associated Press, United Press International, and NBC. Washington, D.C. showings were arranged for Forest Service, Congressional and White House staff. The Committee sold or loaned twenty-eight copies of the film to such groups as the Forest Service, the Minnesota Conservation Commission, the University of Minnesota Extension Service, the Minneapolis Public Library, the Sierra Club, the Wilderness Society and the American Forestry Association.[42]

"Wilderness Canoe Country" was a big success. The director of Minnesota's Bureau of Information said his agency's copy was booked three months in advance, and he had "never witnessed a more enthusiastic reception of an outdoor film." With Olson's permission, Detroit TV station WXYZ aired the film, and viewers began writing to Olson asking how they could help ban planes from the wilderness. But most important was local reaction. Because of the film, Olson wrote, seventy-five organizations in northeastern Minnesota had gone on record in favor of the airplane ban. Only ten had opposed.[43]

117

It was perhaps the best organized and financed wilderness campaign up to that time. By making extensive use of the mass media, wilderness supporters were able to give social strength to the image of the canoe country as a sanctuary. The publicity, in turn, generated political strength. Six months after Olson began working, the campaign achieved its first goal. On June 23, 1948, President Harry S. Truman signed into law the Thye-Blatnik Act, which gave the Forest Service its first authority to purchase land for recreational purposes. It was the second time — the first was when the Shipstead-Nolan Act passed in 1930 — that Congress had taken steps to preserve wilderness. And for the second time, the wilderness that had stirred Congress to action was the Quetico-Superior. Blatnik told Olson, "The publicity which you gave this through your excellent magazine and newspaper articles certainly brought results, for so many Congressmen told me of receiving letters and wires from interested organizations and individuals."[44]

Those who supported the image of the Quetico-Superior as a sanctuary achieved their other campaign objective late in 1949, when President Truman signed an executive order creating an airspace reservation over the three roadless areas. The order barred pilots from flying over the protected area at an altitude of less than 4,000 feet, and prohibited landings. It was the first airspace reservation set aside for reasons other than national security, and the courts, in upholding the order, gave wilderness preservation its first legal backing as a legitimate government purpose. Years later, in the 1960 Multiple Use Act and the 1964 Wilderness Act, Congress extended that recognition nationwide.

After the U.S. Supreme Court refused to grant a final appeal to several fly-in resort owners, they started avoiding the law by making use of political boundaries. They began landing their planes in Quetico Park and taxiing to their border lake resorts. In response, Ontario established its own air ban in 1955. It had become obvious that international cooperation was necessary if either side of the Quetico-Superior was to be preserved as wilderness.

But there was another, unintended effect of the wilderness campaign:

it fueled local animosity toward outsiders. A deteriorating rural economy made this inevitable. In 1927, nearly 80 percent of the rural land in northeastern Minnesota had been on the tax roles. By 1945, more than 60 percent was delinquent. Many local citizens believed all sources of economic development should be encouraged. The *Ely Miner* advocated this viewpoint, arguing that it couldn't see any sense in "closing established resorts and discouraging new wilderness endeavors."[45] But local economic worries seldom received sympathetic coverage by non-local media. Unable to draw attention to their side of the story, and highly aware of the favorable treatment given to wilderness supporters, many local citizens grew resentful.

Their frustration was reflected in the letters they wrote and the publications they produced. John Smrekar, an Ely Chamber of Commerce spokesman, sent out a form letter trying to arouse protest against the proposed airspace reservation. "IT'S UN-AMERICAN, IT'S UN-DEMOCRATIC...IT'S A CHALLENGE TO FREE ENTERPRISE," he cried. "WE NEED YOUR HELP BADLY." Another Ely resident wrote to Agriculture Secretary Charles Brannan, saying local citizens "should be given preference to any other groups living outside the area who are not familiar with the problems and do not know what is best for the area."[46]

As the conflict grew intense, some local citizens spread rumors of outside conspiracy. Most notable was a publication by Basswood Lake resident Leo Chosa. In a booklet called *Isolate and Exploit,* Chosa argued that wilderness proponents were "stooges" of the timber industry. The federal government, he said, was planning to get people out of the roadless areas — isolate them — so that the power and timber companies, assisted by the U.S. Forest Service — "four words that cover more skuldugery [sic] than any other four words in the English language" — could exploit it.[47]

"With cleverly loaded moving pictures (like loaded dice in a crap game) some taken in Canada for purposes of deception," Chosa wrote, "glib talking stooges have bustled about the country, far from the scene of exploitation to distract the attention of public spirited men and women." Banning the plane was essential to the government's purpose, he claimed, because the ban eliminated 98 percent of the area's use, and because "the airplane is the eyes of the public:" if people continued flying over the area they would see the big companies moving in and destroying the land. The Ely Chamber of Commerce printed seventy-five thousand copies of the eight-page booklet, and distributed them at Midwest sport shows and fly-in resorts.[48]

The airplane conflict turned local fears of outside control into almost a paranoia. When the owner of Ely radio station WXLT broadcast a news story about the crash of an airplane that was hauling dozens of fish over the legal limit, fly-in supporters responded with physical threats until he sold the station to them. Frank Hubachek also reported receiving death threats, and a small bomb exploded in the backyard of an Ely canoe outfitter.[49] This near-paranoid hatred of those who didn't toe the legitimized Ely Chamber of Commerce line was the local legacy of what area residents called "the air ban war." And the insider-outsider ethos colored canoe country debate for decades to come.

CHAPTER 7
SACRED PLACE

Unless we can preserve places where the endless spiritual needs of man can be fulfilled and nourished, we will destroy our culture and ourselves.

— *Sigurd F. Olson (1965)* [1]

On or about August 1945, to paraphrase Virginia Woolf, human character changed. The nuclear explosions at Hiroshima and Nagasaki jarred the perceptual boundaries of millions of people all over the world, perhaps especially in the United States, where citizens for the first time felt a chilling sense of vulnerability. As James Reston wrote in the New York Times, "In that terrible flash 10,000 miles away, men here have seen not only the fate of Japan, but have glimpsed the future of America."[2]

The sprawling, eerily beautiful mushroom cloud became the symbol of the modern dilemma: Scientific and technological advances could bring about the happiness and prosperity of the millennium, or a meaningless existence culminating in the irrevocable destruction of Armageddon. In the two decades after the war Americans seemed, on the surface, to be enjoying the former; the United States became the world's richest nation, and its population grew at an unprecedented rate. But Americans swallowed more than a million pounds a year of newly marketed tranquilizers, and most psychiatrists believed that mental illness had dramatically increased. Such problems showed the strain of participating in an increasingly complex and secularized technological order — a consumer culture — that could be destroyed slowly from within by mindless conformity and materialism, or at any moment from without by clouds of fire.

The fear of civilization's decline underlay the broad intellectual and cultural trends of nuclear age America, from the glittering skylines of

121

the largest cities to the sparkling waterways of the Quetico-Superior. One of the most significant developments was a growing concern for identifying absolute values.[3]

Americans were searching for meaning, and some of them found it in wilderness. Though relatively small in number, they were highly influential, and dominated the leading preservationist organizations. To these people, the canoe country was a sacred place. By paddling its waterways they not only escaped temporarily from the tensions of modern existence, but discovered cosmic truths that gave life purpose. After World War II they used their influence to force the Forest Service to adopt an increasingly strict interpretation of the sanctuary image. By 1980, the wilderness resorts were gone, logging was banned, and outboard motors and snowmobiles were greatly restricted.

The fight to ban airplanes from the canoe country had demonstrated widespread public appeal for the image of the area as a sanctuary. The case had attracted attention in newspapers and magazines across the United States and Canada, and editorials consistently emphasized the need for preserving remoteness and solitude. "The gift of tranquility, wherever found, is beyond price," said the *New York Times* in an editorial supporting the airplane ban.[4] The response undoubtedly reflected weariness over post-war tension, as well as a realization that America's record production of quantity was not necessarily yielding a life of quality.

After the courts upheld the presidential order in 1952 and 1953, local tourist promoters used the new boundary as proof of the canoe country's wildness. The Minnesota Arrowhead Association told prospective visitors that off the main canoe trails they could "gaze upon a scene never before witnessed by human eyes...because federal laws have declared parts of it [the Superior National Forest] cannot be entered for commercial venture." Wilderness Outfitters of Ely emphasized that "this is the only Lake Region in which the airplane is prohibited, making it truly a Canoeist's Paradise." And the Boundary Waters Canoe Outfitters, also of Ely, said in its brochure, "Airplanes are banned in the area, leaving it accessible only by canoe.... Peace and quiet prevails — a welcome change of pace from the hustle and bustle of everyday city life."⁵

The leading outdoor writers also used the airplane ban to demonstrate the canoe country's wildness. "It's an air-conditioned, evergreen wilderness that will always remain a wilderness, thanks to joint legislation both in Canada and the United States that prohibits even air travel *over* the area," wrote Erwin A. Bauer in *Sports Afield. Field and Stream's* Mel Ellis agreed: "Here, by Presidential edict, tranquility has been preserved, it is hoped forever....the only man-made sound is the slapping of a canoe in fast water or the ring of an axe as a camper cuts firewood."⁶

These comments continued the forty-year-old tradition of exaggerating the Quetico-Superior's wildness. Resort ads still spoke of "virgin fishing," the city of Ely still advertised itself as "where the wilderness begins," and outfitters and feature writers still implied that all travel into the area was by canoe.⁷ But such statements — at least insofar as they suggested conditions on the American side of the border — were even more an exaggeration after World War II than in the 1920s. In 1951 there were more than thirty resorts in the Superior Roadless Areas, and about fifty private cabins. Outboard motors were common on all of the major water routes. About fifty-seven thousand people visited the roadless areas that summer — nearly thirty times the number just ten years earlier, and almost sixty times the number of voyageurs and Ojibway using the area at the peak of the fur trade.⁸

But that was only the beginning. The number of visitor days spent in the American portion of the Quetico-Superior skyrocketed from thirty-eight thousand in 1942 to more than six hundred thousand in 1966, which was far greater than the use of any other national forest wilderness.⁹ Some anglers used all-terrain vehicles to reach remote lakes, while others used dollies to pull boats across portages. Resort owners and guides cached boats along chains of lakes, with as many as ten at a portage. Canoeists encountered water skiers as far back as Knife Lake, and half a dozen two-story houseboats on Basswood Lake. There were traffic jams on portages, litter at campsites, and tests indicated unhealthy levels of coliform bacteria in nearly two dozen lakes. Even city-type violence reached the canoe country. In July, 1962, one man shot at two fishermen on Wood Lake and, with a partner, later robbed three anglers on the portage to the lake, forced them back to the road and stole their car.

A 1958 survey conducted by University of Minnesota sociologists showed that canoeists frequently were disappointed by the numbers of people they encountered. "They had apparently developed an image of the area which would provide them with more elbow room than that which many actually found," the researchers concluded.[10] For many years, articles and advertisements had proclaimed the Quetico-Superior a virgin wilderness. By the late 1950s many canoeists disagreed, and a number of them were ready to do something about it. If the canoe country *wasn't* a wilderness, they were going to make it so.

Their first objective, shared by the Forest Service, the President's Quetico-Superior Committee, and — at least at first — by the Ely Rod and Gun Club, was to get rid of the roadless area resorts and private cabins. But completing the task proved exceedingly divisive, partly because of political boundaries established in the 1930s, and partly because of a deteriorating local economy.

In 1936, as part of his program to bring relief to counties burdened by tax-default lands, President Franklin D. Roosevelt added 1.3 million acres to the Superior National Forest. This brought the forest's size up to 3.5 million acres and made it the nation's largest. Most of the added land was in the Basswood Lake cutover region — everything from the west end of the lake east to Saganaga Lake and north of the Kawishiwi River. The major canoe routes of the American side twisted through this section, and Roosevelt's action gave the Forest Service an unexpected opportunity to include the routes within the boundaries of what it at the time called the Superior Wilderness Area.

There was one problem. Basswood Lake already had half a dozen resorts and was the year-round home of several families. While the Forest Service had the power to bring the lake within the wilderness area boundaries, it did not have the authority to purchase the private land. But unless the agency bought the land and removed the buildings, the area hardly could be called wilderness.

The agency based its decision on environmental boundaries. Basswood was crucial to the integrity of the Quetico-Superior wilderness, because it provided the best access. Some of its residents had in 1935 erected tollgates across the Four Mile Portage in an unsuccessful attempt to force the government to build a road to the lake. Worried that the residents eventually would succeed, and realizing that a road to Basswood would make other, wilder lakes more accessible to developers, the Forest Service extended the boundaries of the Superior Wilderness Area to include all of Basswood Lake, including the Four Mile Portage. The agency changed the name, however, to Superior Roadless Area. Robert Marshall, Wilderness Society founder and chief of the Forest Service's Division of Recreation, thought the label "wilderness area" was hypocritical; also, the agency wanted to permit logging there.[11]

The Forest Service did not begin seriously to develop a strategy for buying out roadless area resorts until 1946, a year after it had begun consulting with local government officials to develop an acquisition bill. Working with Ernest Oberholtzer, as well as with Charles S. Kelly and other members of the President's Quetico-Superior Committee, the Forest Service ranked sections of the roadless area for possible purchase. The agency gave highest priority to the land within the Superior Roadless Area extending west from the northwestern edge of Basswood Lake to Lac La Croix, and to the land extending east from the eastern corner of Basswood Lake to Saganaga Lake. Next in priority were the remaining private lands in the Little Indian Sioux and Caribou roadless areas. Because of its extensive development, Basswood Lake ranked last.[12]

When the Thye-Blatnik Act became law in 1948, the Forest Service began purchasing resorts and cabins in the priority areas. By that time there were about twenty resorts and almost that many private cabins on Basswood, and the agency gave no public indication that it

125

intended to buy them. It still had not decided what to do. In 1950 Regional Forester Jay Price told the Ontario Department of Lands and Forests that he hoped to buy all of the undeveloped property so no more resorts and private cabins would be built, but that the Forest Service hadn't committed itself to buying the developed sites:

> The eventual status of Basswood is not easy to predict. It will no doubt depend upon the nature of the public interest that develops over the years. This is likely to be influenced to a considerable degree by what is done or not done north of the border. Personally I feel that the long range program should aim towards some degree of restoration of primitive conditions. As a practical matter, however, it is not likely that a great deal should or can be done about it until higher priority phases of the wilderness program are accomplished, except to prevent additional development through public acquisition of undeveloped tracts.[13]

By the end of 1955 the Forest Service realized that the $500,000 appropriated under the Thye-Blatnik Act would not cover even the priority purchases. The Act had increased property values because it forbade condemnation of developed tracts smaller than five hundred acres, but allowed condemnation of undeveloped sites. This ensured the monopolies of fly-in resort owners, increasing their profits and the eventual cost of acquisition to the government. When the number of people visiting the roadless areas grew from fifty-seven thousand in 1951 to more than eighty thousand in 1955, the Forest Service and the President's Quetico-Superior Committee decided that the public interest required a much more intensive purchase program that would include even the Basswood Lake developments. Congress agreed, and appropriated another $2 million for purchases.

The appropriation attracted little organized opposition in northeastern Minnesota, where the iron mines were producing near-record levels of ore. One of Ely's mines had closed in 1954, but three others still were operating, and International Nickel Company recently had acquired nearly eight thousand acres of land near the city and had applied for a 100- year mining lease. Test drilling had indicated a potentially large deposit of low-grade copper and nickel sulfides, and Ely citizens dreamed of a blossoming economy. The local tourist picture also was bright. Stan Pechaver, secretary for the Ely Chamber of Commerce, bragged to a Minneapolis reporter that four outfitting companies, nine motels, and fifty- five resorts had opened in the Ely area since the war.[14]

The lack of organized local opposition to the appropriation did not mean that the traditional insider-outsider ethos was declining. In the wake of the airplane ban and the Cold War, many Ely residents were susceptible to fears of threats from the outside. The pages of the *Ely Miner* were full of items that expressed these fears. The paper, for example, regularly published Civil Defense articles warning readers of impending doom. "The wide oceans that used to protect us have given way to the global bomber," said one. "Today we face more kinds of attack than ever before, and our danger is much greater."[15]

Fear of Soviet missiles easily translated into fear of socialism at home. "We are being taxed and bribed and lulled into socialism," said one editorial. "We'd better face the ugly facts now, before it is too late.? Editor and publisher Fred Childers decried the income tax as "socialistic...not one of us has a constitutional right remaining to one penny of our income." In case readers found it hard to worry about "a little socialism," the paper reminded them that "a Communist is nothing more than a Socialist in a hurry." The *Miner* published photos of alleged communists wanted by the FBI, even though they had last been seen a thousand or more miles away. Even local advertisements sometimes showed fear of outsiders. "Do Not Cash Checks For Strangers," warned the First National Bank.[16]

As long as the local economy was good, this insider-outsider ethos remained in the background, deep-seated but not intensely displayed. A change in fortune, however, could rapidly bring it to the fore. And as the Forest Service began spending its $2 million to buy roadless area resorts, Ely's optimistic vision of the future vanished into the wilderness. In 1957 the Chandler South Mine closed, pressure from wilderness groups convinced the Interior Department to deny International Nickel's application for a mining permit, and Minnesota Senator Hubert H. Humphrey introduced a bill to establish a national wilderness preservation system.

The mine closing was not a surprise, but the permit denial was, and local citizens blamed it on the pending wilderness bill. Childers wrote an editorial on July 18 calling Humphrey a "Brutus or Judas," and told readers the senator's bill would ban outboard motors, logging and mining.[17] The following week he wrote that the bill "will in its overall effect make Ely a ghost town:

> The curtailment of our three basic industries — mining, lumbering and tourist business — without hope of replacement leaves no other alternative....Who wants to take the risk of investment with the hard work it entails in a town that offers NO POTENTIAL for a reasonable return?[18]

Sigurd Olson, who was among the preservationists consulted for advice when the bill was written, told Humphrey that "the whole town is in an uproar" because of the editorials and because of similar broadcasts over radio station WELY. "The statement that people could lose their homes in Ely should the bill go through and that the whole economy of the area would be threatened is actually believed by many people," he said.[19]

Within days the bill was rewritten to specify that all current uses of the Superior Roadless Areas could continue, and the furor subsided. But the **Miner** continued to run front-page editorials throughout the summer and fall, denouncing the "wilderness craze," and the Ely Rod and Gun Club voted to oppose the bill.[20]

In September, 1958, more bad news hit Ely. The Zenith mine shut down, throwing nearly three hundred people out of work. It was the beginning of a six-year slump in Iron Range production as the industry began importing lower-priced ore from overseas, notably Venezuela. The iron frontier — responsible for nearly half of Ely-area employment — was petering out, and Childers thought it was absurd that the federal government should be buying up local resorts. He wrote an editorial that listed the Forest Service purchases since 1956, thirteen from Basswood Lake and seven from other roadless area lakes. "Count them, gentlemen," he said to Humphrey and other government officials, "there are 20 resorts GONE...and no new ones built to replace them and there has been very little enlargement of the remaining facilities. A terrific loss to Ely."[21]

At the end of 1958 investors told Ely officials they would reopen the Zenith Mine on the condition that the city convince the state legislature to remove the property tax on stockpiled ore. Desperate to bring jobs back, residents pushed the idea, and the legislature removed the tax. The mine reopened in March, 1959, and Ely returned to nearly full employment. But the cost was high — a $2 million drop in taxable valuations. Early in 1960, when Ely residents discovered a 45 percent increase in their property taxes, they fumed.[22]

At this inopportune time Representative John Blatnik asked Congress for another million dollars to help buy out the wilderness resorts and cabins. The Ely Chamber of Commerce, in an open letter to Blatnik published in the *Miner,* charged the government buyout program with responsibility for the plunging property valuations:

> Only a few days ago we were appealed to by one of our mining companies who pleaded they cannot continue operations under Ely's rising tax rates....Yet Ely's tax rate can go in only one direction — UP — because of our steadily declining valuations resulting from depressed business occasioned by the U.S. government's purchase and destruction of so many of our big resorts.[23]

When the appropriation passed in June, the Chamber was even more surprised to find that it included a condemnation clause. Chamber Manager Ted Wynn told *Miner* readers, "Our 'representatives' in

Congress even failed to appraise us that CONDEMNATION POW-
ERS were under consideration. Or did they avoid mentioning it?"[24]

Wynn, hired by the Chamber in 1959 to work full time at improving
Ely's economy, began writing front-page columns for the *Miner*,
blaming wilderness preservation for Ely's financial problems and
stirring insider-outsider resentment:

> Ely suffers from a disease seldom known to any other city,
> anywhere. We seem to be in the grip of "non-residentitus"
> — folks who live miles and miles away who make it their
> business to decide whether Ely prospers or withers....
>
> Don't you get fed up, too, with being pushed around?
> Then let's speak out. Tell the press. Tell our politicians.
> Tell the world. Tell them all to stop trying to mess around
> with our town's future.[25]

Sigurd Olson wanted to counteract the misstatements and resentment
spread by Wynn and the *Miner*, but Fred Childers rarely printed
letters sent to him by wilderness supporters.[26] Frank Hubachek
advised Olson to ignore the *Miner*, because any response would
simply provide the paper with "ammunition for more blasts" against
wilderness preservation:

> The crux of the Ely situation is that the Ely audience,
> almost 100 percent, feels it is losing a bushel of dollars by
> our program. To people in that situation, it is worse than
> useless, it is intensely aggravating, to be told we are
> working for the national good, not the local good. You
> can't expect a man who thinks we have just picked his
> pocket of $1,000 to be placated by being told that we gave
> the money to people in 49 other states.[27]

The buyout program continued unimpeded, and even accelerated in
1962. Congress appropriated $2 million in August — bringing the
total amount granted to $5.5 million — and told the Forest Service to

complete its purchases by June 30, 1963. The agency hadn't yet used its power of condemnation; now it had no choice. By March, 1963, the Forest Service negotiated settlements for seventy-eight properties, and condemned ten others.[28] Meanwhile, Ely's Zenith Mine shut down again, this time for good. The city's sacrifice of the stockpiled ore tax had bought three-and-a-half years of employment for 250 people.

The Forest Service completed the acquisition program on schedule in 1963, except for contested settlements. In July, the Forest Service announced it had condemned the last few resorts left on Basswood Lake. The government had purchased a total of thirty-three resorts and many more private cabins, and workers began tearing them down. They were dismantling Fishing Paradise. "Sounds more like communism than democracy," commented Childers in the *Miner*.[29]

Despite the amount of controversy the buyout program generated in Ely, it received little media attention elsewhere. The Thye-Blatnik Act of 1948 had created the necessary precedent, and the program had Forest Service support, so the extra appropriations approved during the 1950s and early 1960s were relatively routine. Getting the money required persistent work on the part of the Forest Service and leading preservationists, but there was no need for a communication campaign to arouse vast numbers of citizens.

During this period Ely tourist promoters continued working hard to maintain the image of the area as a fishing paradise. The Chamber of Commerce distributed tens of thousands of the city's summer tourist guides during late-winter sports shows throughout the Midwest, and sent them to tourist information bureaus and sporting goods stores. The sports shows often yielded newspaper, television and radio publicity. Ely promoters increased their coverage by giving fishing licenses and other goods to journalists. ABC commentator Paul Harvey regularly received a package of Ely-made hot bologna, and always gave the city a plug in a subsequent national broadcast. The Chamber of Commerce also produced at least two short films about the area that it loaned to interested cities and organizations.[30]

Despite local efforts, however, the Quetico-Superior received much less attention from the outdoor magazines than in the past. The three leading publications — **Field and Stream, Outdoor Life** and **Sports Afield** — had published nearly fifty feature articles about the canoe country during the 1930s. During the 1950s they published just ten. The fishing frontier had moved to northern Ontario; airplanes made it accessible, just as they had the remote lakes of the Quetico-Superior. Northern Ontario contained the "virgin lakes" for a new generation of wealthy anglers, and was covered in dozens of features by the top outdoor magazines. This was especially true after 1960, as Canada's new transcontinental highway opened vast areas of wilderness north of Lake Superior.[31]

While the image of the Quetico-Superior as a fishing paradise was receiving less attention from the outdoor magazines, the image of wilderness as sacred space was becoming the central concept of preservationist organizations. The two leading groups, the Wilderness Society and the Sierra Club, made it clear to their members that wilderness was more than a sanctuary for escaping from civilization. The groups' magazines constantly stressed that humans depended upon wild places for spiritual sustenance:

> Are we not truly and in reality human essentially as spiritual creatures nurtured and sustained — directly or indirectly — by a wildness that must always be renewed from a living wilderness?
>
> Is it not with some such understanding as this that we realize the essential importance of our wilderness areas?
>
> Is it not thus that we can explain the fact that a wilderness vacation is remembered as more than sport, more than fun, more than simple recreation?[32]

Beginning in 1949, the Sierra Club sponsored biennial conferences to discuss wilderness issues and philosophy. Leaders of the major preservationist groups attended, as well as government officials and activists from smaller organizations. The belief that wilderness was a spiritual need dominated these conferences, so much so that in 1955 one participant complained that conservation meant *more* than spiritual values. He believed wilderness supporters were unnecessarily alienating the timber and livestock industries by making preservation a moral crusade.[33]

Preservationists continued to steer away from the Progressive Era definition of conservation, which was based on utilitarianism and which stressed efficient resource extraction as the best way to meet social needs. David Brower, the executive director of the Sierra Club, redefined "conservationist" to mean "the man...concerned with what natural resources do for his spirit, not his book balance."[34] Wilderness conservation, then, according to another article in the **Sierra Club Bulletin,** "means, primarily, conservation of the spiritual values of the wild lands, for human beings."[35]

The growth of the Sierra Club and the Wilderness Society during the thirty years after the war indicates the popularity of the spiritual brand of conservation among wilderness supporters. The Sierra Club expanded from seven thousand members in 1950 to one hundred forty-seven thousand in 1966, a 2,000 percent increase. The Wilderness Society grew nearly as fast, from fewer than five thousand members in 1950 to eighty-seven thousand in 1966, a gain of more than 1600 percent.[36]

To those who believed that spiritual benefits were the primary reward of a wilderness excursion, the Quetico-Superior was a sacred place. This image of the canoe country was presented mostly in such publications as **Living Wilderness** and **Naturalist,** primarily subscribed to by true believers in the wilderness faith. The outdoor magazines and newspapers tended to combine editorial support for the sanctuary image with action features that gave *de facto* support to the fishing paradise image. **Sports Afield,** for example, claimed credit for preserving the roadless areas, and strongly supported the Wilderness Act of 1964, but four of its five features on the area between 1950 and 1965 focused on fishing above all other wilderness activities, and in three of the five articles the authors used outboard motors.

The leading proponent of the canoe country as a sacred place was Sigurd Olson. Exposed to the modern scientific world view while attending the University of Wisconsin just after World War I, Olson had lost confidence in the fundamentalist beliefs of his Baptist faith, but years of paddling canoes in the Quetico-Superior convinced him that a spiritual force was inherent in evolution. The great humanists of the twentieth century helped Olson build a core of belief. Among the many whose works he read were Pierre Teilhard de Chardin, Ghandi, Lewis Mumford, Bertrand Russell, Aldous and Julian Huxley, Albert Schweitzer and Albert Einstein. They were amazed, as was Olson, that the chance processes of selection, mutation and adaptation had led to an animal that could create such concepts as beauty, love, morality and God. Here was something that analytical scientists could not measure: through man, the cosmic process of creation had become aware of itself. "If we must have a God to worship," wrote Olson, "then why not worship this new spirit, this awakened consciousness, this awareness."[37]

Olson's long search ended in a faith that allowed a reconciliation between technological society and wilderness. If, as Olson believed, evolution was proceeding toward a mystical union with God, then nature was a symbol of God, a place from which mankind's biological and spiritual roots were derived. By spending time in the outdoors, Olson believed, people could reawaken their sense of cosmic purpose that had been lost with the destruction of ancient religious beliefs and the simultaneous abandonment of civilization's ties to nature. Wilderness, in particular, provided opportunities to experience nature as it always had been and always would be. In wilderness people could rediscover the timeless, creative force of the universe, and regain a sense of being part of that force. If society ignored the spiritual value of wild places, Olson warned, "the holocaust of atomic war might be the end of the long dreams of man and his endless search for beauty and meaning in the universe."[38]

During the Quetico-Superior airplane conflict, Olson had established

134

close ties with top officials in the Forest Service, the White House, and Congress. His long list of government contacts, combined with his extraordinary ability to generate enthusiasm, propelled Olson into a leadership role in the wilderness preservation movement. He became the vice-president of the National Parks Association in 1951, and served as its president from 1953 to 1959. The Wilderness Society elected him to its council in 1956; he became its vice-president in 1963 and its president in 1968. From 1959 to 1966 he served on the Interior Secretary's Advisory Board on Parks, Monuments, and Historic Sites. He also was the wilderness ecologist of the Izaak Walton League and a consultant to the President's Quetico-Superior Committee.

As a representative of these groups, Olson spoke about the spiritual values of wilderness preservation at colleges, universities, conservation group meetings and conferences. He testified at many House and Senate hearings to preserve such places as Dinosaur National Monument and to establish the national wilderness preservation system.

But Olson became best known for his books of essays about the Quetico-Superior wilderness. Olson's books helped attract to the canoe country not only those who were looking for a sanctuary, a place to escape civilization, but those who sought an essentially spiritual experience in a sacred place. In his best-selling first book, *The Singing Wilderness,* Olson showed what the latter could find:

> The sun was trembling now on the edge of the ridge. It was alive, almost fluid and pulsating, and as I watched it sink I thought that I could feel the earth turning from it, actually feel its rotation. Over all was the silence of the wilderness, that sense of oneness which comes only when there are no distracting sights or sounds, when we listen with inward ears and see with inward eyes, when we feel we are aware with our entire beings rather than our senses. I thought as I sat there of the ancient admonition "Be still and know that I am God," and knew that without stillness there can be no knowing, without divorcement from outside influences man cannot know what spirit means.[39]

Those who sought spiritual perspective in the Quetico-Superior wanted most of all to *feel* — if even just for a moment — a universal power that was still beyond the ability of modern science to quantify and explain away. "Wilderness offers [a] sense of cosmic purpose if we open our hearts and minds to its possibilities," said Olson:

> It may come in such moments of revelation as Aquinas, Chardin, and others speak about, burning instants of truth when everything stands clear. It may come as a slow realization after long periods of waiting. Whenever it comes, life is suddenly illumined, beautiful and transcendent, and we are filled with awe and deep happiness.[40]

In their canoes such people as Olson paddled through space *and* time; they needed to sense the forces at work in several billion years of evolution, the quiet of the centuries, and to feel they were part of it all. Anything that interrupted — resorts, logging, motors, and to some extent even other canoeists — was out of place in a sacred wilderness. "At times in quiet waters one does not speak aloud but only in whispers, for then all noise is sacrilege," wrote Olson.[41]

Those who perceived the area as a fishing paradise or as a sanctuary would not necessarily deny that their wilderness trips had any spiritual value, but they emphasized something else. Those who saw the canoe country as a fishing paradise came primarily to fish in a scenic environment, where remoteness guaranteed a big catch. They wanted to experience the freedom and vitality of frontier life, but welcomed any modern conveniences that would make their wilderness trip a comfortable one.

Those who saw the Quetico-Superior as a sanctuary wanted to experience peace and quiet more than abundant fishing or modern comforts. In this respect they had much in common with those who perceived the area as a sacred place. The key difference was that the former sought primarily simple escape and relaxation from the tensions of modern life, while the latter sought primarily a sense of oneness with nature that gave them spiritual sustenance. In practice,

136

this difference in priorities was reflected in the kinds of regulations each group considered appropriate for the Quetico- Superior. Those who saw the canoe country as a sanctuary opposed wilderness resorts and seaplane travel into the area, but did not necessarily oppose logging, outboard motors or snowmobiles. Those who perceived the Quetico-Superior as a sacred place opposed all of these, and they unwittingly were assisted by the Forest Service in 1958, when the agency decided to give the Superior Roadless Areas a new name.

Under the 1948 management plan for the roadless areas, about half of the land was slated for logging. Pulpwood companies already had been clearcutting on 155,000 acres in the southern portion of the Superior Roadless Area, and were pressing north. Modern logging required high- grade tote roads; soon a network of them crossed roadless area canoe routes. The Forest Service found it increasingly hard to explain that logging roads were not really roads just because they were not open to the public. The agency was not about to ban logging in the canoe country, so it decided to change the name.[42]

The Forest Service wanted a name that would capture the public image of the area without implying that logging was prohibited. Officials considered "Superior Waterway Wilderness" and "Superior Wilderness Canoeing Area," but decided the public would make no distinction between such a label and "wilderness area." They ultimately chose the name "Boundary Waters Canoe Area," because it seemingly avoided the wilderness connotation, and promoted the form of recreation to which the agency gave priority.[43]

However, the new name convinced many who paddled canoes that the BWCA was meant exclusively for their kind of recreation. By 1963 the Ely Chamber of Commerce was so worried about the increasingly restrictive meaning being attached by canoeists to the label "Boundary Waters Canoe Area" that it tried to get the name changed to "Boundary Waters Recreation Area." The tactic failed, but the public response showed the importance of labels in creating images of a place. "I can't help but believe the word 'canoe' was used in the official title to the property for a definite purpose," said one writer to the editor of the

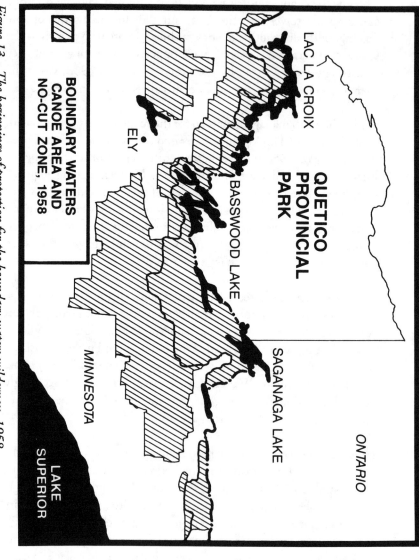

Figure 13 - The beginnings of protection for the boundary waters wilderness, 1958.

BOUNDARY WATERS
CANOE AREA AND
NO-CUT ZONE, 1958

ELY

LAC LA CROIX

QUETICO
PROVINCIAL
PARK

BASSWOOD LAKE

SAGANAGA LAKE

MINNESOTA

ONTARIO

LAKE
SUPERIOR

Minneapolis Star. "I believe they strongly felt that this wilderness should be pierced only by those humans, who like the Indian and Voyageur, could come in only under their own human power — using ski, snowshoe, light boat, canoe or foot — but NOT by motor." Another wilderness supporter agreed: "The whole reason for being of this superb area...is precisely that it IS a CANOE AREA...WHY, IT WOULD BE ALMOST A SACRILEGE TO REMOVE THAT LITTLE WORD *CANOE*."[44]

And the paddlers had the numbers on their side. In 1948 about a third of all those visiting the roadless areas were canoeists; by 1961 canoeists were in the majority. The airplane ban had eliminated a significant number of non-paddlers, and the advent of lightweight aluminum canoes, combined with a nationally increasing interest in wilderness recreation, helped these modern-day voyageurs become the dominant group of BWCA visitors. During the same time, however, total numbers of people relying on outboard motors also were increasing, and logging companies were moving deep into the area. Conflict was inevitable.

Perhaps the most widespread animosity was that directed by paddlers toward those who used outboard motors. While they despised motorboats most of all, the main conflict was with other canoeists who used small outboard motors. A single portage stopped about 80 percent of those using motorboats, but motorized canoes could be found anywhere along all of the major routes in both the BWCA and Quetico Park. Such use was light over much of the area, under one group per day per lake in 1961, but lakes visited by one to five motorized canoes per day extended deep into the Quetico.[45]

Nearly 40 percent of paddling canoeists disliked meeting *any* motorized canoe, but political and environmental boundaries made it inevitable that the two groups would come into frequent contact. More than half of all paddling canoeists entering the BWCA started at Moose Lake. Out of sixty-one other access points, only one received as much as 8 percent of the total use. Moose Lake provided the quickest access to the Canadian Customs station at the eastern end of Basswood

Lake. This was the only customs station near the heart of the Quetico, so nearly everybody who entered the park stopped at the small white house at Prairie Portage — not only the paddling canoeists, but canoeists using motors, and also the many motorboat users who wanted to fish the Canadian side of Basswood.[46]

The environmental boundaries of the waterways prevented quick dispersal of these great numbers of people. Paddling canoeists leaving Moose Lake for either Quetico Park or the BWCA had a practical choice of five routes. Four of the five commonly were used by motorized canoes, and three of them required at least two days' travel — four days on round trips — along lakes used by motorboats. Researchers found that more than half of the paddling canoeists using Moose Lake later said they had seen too many people during their trip. Less than a fifth of those using motors — either on canoes or on boats — felt crowded.[47]

Motor users and paddlers were completely different kinds of people. Those who used outboards were four to nine times more likely than paddling canoeists to say their most important wilderness activity was fishing. They saw the Quetico-Superior as a fishing paradise, while those who paddled canoes saw it as a sanctuary and a sacred place.[48]

The conflict between BWCA visitors and logging was less obvious. Most logging occurred during the winter months, when there were almost no tourists. None of the logging occurred in the most heavily used portions of the BWCA, so relatively few people encountered any tote roads or culverts. The Shipstead-Nolan Act of 1930 mandated a 400-foot-deep strip of timber along lakes and streams, so few saw the clearcuts. In fact, most traveled within a 362,000-acre zone from which the Forest Service had banned logging. (A large portion of this "no-cut" zone, established in 1941, consisted of the Basswood Lake region that had been clearcut for its tall pines early in the century.)

Still, a significant number of wilderness activists were bothered by the mere *knowledge* that logging was taking place in the BWCA. These were the people who saw the canoe country as a sacred place, and they considered any disruption of the natural processes of evolution there to be a sacrilege. As the magazine *Naturalist* editorialized, "In a wilderness forest management by logging can have no place....In a wilderness forest a natural condition that appears untidy to a forester is one of maximum health for the long term well-being of the forest and all its wild inhabitants; it may well be so even for the well-being of man himself if the perspective is broad and deep enough."[49]

Logging, rather than motorboats, caused the next political conflict. Late in 1963, Bill Rom, an Ely canoe outfitter, published an article in *Naturalist* that charged logging practices were destroying the BWCA. "The lower fourth of the Canoe Country has been almost completely logged out in the past two decades," he wrote. "What was once a choice two week canoe route in completely virgin wilderness, the Kawishiwi-Isabella loop, is now a cut over, road - riddled shambles." Rom recalled a 1961 canoe trip he took with his wife, during which they were forced to stop just east of Maniwaki Lake: "The portages and area were completely obliterated by logging operations. A gravel highway and bridge crossed this canoe route just west of Maniwaki, destroying all vestiges of wilderness along this hitherto primitive route."[50]

In 1964, as the scope of BWCA logging became widely known and graphically described in preservationist publications, the Izaak Walton League, the Wilderness Society, the Minnesota Wildlife Federation and six other organizations joined as Conservation Affiliates to demand the BWCA's preservation under the wilderness bill that was nearing passage in Congress. They asked for a logging ban, and for the Forest Service to enforce its policy that allowed outboard motors only in areas where they had become well established by 1948.

Calling for an end to logging meant breaking with the President's Quetico-Superior Committee. For thirty years the Committee, led by Charles Kelly and Ernest Oberholtzer, had pursued a treaty establishing an international land management program that would zone ten million acres for wilderness recreation and resource exploitation. If Canada and the United States had endorsed the proposal and signed the treaty, most of the region would have been designated as wilder-

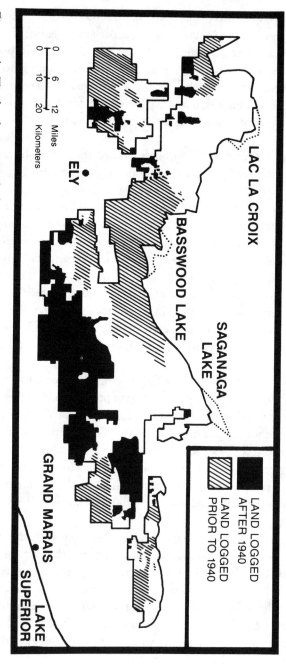

Figure 14 - Timber harvest in the boundary waters canoe area.

ness. Political realities, however, had reduced the amount of land under consideration to the two million acres within Quetico Park and the BWCA, and had dashed all hopes of a treaty. To many wilderness supporters, it no longer made sense to apply the zoning concepts intended for the entire watershed to one-fifth of the area, especially in light of the increasingly heavy recreational use.

Sigurd Olson, long a consultant to the President's Committee, joined the call for full wilderness status. "We are not living in the same era as when the first controversies arose over this area," he said:

> Trees do not mean the same. They have different values when they are part of an ancient ecology of great social value....Wilderness is more than lakes, rivers, and timber along the shores, more than fishing or just camping. It is the sense of the primeval, of space, solitude, silence, and the eternal mystery. It is a fragile quality and is destroyed by man and his machines.[51]

The preservationists did not succeed in changing the wilderness bill. When it became law later that year, the only exceptions allowing logging and motor travel to continue applied to the BWCA. The preservationists *did,* however, convince Agriculture Secretary Orville L. Freeman, a former governor of Minnesota, to appoint a committee to decide the area's fate. The Boundary Waters Area Review Committee, chaired by George A. Selke, former state conservation commissioner under Freeman, held hearings during the summer of 1964 in Ely, Orr, Grand Marais, Duluth and St. Paul, collected written testimony, and visited the BWCA.[52]

In Ely, it was common knowledge, although not officially announced, that the city's last mine was nearing the end of its days. The Pioneer Mine employed five hundred. Many thought it preposterous that the government should ban logging at the expense of an already distressed community — even if logging accounted for less than 2 percent of Ely area employment — and the *Miner* whipped up animosity toward the outsiders:

> The "do-gooders" are at it again: — organized groups of
> birdwatchers and flower sniffers have proposed in the
> Superior National Forest that the "no-cut" area be ex-
> tended, that the Boundary Waters Canoe Area be broad-
> ened and that the existing logging companies in the area
> be expelled. Not content to cutting our tourist business
> by getting rid of our boundary waters resorts, they are
> now out to further reduce our economy by getting rid of
> the loggers in the area.[53]

Northeastern Minnesotans found it hard to understand the preservationist argument against logging. To most natives, logging created at
worst a temporary eyesore. Miles and miles of forested land surrounded them; logged-over areas were one small part of a great, green
mosaic. From their perspective, the unsightly aspects of a stump-filled
clearing were overshadowed by the positive aspects. To many loggers,
the clearing represented a sense of autonomy, closeness to the land,
family tradition and food on the table. To the community, the clearing
meant greater employment, lower property taxes, local tradition and
less dependence upon government handouts. Natives resented being
called wilderness destroyers. "We haven't lived here because the life
was easy, or because we made a lot of money," said a man who lived
near the eastern edge of the BWCA. "I would say the real reason is our
love for our beautiful area:

> The mainstay of our livelihood has been logging and
> fishing, with tourist trade adding tremendously, for the
> few short months we have it. We would like to keep it that
> way....Just ask yourself this question; Would you as a
> county, town, or whatever, like to have your main
> economy voted out by another part of the country, whose
> only interest in you was a playground for themselves for
> a day or two, a year?[54]

Before the Selke Committee wrote its report, preservationists discovered a publicity bonanza: loggers had bulldozed a road right over one
end of Finn Lake, within the BWCA and just south of the Gunflint

Trail. The lake was not on any canoe route, and was on state land. Forest Service employees were unsure of their authority over BWCA logging operations that occurred off federal property. Nevertheless, *Naturalist* ran twelve pages of photos in its fall, 1964 issue, and dramatized the Finn Lake episode as typical of Forest Service management:

> We know from the evidence available to our own eyes and documented by photography that wide areas in the BWCA are now being reduced to a shambles, a cut over mess of stumps and debris, of logging roads and slash completely destroying the wilderness quality of the wilderness forever.[55]

Such publicity imposed limits on the range of politically-acceptable alternatives available to the Selke Committee and to Agriculture Secretary Freeman. In the end, they gave those who saw the canoe country as a sacred place a significant but incomplete victory. The proposed regulations released by the secretary in January, 1965, placed 60 percent of the BWCA's acreage and 90 percent of its lakes and streams into the no-cut zone, banned snowmobiles, and designated zones for large and small outboard motors. The motor zones, however, covered more than 60 percent of the BWCA water surface, and coincided with the most heavily used paddle canoe routes.

Freeman's proposals were intensely opposed by many northeastern Minnesotans. The *Ely Miner* accused the Selke Committee of tricking local citizens into believing they would have a fair hearing, and then ignoring their opinions. Now, with nine months for public comment before the secretary drafted final regulations, area residents were determined to be heard. The Minnesota Arrowhead Association quickly formed a series of Boundary Waters Resources Committees to fight the proposals, using the slogan, "Protect Our Wilderness With Multiple Use."[56] BWRC pamphlets stirred insider-outsider conflict:

> How would YOU like to see the boundary waters area used?
> — For three or four months of the year, or year around?

— Inner areas accessible only to the select group physically able to portage, or to ALL AMERICANS who support it with their taxes? — With the inner areas available only to those who can afford unlimited time, or available to all in a reasonable length of time through the use of a small motor.

— Managed by proper and modern Forestry techniques, or left to the fire cycle?[57]

By July, local opposition was generating political pressure, and Freeman decided to visit Ely, ostensibly to dedicate the Forest Service's new Voyageur Visitor Center. Appearing with him at the July 24 ceremony was Lynda Bird Johnson, the twenty-one-year-old daughter of the president. She had just completed a highly publicized, four-day canoe trip in the BWCA, accompanied part way by Freeman. While the two were in Ely, the city sponsored a "Multiple Use Parade" to protest Freeman's proposed regulations. Twenty-four northeastern Minnesota communities participated in the parade, in which trucks with sawlogs and pulpwood took the place of more traditional floats. One popular entry consisted of four teenagers pushing a boat and motor with a portage wheel, or dolly. The boat displayed a sign saying, "Don't Lock Us Out." The protest, however, failed to get any favorable response from Freeman, and Johnson told reporters at a press conference that, on her canoe trip, she was "not enthused to see people with motorboats after a long day's paddling." She apparently neglected to tell reporters that the Forest Service had widened the portage trails for her, sprayed them with insecticide, and flew in fresh food and water.[58]
The *Ely Miner* decided the city had once again been taken:

> We rather get the impression that the primary purpose of her visit...was to Sell the BWCA Idea to America. In interviews granted after the conclusion of the four-day canoe trip, the remarks of Miss Johnson, the Freemans and other members of the party were loaded with those old cliches on the serenity and peacefulness of the wilderness, the call of the loons and the songs of the birds and those horrible outboard motor noises.[59]

The Wilderness Society and the Izaak Walton League drummed up mail support for Freeman in response to the outcry from northeastern Minnesota. Once again, it was a battle for public opinion. The secretary, editorialized in *Living Wilderness,* had been "bitterly and indeed, viciously criticized by timber and commercial interests, and certain local communities....Wilderness supporters realize that the Secretary has moved about as far as the temper of local public opinion at present seems to allow." The *New York Times* also told readers that Freeman was "under heavy fire in his home state," and urged "the strongest public support" for his stand. The Forest Service later reported that the "overwhelming proportion" of the mail favored regulations even more stringent than those proposed.[60]

On December 16, 1965, Freeman issued his final directive. It added two motorboat routes, but deleted twenty-three lakes originally proposed for motors. The logging restrictions remained unchanged. The only major concession to local interests was Freeman's removal of the snowmobile ban; he decided to allow them to travel over all routes open to motorboats.

The pressure brought on by a tremendous increase in the number of people using the BWCA, combined with the political power wielded by wilderness activists who saw the BWCA as a sacred place, had forced Freeman and the Forest Service to adopt a restrictive interpretation of the sanctuary image. In a statement for the press, the secretary confided that this had been his most difficult cabinet-level decision:

> If the Boundary Waters Canoe Area were a wilderness area in the sense of other remote and wild areas, the task of developing regulations would be relatively easy since there is a history of established patterns of how such areas are treated. But this is not the case.

> If the Boundary Waters Canoe Area were simply a part of the National Forest System, and no more, then the regulations could be developed within the Multiple-Use framework which guides National Forest management.

But this is not the case either.

There is no pattern other than judgments carefully weighed to guide the management policy of the Boundary Waters Canoe Area because there is no other area like it.[61]

It was not the Christmas present that many local citizens had hoped for, but they resigned themselves to it. "The directive is now a fact and we'll have to live with it," wrote Childers in the **Miner.** "And it's our prediction that further restrictions will be added in the years to come."[62]

Childers was right; ambiguity in the 1964 Wilderness Act ensured continuing controversy. The BWCA was not mentioned in the Act's appendix that named the nation's wilderness areas, and was the only place the Act highlighted by name for the purpose of allowing logging and motorized travel. Furthermore, the management rules mandated by Freeman conceivably could be changed by Freeman or a successor at any time. In the late 1960s, as federal courts and the U.S. Congress began to give environmental groups the legal standing to sue government agencies, some of them began to apply this new strategy to the BWCA. Between 1969 and 1977, as Ontario officials were banning logging and outboard motors from Quetico Park, the U.S. Forest Service constantly was in court defending its BWCA management policies. The Minnesota Federation of Ski Touring Clubs fought to ban snowmobiling, and the Sierra Club and the Minnesota Public Interest Research Group stymied BWCA logging.

Because of this constant litigation and heated conflict, Representative James Oberstar introduced federal legislation in 1975 to settle BWCA management issues. A long-time aid to John Blatnik and a fellow member of the Democratic Farmer-Labor Party, Oberstar had won the 1974 election for the retiring congressman's northeastern Minnesota seat. Oberstar's bill proposed to reclassify about 40 percent of the BWCA as the Boundary Waters National Recreation Area, allowing logging, motorboating, and snowmobiling. The remaining 60 percent

— divided into three sections — was to be given complete wilderness protection, and renamed the Boundary Waters Wilderness Area.

Wilderness activists strongly opposed the formal dedication of more than 400,000 acres of BWCA land to multiple use management. In May, 1976, representatives of the Sierra Club, the Wilderness Society, the Izaak Walton League, the National Audubon Society and other state and national groups formed a lobbying coalition called the Friends of the Boundary Waters Wilderness. At their request, Minneapolis DFL Representative Donald Fraser soon introduced into the House an alternative bill providing complete wilderness protection for the entire BWCA.

The preservationists also started a communication campaign to enlist public support for the Fraser bill, sending out booklets and newsletters, requesting donations, and placing articles in environmental group magazines. "Your Boundary Waters Canoe Area Wilderness needs help, Now!" exclaimed the cover of a pamphlet published by the Friends. The Wilderness Society called the situation a "Crisis in the Canoe Country," and the Izaak Walton League told its members, "It's 'high noon at the OK corral.'"[63]

In northeastern Minnesota, most residents did not support *either* bill. They had adjusted, grudgingly, to the Freeman Directive, and believed that Congress had given its final word in the 1964 Wilderness Act. Although the primary purpose of Oberstar's National Recreation Area was to allow logging and motorized recreation to continue in areas where they had been established, local citizens noticed that the NRA's boundaries would encompass private land that was currently outside of the BWCA, and worried that it might be just another attempt to get resorts out of the area. As one Ely resident stated, "We have been asked to compromise over the BWCA for 20 years. Now we are being asked to compromise between being shot and being stabbed."[64]

Local citizens who opposed further wilderness restrictions found their side of the story most vigorously championed in the *Ely Echo,* a weekly newspaper that had begun publishing in 1972. Managing Editor Bob

Cary, a former outdoor writer for the *Chicago Daily News* and a local outfitter, helped propel the *Echo* past its long-established competitor, the *Miner,* with his outspoken coverage of the BWCA conflict.

Cary reflected the deep distrust that many northeastern Minnesotans felt toward the federal government when he suggested that Oberstar's bill was part of a Forest Service/environmentalist conspiracy. He wrote that the Forest Service, which had advised Oberstar on how to write his bill, had "'set [Oberstar] up' with a piece of legislation which was bound to raise the ire of environmental groups and which could be used as a club to get the Fraser legislation passed." As evidence, he told how the Friends of the Boundary Waters Wilderness had gotten its mailing list from the Forest Service's BWCA camping permit records. To Cary, this suggested collusion.[65]

Cary wrote article upon article calling into question key preservationist arguments. In response to the assertion that BWCA logging should be replaced by careful management of lightning-caused fires, he said that many people considered burned areas as ugly as clearcuts, and pointed out that "canoe campers have never been asked if they wish to travel in a burned-off area." He also noted that "a runaway fire might barbecue a large number of canoe campers who are in the BWCA during the summer," but facetiously suggested that Ely residents wouldn't mind if this theory were put to the test.[66]

Preservationists routinely cited the research of Forest Service geographer David Lime, who found that 93 percent of paddling canoeists were irritated by encounters with outboard motors, and that the situation was worsening. To this, Cary replied, "There is an impression that the 90,000 or so people who take their vacation in the BWCA are having a lousey [sic] time. What is amazing is that they keep coming back every year to have their 'wilderness experience...destroyed.'"[67]

Most northeastern Minnesotans simply could not understand how outboard motors could wreck anyone's wilderness experience, and they derided the sacred place imagery that dominated the arguments preservationists used to promote Donald Fraser's bill:

> Donald the Messiah walks through the halls of Congress
> reciting the poetry of Sigurd [Olson] and displaying the
> lists of people baptized in the pristine wilderness
> coalition....The local Ely people cry let us use motors to
> go fishing but Donald the Messiah says, "How can we
> have a pristine wilderness with the putt, putt of outboard
> motors. I say unto thee the motors will desecrate our
> sacred place....The BWCA is our sacred place and you
> cannot enter in until you have been baptized in the name
> of Sigurd."[68]

The preservationists, however, had two key advantages over local citizens in their lobbying efforts. First, they had many years of experience, and better understood the nuances of the political process. Second, national support for wilderness preservation was at an all-time high. A study of attitudes commissioned by the American Forest Institute showed that one-third of Americans thought the country needed *more* land preserved as wilderness; only seven percent thought too much had been set aside. Almost *one-half* of adults under the age of 30 wanted the government to establish more wilderness.[69] With such broad national support for preservation, it was easy for downstate and national media to take a popular stand on an issue that did not affect the economy of the regions they represented. As the major newspapers began to editorialize on behalf of the Fraser bill, northeastern Minnesotans came to believe that their legitimate concerns once again were being ignored.

By May of 1977 it was clear to Oberstar supporters that they needed a new organization to engage effectively in the battle for public opinion. They formed the Boundary Waters Conservation Alliance, and appointed a former Oberstar staff member as its executive director. Because many local residents did not support either bill, however, the Alliance was unable to present a united front. Eventually, it became dominated by the most outspoken opponents of the Fraser bill, those who agreed with the **Duluth News-Tribune** that passage of the bill would "trigger a backwoods revolution."[70] And some of them were ready to start one.

The warning signs were evident during a congressional hearing in Ely on July 8, 1977, that attracted more than a thousand people. Local citizens took a step toward confrontation by hanging in effigy a figure that the Associated Press said represented Sigurd Olson, but that a Duluth paper said was labeled "Sierra."[71] Olson, who at the age of 78 still was a powerful spokesman but not healthy enough to lead a wilderness campaign, was jeered and cursed by Ely residents when he took his turn to testify against the Oberstar bill.

Organized resistance to environmentalists in general and the Fraser bill in particular grew during the following year. On January 15, 1978, for example, more than 400 people defied BWCA snowmobile regulations by riding into Trout Lake; angry words were exchanged and at least one scuffle broke out as Forest Service employees issued 15 citations. In May, Ely residents stopped carloads of tourists arriving in town for the opening day of the fishing season, and claimed to gather 10,000 signatures opposing the Fraser bill. In June, more than a thousand Alliance members picketed the Democratic Farmer-Labor Party convention in St. Paul, and made enough noise to prevent Fraser from speaking until Oberstar intervened and asked them to stop.

From the Alliance point of view, these tactics successfully turned the BWCA issue into an election-year hot potato for Minnesota's Democrats. Fraser, who was running to fill the remaining four years of the late Senator Hubert Humphrey's term of office, could not gain support at the convention for a BWCA resolution he endorsed, and barely won the Democratic nomination. He was defeated in the September primaries. Minnesota Senator Wendell Anderson, a Democrat running for reelection, originally gained favor with Alliance members. He played up the insider-outsider resentments, saying, "The people from the *Minneapolis Tribune* come up here only 10 days a year. They don't like me, and they don't like you."[72] Later, after he supported a compromise unacceptable to the Alliance, the group turned sharply against him. Anderson lost his Senate seat in November, and the Alliance claimed responsibility. Minnesota Governor Rudy Perpich, another Democrat, lost on election day to Al Quie; he blamed the BWCA controversy for the clean sweep by Independent

Republicans of the state's three most powerful offices.

Congress usually is reluctant to pass a bill that is opposed by a representative of the area affected by that bill, so the strong pressure put on the Minnesota delegation by the Alliance ensured a series of compromises. By July of 1978 this much was clear: there would be no National Recreation Area, logging and mining would be banned from the entire BWCA, and *some* of the BWCA would remain open to snowmobiles and outboard motors. The last — and most bitter — question, was *how much?*

At the request of North Dakota Senator James Abourezk, who chaired the subcommittee examining the Senate version of the BWCA bill, the Alliance and the Friends of the Boundary Waters Wilderness each appointed an attorney to negotiate motor restrictions. The Alliance chose Ronald Walls, of Ely, and the Friends chose Charles Dayton, of Minneapolis. With an Abourezk aide as mediator, the two men met in Washington, D.C. for three days at the end of July. They agreed to cut in half the percentage of BWCA water surface area open to outboard motors, and mandated future reductions. They also agreed to eliminate six of eight snowmobile routes by 1984.

Alliance members, stunned by what they saw as a giveaway of their interests, overwhelmingly rejected the compromise. They felt further betrayed when Senator Anderson took no action to intervene on their behalf, despite his strategic position on the Senate Parks and Recreation Subcommittee, which put together a new bill based upon the compromise. Feeling completely locked out of the system — and out of the BWCA — some of them agreed with the sentiment expressed by one local citizen? "If a bill like this passes...the people of Ely should make tourists feel damn unwelcome."[73]

Before sunrise on August 5, Alliance members from Ely set up roadblocks at six key BWCA access points and prevented tourists from entering the area until early in the evening. Those coming out of the wilderness were prevented from leaving until early afternoon. While there were no reports of violence, angry exchanges took place at all six sites. One Ely citizen told a reporter, "Well, we proved one thing for sure...we can shut this whole thing down if we want to." A week later, about a hundred Ely residents marched to the downtown store of a local canoe outfitter, then hanged and burned him in effigy. His crime — opposing the roadblock of the previous weekend, and testifying to Congress in favor of the bill supported by "the outsiders," the wilderness preservationists.[74]

Intimidation, a tactic of desperation, worked against the interests of the Alliance. It generated media coverage that portrayed Alliance members and sympathizers — especially those in Ely — as rude, small-minded people who turned to violence if they didn't get their way. Perhaps the most negative piece was a story in the **Minneapolis Tribune** called "Fear Stalks the Ely 'Resistance.'" It reported that intimidation went well beyond the anonymous threats made against Ely residents who publicly supported the Fraser bill; those who tried not to take *any* stand were viewed with suspicion:

> They are asked if they or members of their families belong to the Sierra Club; they are asked why they did not attend a meeting of the Boundary Waters Conservation Alliance....They are refused service in some business establishments because it is rumored they sympathize with the wilderness advocates.[75]

Bob Cary said many reports about tourist's cars being vandalized and about physical threats were simply lies, and he accused the media of conspiring against Ely. "There is considerable suspicion," he wrote, "that some of these stories have been engineered just to provoke violence and vandalism in order to portray the people of the area as unprincipaled [sic] and unlawful." Cary said downstate reporters were too quick to blame Alliance supporters for vandalism, rather than examine the possibility that a given incident had nothing to do with the wilderness conflict. He noted that some of the vandalism at BWCA entry points had been committed against cars with boat trailers, and that downtown Ely businesses also had been vandalized during the summer, but local residents didn't automatically assume that these misdeeds were performed by wilderness preservationists.[76]

To many Ely residents, the negative media portrayal of their town simply verified that nobody was willing to listen to their side of the story. Being portrayed as antiwilderness was bad enough, considering that a number of Ely residents regularly volunteered to clean BWCA campsites and trails, and risked their lives fighting BWCA forest fires. But being portrayed as greedy and antidemocratic was more than some could stand, as the following statement from a local resort owner shows:

> You have the utter gall to accuse the people of Ely of being rude, ugly, selfish and irresponsible — we who have been harrassed by your well-heeled purists for years...we who have gone to hearing after hearing and testified — have written our Congressmen, gone to Washington; we who have protested peaceably, formed committees, we who have watched our rights dwindle, our business shrivel, and our area become congested with youth groups who have been brainwashed by pressure groups throughout the country; we who have been fed lip service by our representatives, lied to by the Forest Service, ignored by the Department of Agriculture; we who have been fined for using snowmobiles on routes the forest service themselves cut; we who have been told when, where and how to live, and when to enter here and when not to enter there; we who have outnumbered and out-testified you time and time again only to end up with the short end of the stick. HOW DARE YOU![77]

Despite the public outrage in northeastern Minnesota, the bill constructed around the Dayton-Walls compromise was passed by the Senate without any debate late in the evening of October 9, 1978. The House of Representatives passed it by a two-to-one margin five days later. Ignoring a request for a veto from Representative Oberstar, President Jimmy Carter signed the Boundary Waters Canoe Area Wilderness Act into law on October 21. It eliminated logging and mining in the BWCA, and, by 1999, will have banished outboard motors from three-fourths of the water surface area. It also banned all interior BWCA snowmobile routes; the two routes allowed connect the northeastern and northwestern edges of the BWCA to nonwilderness land in Canada.

More than anything else, the Act reflected shifting boundaries in American culture. The nation's prosperity, increasingly dependent upon building weapons of annihilation and upon encouraging materialism, was producing a growing generation of antimodern modernists — people whose perceptual boundaries accepted the academic knowledge that made them doubt their religious traditions, but who were determined to search for cosmic truths that could give meaning to a self-destructing world.[78] Some of them believed they caught glimmers of these truths in wilderness; they dominated such groups as the Wilderness Society and the Sierra Club. The 1978 BWCA Wilderness Act codified much of their perceptual outlook into a new set of political boundaries.

To many local citizens, however, these new perceptual and political boundaries gave control of *their* land to outsiders. Changing environmental boundaries added to this feeling. The fishing frontier had moved to Canada, and the iron frontier had moved to the Third World. Even Ely's Pioneer Mine, which had employed five hundred and paid 60 percent of local property taxes, had closed in 1967. It was the last mine in a city that was born to mine.

Changing times and changing boundaries had caught up with Ely. The situation faced by local residents was similar to that faced by the Dacotah three hundred years earlier on the same land. The environmental boundaries supporting the tribe's hunting economy had changed, as tall pine forest replaced the open grasslands. During this period the Anishinabe — outsiders — began arriving, and the tribes fought for control of the land. Over the long run, the Dacotah migrated southwest rather than adapt to changing environmental and social conditions.

In Ely, the environmental boundaries supporting the city's mining economy had produced a limited amount of usable ore. As the city approached this limit, recreationists — outsiders — began arriving, and Ely residents fought for control of the land. Would its citizens adapt to changing conditions, or would they, like the Dacotah, migrate in search of the good life? Ely's population had peaked in 1930 at just over six thousand; by 1981, when the U.S. 8th District Court of Appeals upheld all provisions of the BWCA Wilderness Act, it had declined to less than five thousand. Bob Cary was philosophical:

> There is no such thing as a "final" solution to the BWCA issue, only a continuation on different levels.
>
> This is not to say that the people in the northeast cannot adjust to whatever is going on. We will. We will continue to make the best of whatever the situation may be. There is also a strong feeling that a lot of the current provisions of the BWCA will change with time, simply because they won't work....
>
> We are patient folk. We will watch and see.[79]

EPILOGUE

Several years ago, I visited the site of an abandoned resort near Ely. The resort was one of more than twenty in the Ely area — all financially dependent to some extent on motorized travel within the BWCA — that have been bought by the federal government under a hardship clause of the BWCA Wilderness Act. But this one was special to me; my family had visited it for a couple of weeks every summer for about ten years. And now the log cabins were empty, and weeds were sprouting everywhere.

When I was a child, I would spend most of the summer dreaming about the trip to this resort; I'd pack special games and fishing equipment weeks in advance. And finally the day would arrive, and for two weeks I'd be immersed in the northwoods. Not literally, perhaps, because except for an occasional overnight campout on a favorite island, we stayed in very comfortable quarters, and all of our outdoor excursions were by motorboat or motorized canoe. But these childhood vacations made me *love* the canoe country. I delighted in the smell of balsam, and felt a magical presence every evening when the setting sun cast a quivering golden glow on the trunks of shoreline cedars. Something stirred within me every time I heard a loon, or caught a glimpse of northern lights. Were those intangible experiences any less valuable because of their surrounding context of cabins and outboard motors?

As I sat on the edge of the abandoned resort's main dock, I realized that without those childhood experiences I might never have read the works of Sigurd Olson, never have taken a canoe trip, never have become an advocate of wilderness preservation. And yet, as an advocate, I had supported the law that led to the demise of the resort that had provided the experiences necessary for me to become a preservationist. Had I been wrong?

This is a question I often asked in the past few years, as I researched the area's past and wrote this book. My answer, ultimately, was no — I believe the 1978 BWCA Act was, by and large, a good piece of legislation. But my purpose in this epilogue is not to defend wilderness preservation, for that has been done many times. I wish instead to raise difficult issues and questions that I hope will prick the consciences of readers on both sides of the ongoing BWCA debate.

First, let's examine the long-term economic role of the BWCA in northeastern Minnesota. The local economy, perhaps especially in the Ely area, was built upon the rapid extraction of natural resources. First there was tall pine logging, and such villages as Winton prospered briefly, then withered as the forest was leveled. Then the discovery of iron ore led to an explosion of cities along the Mesabi and Vermilion Ranges. Early logging and iron mining companies extracted their respective resources quickly to take advantage of existing markets. This intense form of resource use soon ran against the environmental boundaries limiting the resource's supply. Tall-pine loggers exhausted their supply within several decades. The half-dozen iron mines that built Ely were used up within eighty years. Meanwhile, however, Ely had grown to a size that at one point exceeded six thousand people. And other cities had similarly grown because of rapid resource extraction.

Such an economy is inherently unstable, but most local residents seemed stuck on the idea of intense resource use as the best means to achieving the good life. They quite naturally did not want their communities to decline, but did not seem to perceive the inevitability of decline. There were two choices: 1) continue intense resource use as long as possible, spreading such use out onto the undeveloped canoe country; or 2) slow down the rate of resource use and develop some form of low-intensity economy to gradually replace the existing economy. Either choice ultimately would force a significant drop in the local population; it was just a matter of timing.

Most Ely citizens seemed to favor the first choice. To them, it made sense to exploit the untapped sections of the Quetico-Superior, to cut pulpwood there, to search for economically valuable deposits of copper- nickel sulfides, and, most notably, to develop a strong resort industry with a focus on wilderness fishing.

It might seem that the resort industry was a low-intensity use; it was not. The rapid growth of resorts in the 1930s and 1940s depended upon two resources: significant numbers of large fish, and enough undeveloped lakeshore to give anglers a feeling of being part of the frontier. By the late 1940s, it was clear that the unrestricted resort industry was destroying both resources, particularly with the development of fly-in fishing. The Quetico-Superior was too small an area to retain its wild feeling in the face of unrestricted resort growth, and, while stocking fish could ensure adequate supplies of desirable species, it could not replace the numbers of trophy fish that anglers had caught before 1950.

Perhaps this wouldn't have mattered, except for one other factor: The way people perceived and used the Quetico-Superior also depended upon the way they perceived and used other places. When the untapped lakes of northern Ontario became accessible in the 1950s, Fishing Paradise moved farther north. The Quetico-Superior could not match the wildness or the fishing of the land north of Lake Superior.

There was no place on the continent, however, that could match the Quetico-Superior as a place for wilderness lakeland canoeing. And as wilderness canoeing grew in popularity, its supporters — outsiders, mostly — demanded new political boundaries to preserve the canoe country. Boundaries were drawn to demarcate the wilderness, airplanes were banned, resorts were purchased and torn down, and new boundaries were put in place to designate zones in which logging and motors were prohibited. The outsiders were, in essence, forcing a low-intensity economy upon the insiders before the high-intensity economy was completely played out.

Wilderness supporters were not completely in tune with the local environmental boundaries, either. Unrestricted wilderness recreation also imposed a rate of use that exceeded the supply of the key resource: wildness. The Forest Service began to recognize this by the early 1960s, and in 1966 the BWCA became the nation's first wilderness area to use a visitor permit system. Today, however, visitor use of the BWCA is twice as great as in 1960, when people were beginning to complain about overcrowding — an issue I'll come back to later.

Much of the local animosity toward wilderness preservation has been expressed through an insider-outsider ethos. The insiders have considered themselves as long-term residents, and the outsiders as newcomers. Environmentally speaking, however, they *all* are newcomers, whose roots to the land are shallow. The Dacotah, the Anishinabe, the voyageurs, the iron miners, the loggers, the resort owners — they all came and lived off the Quetico-Superior for a while, made their mark, and moved on. Perhaps the same will be true of the canoeists. The insider-outsider ethos, no matter how understandable in the light of local history, was —and still is — self-destructive. It has focused local concern upon the political boundaries delineating and governing the BWCA, and blamed these for the poor local economy. This single-minded focus on the BWCA has obscured the local residents' vision; they have not understood adequately the environmental boundaries that placed the real limits upon the local economy. In fact, the creation of the BWCA has given local citizens a longer period of time than they would have given themselves to make the difficult transition from a high-intensity economy to one that does not exceed the renewability of its resources. For that, they can thank Sigurd Olson, Ernest Oberholtzer, Frank Hubachek, Charles Kelly and many others who too often have been reviled.

This is not to say that wilderness preservation has caused local citizens no pain. Of course it has, and preservationists need to face that fact more openly. While I am arguing that the BWCA has been good for the local economy in the long run, individual businesses have been closed and people have been hurt with every BWCA battle. Short-term economic problems have been at least partly counteracted by government programs designed to help the local economy, but try telling that to the resort owner whose joys and sorrows of a lifetime have been wrapped up in a few acres of land and half a dozen or so cabins. Even if the government pays a fair price, the owner can't help but feel violated, for something deeply personal has been taken from him.

This does not mean, of course, that just because a given law has led to resort closings it is a bad law; sometimes the broader public good requires decisions that hurt individuals. But each time preservationists propose such a law they need to face honestly the following difficult questions: Have we adequately defined the public good? How serious is the threat to the public good? And, if action is necessary, have we sought to protect the public good while hurting as few individuals as possible? When preservationists automatically throw out such phrases as "greedy resort owners" and "shrill demands from the local Ely area," it is unlikely that they are sincerely seeking fairness.

I can hear the preservationists' response: "But *they* stereotype *us*, too!" True enough. Local citizens typically portray wilderness supporters as wealthy, selfish elitists. In terms of education, of course, wilderness visitors *are* the elite. Half or more have at least some college education, and 20 percent have done graduate work. But they're not economically elite. First of all, most of them are either in school or not too far along in their careers. Secondly, the careers they choose most often are not high-paying ones — the leading occupational categories are education, research, social service and religion. Local citizens who complain about preservationists as being wealthy are not only wrong, they are tossing out a red herring. If they don't want "wealthy tourists," then the first thing to do is eliminate all resorts. A week in the wilderness is still more affordable to many more people than a week at a rustic lodge.

The more difficult charge is that of selfishness. People on both sides, not wanting to understand the legitimate concerns of their opponents, inflict this term upon each other. The burden of defense, however, should fall upon the group that is trying to change BWCA management in its favor, because it is the others who stand to suffer. Today, this burden belongs to the preservationists. They are the ones who need to make the extra effort that is necessary to ease tensions.

The preservationists should be in a particularly good position to do this, because they champion spiritual values as central to the wilderness experience. I am concerned, however, for as the wilderness movement has become institutionalized, with its own professional bureaucracy, the living philosophy once espoused by such people as Sigurd Olson, Aldo Leopold and Bob Marshall too often has become rigid dogma. Too often these days anyone who questions a wilderness proposal is excommunicated into the enemy camp. In every wilderness battle there are gray areas; the issues are not all black and white. Why do preservationists so often brand as traitors those who point out the gray areas? If wilderness — as preservationists such as myself often claim — is meant to help those who are searching for meaning, for spiritual truths, how can we justify condemning those who see differently? In doing so, we prove that we do not seek pure truth in wilderness, but only justification for our selfishness and prejudices. To paraphrase Thomas Merton, the Trappist monk best known for his book *The Seven Storey Mountain,* we promote an us vs. them attitude because if we can convince ourselves that they are wrong and we are right, then our lies and partial truths become whole truths, and our intolerance and greed become virtues.

As the 1990s begin, two issues dominate BWCA management. First is the question about the Four Mile Portage and two other truck portages in the BWCA. The Friends of the Boundary Waters Wilderness and seven other groups have taken the Forest Service to court, charging that the 1978 BWCA Act requires these portages to be closed. Actually, the Act said that the Secretary of Agriculture had to close these portages by 1984 unless he decided "that there is no feasible nonmotorized means of transporting boats across the portages to reach the lakes...." The court argument revolves around the definition of feasibility. There is no doubt that it is possible to reach the two lakes in question by putting the boat on a dolly — called "portage wheels" — and pulling it over a portage. But the courts will need to decide if Congress meant the term "feasible" to mean "possible," "practical," or "ideal."

The whole issue, however, seems a false one. Since the BWCA Wilderness Act allows motorboats on the two lakes in question, why does it matter how those boats get there? If the preservationists are trying to cut motorboat use of these lakes, then they should present their case honestly. If they are not trying to cut motorboat use, then they need to explain why the portages are more harmful to the wilderness than motorboats.

The other hot issue is that of overcrowding. The Friends say "too many people currently visit the BWCA," and the organization is calling for reductions. As evidence of overcrowding, the Friends cite a recent study showing that 59.9 percent of BWCA canoeists said "meeting too many other groups was a problem." However, the study also showed that only 12 percent of these canoeists identified the problem as serious. Also, 59 percent of BWCA visitors rated their experience as very good — the top choice of five alternatives — while a total of only 1 percent ranked their trip as either poor or very poor.[1]

I don't mean to say that the BWCA is not overcrowded. I know that at times *I* have encountered far more people in a day than I either wanted or expected to see. I *am* suggesting that the Friends' use of the recent survey to prove its case is misleading. If the BWCA has too many canoeists paddling its waters every summer, then those of us who don't like it should be able to make a straightforward case that doesn't rely on a pseudo- objective set of statistics. Use of such a survey also sets a poor precedent, for it implies that what the majority wants, the majority should get. That is the kind of reasoning that wilderness activists — a longstanding minority — have been fighting against from the very beginning.

In any case, anyone who wants the Forest Service to cut back on the number of people who can enter the BWCA should first think about this question, regularly posed by Bob Cary of the ***Ely Echo:*** Are you saying that you will give up your permit and stay home to make more solitude for me, or are you saying that I should stay home and make more solitude for you?

While these two issues currently dominate public attention, a much more serious one looms in the background — acid rain and other forms of air pollution. The BWCA is more sensitive to acid rain than is any other part of Minnesota, and many lakes are threatened. Less widely known is the human health threat posed by mercury contamination. Coal-burning electric power plants, waste incineration, and latex paint have contributed to atmospheric deposition of mercury into the BWCA, and it is getting concentrated in the fish. Health officials recommend eating no more than one meal per week of BWCA fish, and no more than one large fish of twenty inches or so per month. While local fishing guides still cook walleye shore lunches for their guests, they can't afford to participate regularly in the feast. The Friends of the Boundary Waters Wilderness have, appropriately, labeled this the number one issue for the 1990s.

I thought of both past and future problems during a week-long canoe trip in 1986 on Basswood Lake, which, because of its central access, has been at the heart of canoe country conflict. I traveled the Four Mile Portage, saw the unmarked graves of settlers, the ceremonial grounds of the Ojibway, the old resort sites. The latter are easy to spot if you know the area's past. Just look for uniform stands of red and white pine; they were planted by the resort owners who moved onto the land after it had been logged and burned.

Although the resort and cabin owners on Basswood Lake had a different image of the area than did the preservationists, they felt just as attached to it. To a few Ojibway it was their lifelong home; they had been born on Basswood, and their ancestors were buried on its islands. They were outraged to be forced into signing a document that would not let them pass on their property to their children. White families who had owned cabins for decades felt much the same. One family, whose several cabins on an island were torn down by the Forest Service, installed a bronze plaque in a huge boulder, commemorating their decades of attachment to this place.[2] Many Basswood Lake resort owners felt betrayed, because when they had built their resorts there had been no indication of an eventual buyout. One resort owner on Pipestone Bay undoubtedly spoke for many:

> If I and others like me had known of federal intentions in
> this area in 1946, where might we be now? Completed

education under the GI Bill? Where? It seems to have
been our misfortune to pursue a course that has us
continually bumping heads with federal purpose. We do
not stand the knocks as well as Uncle Sam....My feeling
for the wilderness is genuine. Any sacrifice of principle on
my part will be for the sake of four children to raise and
educate....Each year is a most vital commodity. We do
not wish them lightly trifled with. We wish to make the
most of our passage.[3]

When Sigurd Olson first traveled Basswood Lake in 1921, it was nearly
impossible to get lost because the American side consisted of tree
stumps and the Canadian side was dominated by tall pine. Today, it
is easy to get lost; the forest is thick on both sides of the international
boundary, and all the resorts are gone. Motors are banned on the
Canadian side and on half of the American side, but there have been
a number of violations — I witnessed two during my short trip.

Camped near the burial site of an Ojibway chief one evening, I thought
about some of the ironies of wilderness travel, how so many of us try
to get away from civilization and yet take so many products of modern
technology with us: aluminum canoes, kevlar canoes, freeze-dried
foods. We try to escape the mentality of the consumer culture, but look
askance at those who wear old rubber raincoats instead of gore-tex,
who wear hole- strewn sneakers instead of the latest footwear. I had to
laugh when, at the Quetico Park Ranger station in the middle of the
wilderness on Basswood Lake, I was asked if I wanted to pay my
camping fees with MasterCard.

As I thought about these things and listened to the loons and watched
the stars, I couldn't help but watch the satellites zip soundlessly across
the sky. My thoughts drifted back to something else the owner of the
Pipestone Bay resort had said, a statement that certainly didn't fit the
stereotype of a resort owner: "Since the earliest days," he said,

the tread of the white man has been heavy upon this land;
all the while gathering momentum until now we seem

gripped in one mad rush to consume everything. A materialistic concept has us by the throat. How many tons of ore, coal; how many cords of pulp, board feet of timber; how many bushels to the acre, kilowatts from the river? Our needs are even outrun by hucksters creating false needs. Certainly directives are in order and much is begging to be done. But — how are you going to reverse the going concepts at the border of the BWCA?[4]

I reached into my pocket and pulled out a small piece of greenstone that I had been carrying all week. I turned it slowly, over and over, three billion years in the palm of my hand. A cool breeze stirred; I shivered. Ripples spread down the sweep of Basswood, glistening in the starlight, framed by the silhouetted shores of two countries. And then I knew: To the greenstone, to the shores, and to the lake itself, this was just another evening. The motorboats, the satellites — even I — were but ripples in the fathomless river of time. Perhaps, I thought, we cannot "reverse the going concepts" when we enter the canoe country. But then, perhaps the land itself renders them insignificant.

REFERENCE NOTES

Chapter 1 / *Wilderness Bound* / pages 1 - 24

[1] Nicholas Garry was deputy governor of the Hudson's Bay Co. in 1821, when he made his first trip through the Quetico-Superior. Quoted in Grace Lee Nute, *The Voyageur,* Reprint ed. (St. Paul, Minn.: Minnesota Historical Society Press, 1955 [orig. 1931]), p. 59.

[2] The term "cultural animal" comes from Robin Fox, "The Cultural Animal," *Encounter,* July 1970, pp. 31-42.

[3] Clifford Geertz, *The Interpretation of Cultures: Selected Essays* (New York: Basic Books, 1973), pp. 49-51; Peter L. Berger, *The Sacred Canopy: Elements of a Sociological Theory of Religion* (Garden City, N.Y.: Doubleday & Co., 1967), pp. 4-22.

[4] The twin concepts of space and place, which are used throughout this book, are derived from a course I took from geographer Yi-Fu Tuan at the University of Wisconsin-Madison in the fall of 1985. They are developed at length in his book, *Space and Place: The Perspective of Experience* (Minneapolis, Minn.: University of Minnesota Press, 1977).

[5] This is known today as glacial Lake Agassiz, which spread from what is now northwestern Saskatchewan across most of Manitoba and western Ontario, and south across northern Minnesota, down western Minnesota and eastern North Dakota to the head of the Minnesota River. Lake of the Woods, Lake Winnipeg, and Lake Winnipegosis are parts of the ancient lake. See Charles L. Matsch, *North America and the Great Ice Age* (New York: McGraw-Hill, 1976), pp. 88-90; Grace Lee Nute, *Rainy River Country* (St. Paul, Minn.: Minnesota Historical Society Press, 1950), pp. 2-4.

[6] The lake, of course, is known to us today as Lake Superior. But, as this book will often show, labels help create particular images. To keep from foisting modern images on earlier times, I will try to use only those labels that are historically appropriate. There is one important exception, which first occurs at the end of the next paragraph, and that is my use of the term Rainy Lake watershed.

[7] Bruce Nelson, *Land of the Dacotahs* (Minneapolis, Minn.:

University of Minnesota Press, 1946), p. 10; Clifford Ahlgren and Isabel Ahlgren, *Lob Trees in the Wilderness* (Minneapolis: University of Minnesota Press, 1984), pp. 80-81.

[8] The Hochelaga eventually came to be known as the St. Lawrence. Cartier had given the name to a bay near the mouth of the river, where he had been windbound on the saint's feast day (August 8).

[9] William Cronon, *Changes in the Land: Indians, Colonists, and the Ecology of New England* (New York: Hill and Wang, 1983), p. 83.

[10] This argument also has been made by Cronon in *Changes in the Land*, pp. 91-107.

[11] The following discussion of the fur trade and native Americans relies largely on these sources: Cronon, *Changes in the Land;* Edmund Jefferson Danziger Jr., *The Chippewas of Lake Superior,* The Civilization of the American Indian Series, vol. 148 (Norman, Okla.: University of Oklahoma Press, 1978); Bernard DeVoto, *The Course of Empire* (Lincoln, Neb.: University of Nebraska Press, 1952); and, especially, Harold Innis, *The Fur Trade in Canada: An Introduction to Canadian Economic History,* revised ed. (New Haven, Conn.: Yale University Press, 1962 [orig. 1930]).

[12] Danziger, *Chippewas,* pp. 36-37.

[13] Ibid., p. 74.

[14] Ahlgren and Ahlgren, *Lob Trees,* pp. 80-84.

[15] Ibid.

[16] Grace Lee Nute, *The Voyageur's Highway* (St. Paul, Minn.: Minnesota Historical Society Press, 1941), pp. 7-8, 62; William E. Lass, *Minnesota's Boundary With Canada: Its Evolution Since 1783* (St. Paul, Minn.: Minnesota Historical Society Press, 1980), p. 5; Innis, *Fur Trade,* p. 237; Danziger, *Chippewas,* p. 79.

[17] Robert V. Hine, *The American West: An Interpretive History* (Boston: Little, Brown & Co., 1973), p. 45; William Watts Folwell, *A History of Minnesota,* 4 vols. (St. Paul, Minn.: Minnesota Historical Society Press, 1921), 1: 66-67; Ahlgren and Ahlgren, *Lob Trees,* p. 86.

[18] The following discussion about Mitchell's map and border disputes is based upon Lass, *Minnesota's Boundary.*

[19] Quoted in Lass, *Minnesota's Boundary,* p. 61.

[20] Quoted in Lass, *Minnesota's Boundary,* p. 68.

[21] Quoted in David A. Walker, *Iron Frontier: The Discovery and*

Early Development of Minnesota's Three Ranges (St. Paul, Minn.: Minnesota Historical Society Press, 1979), p. 74. See also Ahlgren and Ahlgren, *Lob Trees,* pp. 46, 95, 116-117.

[22] Ahlgren and Ahlgren, *Lob Trees,* pp. 96-99; G.H. Good, "Fall-Basswood Lake Logging Railroad," June, 1952, unpub. mss., copy at Vermilion Interpretive Center, Ely, Minn.

[23] Agnes M. Larson, *History of the White Pine Industry in Minnesota,* Use and Abuse of America's Natural Resources, ed. Stuart Bruchey and Eleanor Bruchey (New York: Arno Press, 1972 [orig. University of Minnesota Press, 1949]), pp. 254-256.

[24] George Michael Warecki, "The Quetico-Superior Council and the Battle for Wilderness in Quetico Provincial Park, 1909-1960," (M.A. Thesis, University of Western Ontario, 1983), pp. 13, 26-29; Shan Walshe, "History of the Quetico-Superior Country" (unpub. mss., copy at Quetico Park headquarters), Part 5, p. 5, Part 6, pp. 3-5.

[25] Warecki, "The Quetico-Superior Council and the Battle for Wilderness," pp. 16-19, 22.

Chapter 2 / *Saganaga Lake* / pages 25 - 38

[1] T.S. Eliot, "Ash Wednesday," in T.S. Eliot, *Collected Poems, 1909-1962* (San Diego: Harcourt Brace Jovanovich, 1970), p. 85.

[2] Hans Huth, *Nature and the American: Three Centuries of Changing Attitudes* (Lincoln, Neb.: University of Nebraska Press, Bison Books, 1972), p. 2; Lee Clark Mitchell, *Witnesses to a Vanishing America: the Nineteenth-Century Response* (Princeton: Princeton University Press, 1981), p. 58; Samuel P. Hays, *Conservation and the Gospel of Efficiency: The Progressive Conservation Movement, 1890-1920* (New York: Atheneum, 1980 [orig. Harvard University Press, 1959]), p. 22.

[3] Hays, *Conservation and the Gospel of Efficiency,* pp. 2, 266.

[4] Mitchell, *Witnesses,* p. 15; Hays, *Gospel of Efficiency,* pp. 27-33.

[5] Hays, *Gospel of Efficiency,* pp. 47-71.

[6] Ibid., pp. 100-121.

[7] Ibid., pp. 122-125, quote p. 125.

[8] Ibid., p. 176.

[9] Ibid.

[10] The thrust of the following argument about the role of urbanization, technology, the corporate economy and secularization is based on T.J. Jackson Lears, *No Place of Grace: Antimodernism and the Transformation of American Culture, 1880-1920* (New York: Pantheon Books, 1981).

[11] Leo Marx, *The Machine in the Garden: Technology and the Pastoral Ideal in America* (New York: Oxford University Press, 1964), p. 127.

[12] Marx, *The Machine in the Garden*, p. 226.

[13] Daniel J. Boorstin, *The Americans: The Democratic Experience* (New York: Vintage Books, 1973), p. 420.

[14] Ibid., p. 363.

[15] Ibid., p. 369.

[16] Lears, "From Salvation Through Self-Realization," p. 8.

[17] Robert H. Wiebe, *The Search for Order: 1877-1920* (New York: Hill and Wang, 1967), p. 46.

[18] Ibid., p. 47.

[19] Bridgeman quoted in Henry Steele Commager, *The American Mind: An Interpretation of American Thought and Character Since the 1880s* (New Haven, Conn.: Yale University Press, 1950), p. 105. See also Nash, *Nervous Generation*, pp. 122-123.

[20] Quoted in Lears, *No Place of Grace*, p. 41.

[21] The figure on wilderness visitation was calculated from information presented in Marion Clawson and Burnell Held, *The Federal Lands: Their Use and Management* (Lincoln, Neb.: University of Nebraska Press, 1957), p. 408.

[22] The top four were by Gene Stratton Porter: *Freckles, The Girl of the Limberlost, The Harvester* and *Laddie*. In fifth place was *The Winning of Barbara Worth*, by Harold Bell Wright. Owen Wister's *The Virginian* was sixth, and Jack London's *Call of the Wild* was seventh.

[23] Harold Bell Wright, *When a Man's a Man* (New York: A.L. Burt, 1916), p. 11.

[24] James Oliver Curwood, *Honor of the Big Snows* (Indianapolis: Bobbs-Merrill, 1911), p. 285.

[25] Mary Meek Atkeson, "The Religion of the Fields," *Good Housekeeping*, July 1924, p. 190.

[26] Hays, *Gospel of Efficiency,* p. 141.

[27] The quote and Olson's description of the encounter are from an oral history of Olson, the recording and transcripts of which are available at the Audio-Visual Library, Minnesota Historical Society.

[28] Student Volunteer Movement pledge quoted in Emily Rosenberg, *Spreading the American Dream: American Economic and Cultural Expansion, 1890-1945* (New York: Hill and Wang, 1981), p. 29.

[29] Lears, *No Place of Grace,* p. 32.

[30] Olson, "Canoe Tourist."

[31] Ibid.

[32] Arthur H. Carhart, "Live Game and Forest Recreation," *American Forestry,* December 1920, pp. 725-726.

[33] [Arthur H. Carhart], "Recreation Plans, Superior National Forest," May 1922, p. 15, in Carhart, Arthur H., 1922 Report and Photos, Superior National Forest Records microfilm roll 3, Minnesota Historical Society. (Superior National Forest Records at the Minnesota Historical Society are hereafter cited as SNFR-MHS).

[34] Ibid., p. 3.

[35] Donald N. Baldwin, *The Quiet Revolution: Grass Roots of Today's Wilderness Preservation Movement* (Boulder, Colo.: Pruett Publishing Co., 1972), p. 34. See also Roderick Nash, "Arthur Carhart: Wildland Advocate," *Living Wilderness,* December 1980, pp. 32-34.

Chapter 3 / *Canoe Country* / pages 39 - 50

[1] V.K. Brown, "A Vacation in the Superior Forest," *Parks and Recreation,* March-April 1926, p. 466.

[2] Arthur H. Carhart, "Vacation Opportunities in Your National Forests," *American Forestry,* September 1920, p. 551.

[3] On Quetico Park logging, see George Michael Warecki, "The Quetico-Superior Council and the Battle for Wilderness in Quetico Provincial Park, 1909-1960," (M.A. Thesis, University of Western Ontario, 1983), pp. 24-30. See also Sigurd F. Olson, "Explorers," *Naturalist,* Winter 1961, pp. 2-7.

[4] R. Newell Searle, *Saving Quetico-Superior: A Land Set Apart* (St. Paul, Minn.: Minnesota Historical Society Press, 1977), p. 20.

[5] Ely (Minn.) Commercial Club, *Ely, Minnesota, Gateway to the Superior National Forest in "The Playground of a Nation,"* (Ely, Minn., 1929), original at Vermilion Interpretive Center, Ely, Minn.

[6] On gateways, see Yi-Fu Tuan, *Topophilia: A Study of Environmental Perception, Attitudes, and Values* (Englewood Cliffs, N.J.: Prentice-Hall, 1974), pp. 203-204.

[7] Duluth and Iron Range Railroad, *The Playground of a Nation* (Duluth, Minn.: Duluth and Iron Range Railroad, [1921]), Arrowhead pamphlets file, MHS; C[harles] L. Gilman, *The Pack Sack Trail* (Duluth, Minn.: Duluth and Iron Range Railroad, [1916?], St. Louis Co. pamphlets file, MHS. For a map of the timber cut between 1890 and 1925, see Boundary Waters Resources Committee, *Recreational Studies in Correlation With Forest Management and Local Area Economy* (Duluth, Minn.: Minnesota Arrowhead Association, September 1965).

[8] Ely Commercial Club, *Ely, Minnesota, Gateway to the Superior National Forest.*

[9] St. Louis Country Club, *The Vacation Land Supreme: Amid the Pines and Lakes of Northern Minnesota* (n.p., 1923?), in Arrowhead pamphlets files, MHS.

[10] U.S. Forest Service, *A Vacation Land of Lakes and Woods: The Superior National Forest* (Washington, D.C.: U.S.Forest Service, 1919), p. 3.

[11] Sigurd Olson, "Canoe Tourist Finds Joys of the Great Outdoors Through Vast Watered Wilderness of the North," *The Milwaukee Journal,* July 31, 1921.

[12] Donald Hough, "Autocamping Possibilities in Minnesota," *Outdoor Life,* August 1924, p. 134.

[13] C.S. Samuelson, "Minnesota, the Outer's Paradise," *Outdoor Life,* June 1925, p. 476.

[14] Arthur H. Carhart, "Vacation Opportunities in Your National Forests," *American Forestry,* September 1920, p. 551.

[15] A.T. Huizinga, "Wilderness Fish Stories," *Outdoor Life,* August 1927, p. 32.

[16] U.S. Forest Service, *Vacation Land of Lakes and Woods,* p. 4.

[17] Donald Hough, "A Battlefield of Conservation," *Outdoor America,* September 1927, p. 5.

[18] Clifford Ahlgren and Isabel Ahlgren, *Lob Trees in the Wilderness*

(Minneapolis, Minn.: University of Minnesota Press, 1984), pp. 93-115.

[19] W.J. Breckenridge, "A Century of Minnesota Wild Life," *Minnesota History* 30 (1949):129-130; Calvin A. Dahlgren, "Fish and Game in the Superior," *Parks and Recreation,* July-August 1924, pp. 629-634.

[20] Ely Commercial Club, *Ely, Minnesota, Gateway to the Superior National Forest.*

[21] "Facts About the Superior National Forest," *Parks and Recreation,* March-April 1923, p. 322.

[22] Winton Trading Co. advertisement, *Outdoor Life,* April 1924, p. 327; Edgar S. Perkins, "The Care of Canoes," *Outdoor America,* February 1926, p. 60.

[23] Ibid.

[24] Minnesota Arrowhead Association, *Main Highways and Some By-ways: Little Journeys that Should Interest You to Points of Interest in the Famous Minnesota Arrowhead Country* (Duluth, 1928).

[25] Paul B. Riis, "Birth of a Wilderness," *Parks and Recreation,* March - April 1923, p. 313.

[26] Sigurd Olson, "Reflections of a Guide," *Field and Stream,* June 1928, p. 28.

[27] Ibid.

[28] A.L. Skradske, "Vacationing in Superior National Forest," *Forest and Stream,* March 1926, p. 170.

[29] Ely Commercial Club, *Ely, Minnesota, Gateway to the Superior National Forest.* I am indebted to Linda H. Graber for this theme of wilderness as sacred. See her book, *Wilderness as Sacred Space* (Washington, D.C.: Association of American Geographers, 1976).

[30] Ely Commercial Club, *Ely, Minnesota, Gateway to the Superior National Forest.*

[31] Ibid.

Chapter 4 / Insiders And Outsiders: When Images Collide / pages 51 - 79

[1] Julius M. Nolte, "The Call to Battle," *Outdoor America,* April 1928, p. 4.

[2] See Agnes M. Larson, *History of the White Pine Industry in Minnesota,* Use and Abuse of America's Natural Resources series, ed. Stuart Bruchey and Eleanor Bruchey (New York: Arno Press, 1972 [originally University of Minnesota Press, 1949]), pp. 279-284; and Fremont P. Wirth, *The Discovery and Exploitation of the Minnesota Iron Lands* (N.Y.: Arno Press, 1979 [originally Cedar Rapids, Iowa: Torch Press, 1937]), pp. 105-106.

[3] Paul Landis, *Three Iron Mining Towns: A Study in Cultural Change* (Ann Arbor, Mich.: Edwards Brothers, Inc., 1938), pp. 38-41.

[4] Landis, *Three Iron Mining Towns,* pp. 38-41, 106-108.

[5] Ibid., quotes pp. 79, 83. See also pp. 73-86, 104.

[6] See Rev. Karl N. Aho, *Portrait of the Church in an Economic Eclipse: A Study of the Church's Role in Minnesota's Iron Range* (Minneapolis: Minnesota Council of Churches [1964]), pp. 16-17, 76-77 (quote from p. 77); John Sirjamaki, "The People of the Mesabi Range," *Minnesota History* 27 (1946): 203-215; Neil Betten, "Strike on the Mesabi — 1907," *Minnesota History* 40 (1967): 340-347.

[7] Landis, *Three Iron Mining Towns,* pp. 87-94; William Watts Folwell, *A History of Minnesota* (St. Paul: Minnesota Historical Society Press, 1930), 4: 52-53.

[8] Agricultural statistics for 1920 come from *The 14th Census of the United States,* vol. 6, pp. 497-502. Statistics for 1930 are from Committee on Land Utilization, *Land Utilization in Minnesota* (Minneapolis: University of Minnesota Press, 1934), pp. 99-106.

[9] MacCrickart quoted in Minnesota Arrowhead Association, *Come to the Minnesota Arrowhead Country* (Duluth: Minnesota Arrowhead Association, 1929). See also Minnesota Arrowhead Association, *50 Years of Service to the Vacation Travel Industry* (Duluth: Minnesota Arrowhead Association, 1974).

[10] Regional Forester Allan Peck estimated the number of canoeists in 1926 at nine hundred or one thousand. See R. Newell Searle, *Saving Quetico-Superior: A Land Set Apart* (St. Paul: Minnesota Historical Society Press, 1977), p. 29.

[11] Donald N. Baldwin, *The Quiet Revolution: Grass Roots of Today's Wilderness Preservation Movement* (Boulder, Colo.: Pruett Publishing Co., 1972), p. 5.

[12] Quoted in Baldwin, *Quiet Revolution,* p. 34.

[13] Quoted in [Arthur Carhart], "Preliminary Prospectus: An Outline of the Superior National Forest," [1921], p. 4, in Carhart, Arthur H., 1922 Report & Photos, microfilm roll 3, Superior National Forest Records, Minnesota Historical Society Research Center, St. Paul, Minnesota. [File hereafter cited as Carhart Report, SNFR-MHS.]

[14] Carhart, "Carhart Report," p. 51. See also p. 50.

[15] Ibid., pp. 41-46.

[16] Carhart, "Carhart Report," pp. 58, 57. Donald Baldwin used this last quote out of context to argue that Carhart "clearly advocated wilderness preservation." Carhart opposed "urban type" developments, but not such things as rustic log hotels, dams, and motorboat highways.

[17] Carhart, "Carhart Report," pp. 46, 54.

[18] Ibid., pp. 68, 61, 59.

[19] Ibid., pp. 61-62.

[20] Aldo Leopold, "The Wilderness and Its Place in Forest Recreation Policy," *Journal of Forestry,* November 1921, p. 719.

[21] Aldo Leopold, *Round River: From the Journals of Aldo Leopold,* ed. Luna B. Leopold (New York: Oxford University Press paperback, 1972 [originally 1953]), p. 66; Aldo Leopold, "The Last Stand of the Wilderness," *American Forests,* October 1925, pp. 601-602.

[22] Arthur Carhart to William Vogt, November 3, 1964, in Carhart Report, SNFR-MHS. See also Arthur Carhart, *The National Forests* (New York: Alfred A. Knopf, 1959), pp. 121- 122 for another statement supporting logging in the BWCA.

[23] Untitled editorial, *Ely Miner,* August 13, 1926, copy in Road Controversies 1920s file, microfilm roll 9, SNFR-MHS.

[24] Searle, *Saving Quetico-Superior,* pp. 22-23; Baldwin, *Quiet Revolution,* p. 106.

[25] Paul B. Riis, "Birth of a Wilderness," *Parks and Recreation,* March-April 1923, p. 315.

[26] "The Paths of Hokum Lead But to the Grave," *Outdoor America,* September 1926, p. 29.

[27] Ibid.

[28] Quoted in Searle, *Saving Quetico-Superior,* p. 30.

[29] Superior National Forest, "Recreation Policy Statement," May 8,

1926, in Plans of Management 1926, microfilm roll 5, SNFR-MHS.

[30] [William M. Jardine], "The Policy of the Department of Agriculture in Relation to Road Building and Recreational Use of the Superior National Forest, Minnesota," September 17, 1926, in Road Controversies 1920s, microfilm roll 9, SNFR-MHS; Baldwin, *Quiet Revolution*, p. 249, note 12; Searle, *Saving Quetico-Superior*, pp. 31-32; Paul B. Riis, "SNF News," *Parks and Recreation*, September-October 1926, pp. 77-78.

[31] Both Searle and Baldwin presented the resolution of the road fight as a victory for preservationists. For the state of road building in 1928, see the map for that year in Superior National Forest, Genesis of Management Plan, 1931-1934, microfilm roll 3, SNFR- MHS.

[32] Searle, *Saving Quetico-Superior*, pp. 34-39.

[33] Ibid., pp. 47-49. On the International Joint Commission, see Joseph T. Jockel and Alan M. Schwartz, "The Changing Environmental Role of the Canada-United States International Joint Commission," *Environmental Review* 8 (Fall 1984): 236-251.

[34] Donald Hough, "A Battlefield of Conservation," *Outdoor America*, September 1927, p. 8, and October 1927, p. 68; Searle, *Saving Quetico-Superior*, p. 48.

[35] Searle, *Saving Quetico-Superior*, pp. 47-48.

[36] Ibid., pp. 40-41.

[37] Ely Commercial Club, *Ely, Minnesota, Gateway to the Superior National Forest in 'The Playground of a Nation'* (n.p., 1929); Donald Hough, "A Battlefield of Conservation," *Outdoor America*, October 1927, p. 72; Searle, *Saving Quetico-Superior*, p. 52.

[38] Searle, *Saving Quetico-Superior*, pp. 53-56.

[39] Ernest C. Oberholtzer, "Conserving the Public Values of the Rainy Lake Watershed," *Outdoor America*, January 1928, p. 8.

[40] Ibid.

[41] Earle W. Tinker to Arthur Carhart, February 28, 1928, in Carhart, Arthur H., 1922 Report & Photos, microfilm roll 3, SNFR-MHS.

[42] Earl W. Tinker to Forest Supervisor, April 4, 1928; [Bill] Barker, memo to Supervisor Hamel, March 15, 1928, both in Carhart, Arthur H., 1922 Report & Photos, microfilm roll 3, SNFR-MHS.

[43] Searle, *Saving Quetico-Superior*, pp. 70-71.

[44] Donald Hough, "A Battlefield of Conservation," *part two, Outdoor America,* October 1927, p. 16.

[45] Hough, "Battlefield," part two, pp. 16-17.

[46] "Water Power," *Outdoor America,* April 1928, p. 30.

[47] Harry McGuire, "The Divine Right of the Dollar," *Outdoor Life,* September 1929, p. 9.

[48] Sen. Thomas D. Schall, "The De-Creator: E.W. Backus and His Water Power Project," *Outdoor America,* April 1928, p. 6.

[49] Pittenger quoted in Searle, *Saving Quetico-Superior,* p. 83. See also pp. 73-82.

[50] William I. Nolan had replaced Newton after the latter had become Herbert Hoover's secretary.

[51] Searle, *Saving Quetico-Superior,* pp. 101-103.

[52] Ibid., pp. 106-107.

[53] Frank B. Hubachek to Charles S. Kelly, July 15, 1946, Control of Use of Airplanes file 2, Quetico Superior Council Papers, MHS (papers hereafter cited as QSC); Hubachek to Ernest Oberholtzer, August 15, 1946, Charles S. Kelly folders, QSC; Sigurd Olson to Robert Mueller, December 14, 1947, Quetico-Superior files, Sigurd F. Olson Papers, MHS; Hubachek, "Memorandum Re Canadian Border Developments July 1946," August 3, 1946, Kelly folders, QSC; H.R. Scott to Ken Reid, December 18, 1946, Quetico-Superior files, Sigurd F. Olson papers.

Chapter 5 / *Fishing Paradise* / pages 80 - 95

[1] Arthur Hawthorne Carhart, "Trout Lake," *Outdoor Life,* July 1932, p. 46

[2] The quotes are from David E. Shi, *The simple Life: Plain Living and High Thinkin in American Culture* (New York: Oxford University Press, 1985), pp. 217, 219. See also Foster Rhea Dulles, *America Learns to Play: A History of Popular Recreation, 1607-1940* (New York: D. appleton-Century Co., 1940), pp. 366-367.

[3] T.J. Jackson Lears, "From Salvation to Self-Realization: Advertising and the Therapeutic Roots of the Consumer Culture, 1880-1930," in Richard Wrightman Fox and T.J. Jackson Lears, ed., *The*

Culture of Consumption: Critical Essays in American History, 1880-1980 (New York: Pantheon Books, 1983), p. 4.

[4] Hoover quoted in Shi, *Simple Life*, p. 222; Robert C. Mueller, "Let's Go Fishing in 1932!" *Sports Afield*, April 1932, p. 9.

[5] E.G. Stoughton, "The Thirteenth Disciple," *Outdoor Life*, July 1926, p. 32.

[6] W.J. Webb, "The Fifty Greatest Years of Outboarding," *The Antique Outboarder*, January 1977, pp. 14-16.

[7] Webb, "Fifty Greatest Years," pp. 10, 14-15; "History of Outboards," *The Antique Outboarder*, October 1981, p. 59; Waterman Motor Co., advertisement, *Outdoor Life*, August 1915, p. 27A; Gordon MacQuarrie, *Ole Evinrude and the Old Fellows* (Milwaukee, Wis.: Evinrude Motors, 1984 [originally 1947]), pp. 15-16; Evinrude Motor Co. advertisement, *Forest & Stream*, April 1919, p. 186.

[8] Paul Burress, "Outboard Motors and Small Boats," *Outdoor America*, September 1928, p. 62.

[9] Jim Webb and John Van Vleet, "The Johnson Story," *The Antique Outboarder*, January 1979, pp. 3-27; Webb, "Fifty Greatest Years," pp. 14-16; William Voigt, Jr., "Aquatic Hotrodders and Shrinking Shorelines," *Outdoor America*, September 1958, p. 6.

[10] Captain Jack Sparr, "Outboard Motors and Watercraft," *Outdoor America*, October 1930, p. 61.

[11] Robert C. Mueller told one of his *Sports Afield* readers in a 1931 advice column, "I presume you intend to avail yourself of the motorboat tow through Fall and Basswood Lake to Upper Basswood Falls." See Mueller, "Your Vacation: Where to Go and How to Get There," September 1931, p. 3.

[12] On boat catching in Quetico Park, see George Michael Warecki, "The Quetico-Superior Council and the Battle for Wilderness in Quetico Provincial Park, 1909-1960: (MA Thesis, University of Western Ontario, 1983), p. 99.

[13] The numbers of outfitters and resorts operating in the Ely area (as well as their names and locations) can be found in the annual Ely Chamber of Commerce tourist guides.

[14] Jay Price to H(erman) H. Chapman, September 12, 1944, Organizations, Committees files Box 7, Quetico-Superior folders, Aldo Leopold Papers, University of Wisconsin-Madison Archives,

Madison, Wis.

[15] Shan Walshe, "History of the Quetico-Superior Country" (unpublished mss., ca 1984, copy at Quetico Park headquarters), part 7, pp. 12-13; Warecki, "The Quetico-Superior Council," note 65 on p. 120.

[16] Jamieson quoted in Walshe, "History of the Quetico-Superior Country," part 7, p. 14.

[17] Clifford and Isabel Ahlgren, *Lob Trees in the Wilderness* (Minneapolis: University of Minnesota Press, 1984), pp. 161-162; Warecki, "The Quetico-Superior Council," p. 85.

[18] Minnesota Arrowhead Association, Annual Report, December 31, 1931, pp. 3-4, available at MHS; Minnesota Arrowhead Association, *Minnesota Arrowhead Country: The Arrowhead Resort Directory* (Duluth: Minnesota Arrowhead Association, 1933), in Arrowhead pamphlets files, MHS.

[19] Ibid., pp. 4-6.

[20] Ibid., p. 6.

[21] Sig Olson, "Let's Go Exploring," *Field and Stream,* June 1937, p. 44.

[22] Burntside Lodge brochure (n.p., circa 1926), in St. Louis County pamphlets files, MHS; Northern Lakes Guides advertisement, *Sports Afield,* July 1932, p. 5; Wegen's Wilderness Camp advertisement, *Sports Afield,* October 1930, p. 4.

[23] Emil "Ogima" Anderson, "Quetico Bass (The Villains)," *Sports Afield,* June 1935, p. 16; Bert Claflin, "Where Big Ones Lurk," *Sports Afield,* November 1939, p. 18; Arthur Hawthorne Carhart, "The Warriors of Wind Bay," *Outdoor Life,* April 1932, p. 13; Arthur Hawthorne Carhart, "Wilderness Walleyes," *Outdoor Life,* June 1932, p. 12; Paul Gartner, "Lucius the Mihty," *Field and Stream,* August 1933, p. 18; thomas E. Powers, "We Wanted Bass," *Field and Stream,* December 1930, p. 34.

[24] Arthur A. Carhart, "The Great God Smash!" *Field and Stream,* February 1933, p. 11.

[25] Emil "Ogima" Anderson, "Off the Trail in Quetico," *Sports Afield,* August 1933, pp. 20, 24.

[26] Seth Briggs, "Tales of Record Fish," *Field and Stream,* June 1930, p. 43; Beebee, "What's Doing Up North," *Sports Afield,*

October 1930, p. 79.

[27] South Bend Bait Co. ad, *Field and Stream,* June 1930, pp. 56-57.

[28] Emil Anderson, "Quest for Bass in Quetico," *Sports Afield,* April 1936, p. 68; Emil "Ogima" Anderson, "On the Trail in Quetico," *Sports Afield,* April 1937, p. 70 (emphasis his).

[29] Calvin A. Dahlgren, "Fish and Game in the Superior," *Parks and Recreation,* July-August 1924, p. 633. On biological productivity of the area's lakes, see Fritz H. Johnson and John G. Hale, "Interrelations Between Walleye (Stizostedion vitreum vitreum) and Smallmouth Bass (Micropterus dolomieui) in Four Northeastern Minnesota Lakes, 1948-69," *Journal of the Fisheries Research Board of Canada* 34 (1977): pp. 1626-1627.

[30] Fish stocking records up to the early 1940s are in the Minnesota Conservation Department Records, Game and Fish Division: Fisheries Section, Boxes 1-3, Minnesota State Archives, MHS. [Hereafter cited by the appropriate lake or river name, and box number for that record.] The earliest date I fourn was 1909, when Charles Nobowsky planted 10 cans of trout in the Isabella River. See Isabella River, Box 3.

[31] Basswood Lake, Box 2.

[32] Moose Lake, Box 2; Twin and Burntside lakes, Box 1. Twin Lake has since been renamed Ojibway Lake.

[33] Basswood, Snowbank, Fall, Ensign and Moose lakes, Box 2; Big Lake, Box 1.

[34] Dunnigan Lake, Box 2.

[35] U.S. Forest Service, Classification, R-9, Superior Roadless Area, November 15, 1937, p. 12, in Plans of Management BWCA 1926-1939, microfilm roll 5, Superior National Forest Records, MHS.

[36] Robert Page Lincoln, "Fishing in the Last Wilderness," *Sports Afield,* April 1936, p. 16.

[37] Robert Page Lincoln, "Fishermen Three," *Sports Afield,* April 1931, p. 51. "H.B.C." stands for Hudson's Bay Company.

[38] Robert Page Lincoln, "From the Diary of an Angler," *Sports Afield,* October 1930, p. 25; Robert Page Lincoln, "Land-Locked Lake Trout," *Sports Afield,* April 1937, p. 82.

[39] Robert Page Lincoln, "Fishing in the Last Wilderness," *Sports Afield,* April 1936, p. 15.

[40] Quoted in O.R. Tripp, "Tourists and Tall Timber," *Field and*

Stream, July 1931, p. 36.

[41] Canadian Border Lodge brochure (n.p., ca. 1930), in St. Louis Co. pamphlets files, MHS.

[42] Winton Trading Lodge ad, in Minnesota Arrowhead Association, *Minnesota Arrowhead Country: The Arrowhead Resort Directory* (Duluth: Minnesota Arrowhead Association, 1933), p. 7.

[43] Ely Commercial Club, *Rest and Relaxation at Ely, Minnesota: Arrowhead Country* (n.p., 1944), in St. Louis County pamphlets file, MHS.

Chapter 6 / *Sanctuary* / pages 96 - 120

[1] Harold Martin, "Embattled Wilderness," *Saturday Evening Post,* September 25, 1948, p. 22.

[2] Sigurd F. Olson, *Open Horizons* (New York: Alfred A. Knopf, 1969), pp. 81-82.

[3] Olson to Robert Sterling Yard, April 15, 1935, Reflections From the North Country files, Sigurd F. Olson Papers, MHS.

[4] Border Lakes Outfitting Co. ad, *Sports Afield,* September 1931, p. 3.

[5] Border Lakes Outfitting Co. brochure (n.p., undated), viewed at Border Lakes Outfitting Co. office, Winton, Minn.

[6] Ibid.

[7] Samuel Eddy and James C. Underhill, *Northern Fishes: With Special Reference to the Upper Mississippi Valley,* 3rd ed. (Minneapolis: University of Minnesota Press, 1974), pp. 345-346.

[8] Olson to Reid, September 28, 1939, Q-S files, SFO.

[9] I have found only a handful of letters on the subject in Olson's papers. They all are located in the Q-S files. There is no indication in Olson's papers that he or the U.S. Forest Service contacted Quetico Park officials before planting smallmouth in Sarah and Robinson lakes.

[10] "Smallmouth Bass in the Border Lakes," p. 14; Reid to Olson, December 7, 1943, Q-S files, SFO.

[11] Quote from Fritz H. Johnson and John G. Hale, "Interrelations Between Walleye (Stizostedion vitreum vitreum) and Smallmouth

Bass (Micropterus dolomieui) in Four Northeastern Minnesota Lakes, 1948-69," *Journal of the Fisheries Research Board of Canada* 34 (1977) 10:1632.

[12] Peter D. Inskip and John J. Magnuson, "Changes in Fish Populations Over an 80-Year Period: Big Pine Lake, Wisconsin," *Transactions of the American Fisheries Society* 112 (1983): 378-389; Big Lake Gillnet records, Big 69-190 file, Minnesota DNR, Winton, Minnesota.

[13] Inskip and Magnuson, "Changes in Fish Populations," p. 386.

[14] Wynn Davis, "Best Fishing in the Midwest," *Outdoor Life*, April 1961, p. 99. See also Wynn Davis, "100 Best Bass Lakes," *Outdoor Life*, July 1958, p. 33; Hank Bradshaw, "Smallmouth Boom," *Outdoor Life*, July 1962, p. 28; Hank Bradshaw, "Wilderness Smallmouths," *Sports Afield*, September 1963, p. 34; and Bob Cary, "Blizzard Bass," *Outdoor Life*, April 1964, p. 60.

[15] Wynn Davis, "100 Best Bass Lakes," *Outdoor Life*, July 1958, pp. 35, 75 (quote p. 75). See also "Ely Bass 1st in National Fish Contest," *Ely Miner*, March 3, 1966.

[16] Ben East to Olson, March 3, 1948, Lit. Mss. files, SFO.

[17] Anita Diamant to Olson, January 17, 1946, Lit. Mss. files, SFO.

[18] I did not find a published version of "Fishin' Jewelry." Olson's papers contain the manuscript and indicate that *Field and Stream* accepted it for publication on May 9, 1927, but I did not locate copies of the magazine from before 1930. See also Sig Olson, "Cruising in the Arrowhead," *Outdoors*, May 1934, p. 22; Sig Olson, "Spring Fever," *Sports Afield*, April 1931, p. 26; Sig Olson, "The Immortals of Argo," *Sports Afield*, July 1939, p. 36.

[19] Sig Olson, "Search for the Wild," *Sports Afield*, May 1932, p. 51. See also Sigurd F. Olson, *Open Horizons* (New York: Alfred A. Knopf, 1969), p. 185.

[20] Olson, "Search for the Wild," pp. 33, 52.

[21] Sigurd F. Olson, "Interval," January 13, 1941, Lit. Mss. files, SFO.

[22] Leo Marx, *The Machine in the Garden: Technology and the Pastoral Ideal in America* (New York: Oxford University Press, 1964), pp. 16-17.

[23] "A Few Words About Airplane Transportation," *Sports Afield*,

October 1930, p. 72.

[24] Charles W. "Speed" Holman, "Aviation and the Great Outdoors," *Sports Afield*, October 1930, p. 74. For more on airplanes and accessibility, see Charles W. "Speed" Holman, "A Duck Hunter," *Sports Afield*, November 1930, p. 50; and P.W. Ament, "Exploring Inaccessible Lakes by Hydroplane," *Sports Afield*, April 1931, p. 90.

[25] Rob F. Sanderson, "After the War You Can Have Your Own Plane," Outdoor Life, May 1944, p. 17.

[26] Olson to Frank Robertson, May 31, 1945, Q-S files, SFO; Olson to Reid, April 24, 1945, 1020-1-1 Public Law 733 folders, Superior National Forest Records, Duluth, Minn. [hereafter cited as PL 733 folders, SNFR].

[27] George E. Bounds, "How it *Feels* to *Fly*," *Sports Afield*, October 1931, p. 33.

[28] Yi-Fu Tuan, *Space and Place: The Perspective of Experience* (Minneapolis: University of Minnesota Press, 1977), p. 54.

[29] Curtain Falls Fishing Camp advertisement, *Ely* (Minn.) *Fish Facts*, May 28, 1949, p. 4.

[30] Sig Olson, "Wings Over the Wilderness," *American Forests,* June 1948, p. 282.

[31] James N. Diehl, memo, August 12, 1948, 2320 Use of Airplanes folders, Superior National Forest Records, Duluth, Minn. [hereafter cited as Airplanes folders, SNFR]; John E. Ledbetter to Sigurd Olson, May 3, 1949, Quetico-Superior files, SFO [hereafter cited as Q-S files]; Olson to Albert Niss, October 28, 1948, Q-S files, SFO.

[32] The most detailed account of the campaign is in David James Backes, "THE AIR BAN WAR: Sigurd F. Olson and the Fight to Ban Private Planes from the Roadless Area of Minnesota's Superior National Forest," (M.S. thesis, University of Wisconsin-Madison, 1983).

[33] "Construction of New Highway to Open Quetico is Approved," *The* (International Falls, Minn.) *Daily Journal,* March 9, 1946; Galen Pike, memo, March 19, 1946, PL 733 folders, SNFR; Pike, memo, July 9, 1946, PL 733 folders, SNFR. At the end of 1946, after talks with American conservationists and Forest Service officials, Ontario agreed to hold off development within Quetico Park for a year, to give the United States a chance to solve the roadless area problem.

[34] Charles S. Kelly, "Memorandum Re Mr. Wentworth," October

14, 1946, Charles S. Kelly folders, Quetico-Superior Council Papers, MHS. [Hereafter cited as Kelly folders, QSC.]

[35] Hubachek to Olson, November 5, 1947, Olson Activities folder, QSC; Olson to Kelly, December 3, 1947, Olson Activities folder, QSC; Olson, note, April 14, 1947, Lit. mss. files, SFO.

[36] The following quotes are from Sig Olson, "Wings Over the Wilderness," *American Forests,* June 1948, p. 252.

[37] Sig Olson, "Veterans Named," *Christian Science Monitor,* March 22, 1948.

[38] The article was "Quetico-Superior Challenge." Minnesota Rep. John A. Blatnik, who represented the Ely area, put the article into the *Congressional Record* on June 8, 1948. See Blatnik to Olson, June 8, 1948, Q-S files, SFO.

[39] A large reprint of many editorials is contained in the Ralph P. Wentworth folder, QSC.

[40] Among the outdoor magazines, *Sports Afield* led the fight, publishing the Olson articles previously cited. *Outdoor Life* and *Field and Stream* held off editorial comment until the conflict nearly was over.

[41] *Wilderness Canoe Country,* written and directed by Sigurd F. Olson, photography by Grant Halliday, produced by the President's Quetico-Superior Committee. A copy of the film is in the Audio-Visual library, MHS.

[42] For a list of those present at the Chicago showing, see Control of the Use of Airplanes file 6, QSC. [Hereafter cited as Airplanes file.]

[43] Carl Moen to Olson, April 21, 1949, Q-S files, SFO; Olson to Grant Halladay, May 31, 1949, Q-S files, SFO; Jack Van Coevering to Olson, March 5, 1949, Q-S files, SFO; Olson to Van Coevering, ca March 1949, Q-S files, SFO; Van Coevering to Olson, March 21, 1949, Q-S files, SFO; William Dalling to Olson, April 18, 1949? Q-S files, SFO; John Smrekar to Sen. Edward J. Thye, May 31, 1949, Airspace Reservation, Ely Opposition folder [hereafter cited as Ely folder], Edward J. Thye Papers, MHS. [Hereafter cited as EJT.]

[44] Blatnik to Olson, June 8, 1948, Q-S files, SFO.

[45] "Something to Consider, Anyway," *Ely Miner,* May 15, 1948; Samuel Trask Dana, John H. Allison and Russell N. Cunningham, *Minnesota Lands: Ownership, Use, and Management of Forest and Related Lands* (Washington, D.C.: The American Forestry Associa-

tion, 1960), pp. 27-30, 160.

[46] John A. Smrekar, form letter, July 23, 1949, Correspondence and Miscellaneous files, Friends of the Wilderness Papers, MHS; Frank V. Strukel to Charles F. Brannan, August 5, 1949, Airplanes folders, SNFR. [Friends of the Wilderness Papers hereafter cited as FOW.]

[47] Leo Chosa, *Isolate and Exploit* (Ely, Minn., ca. March 1950), in Q-S files, SFO.

[48] Ibid.

[49] Charles W. Ingersoll to FOW, August 29, 1949, Correspondence and Miscellaneous files, FOW; Bill Trygg to Bill Magie, July 2, 1949, Correspondence and Miscellaneous files, FOW; "F.B. Hubachek Makes Statement," *Ely Miner*, August 25, 1949? Bill Rom to Olson, March 9, 1949, Q-S files, SFO; Rom to Olson, March 29, 1949, Airplanes file 6, QSC.

Chapter 7 / *Sacred Place* / pages 121 - 157

[1] Sigurd F. Olson, "The Spiritual Need," in Bruce M. Kilgore, ed., *Wilderness in a Changing World* (San Francisco: Sierra Club, 1966), p. 219.

[2] Quoted in Paul Boyer, *By the Bomb's Early Light: American Thought and Culture at the Dawn of the Atomic Age* (New York: Pantheon Books, 1985), p. 14.

[3] See Merle Curti, *The Growth of American Thought*, 3rd ed. (New Brunswick, N.J.: Transaction Books, 1982), pp. 767-774.

[4] "Endangered Sanctuary," *New York Times*, October 5, 1952.

[5] Minnesota Arrowhead Association, *Your Invitation to Visit the Magnificent Minnesota Arrowhead Country and Canadian Lakehead* (Duluth: Minnesota Arrowhead Association, 1961).

[6] Erwin A. Bauer, "Quetico-Superior Canoe Trip," *Sports Afield*, July 1958, p. 29; Mel Ellis, "Canoe Into Wilderness," *Field and Stream*, June 1957, p. 55.

[7] On virgin fishing, see advertisements by Mittermaier's Evergreen Lodge, Lac La Croix Lodge, and Bill Zup's Curtain Falls Fishing Camp, all in Ely Chamber of Commerce, *Ely, Minnesota: Where the Wilderness Begins* (Ely, 1950), in Ely, Minnesota Chamber of Com-

merce folder, Conservation Printed Materials Files, MHS.

[8] Jay Price to W.D. Cram, February 14, 1950, 2320 Genesis of Management Plan files, SNFR [hereafter cited as Mngmt. Plan folders].

[9] Clifford and Isabel Ahlgren, *Lob Trees in the Wilderness* (Minneapolis: University of Minnesota Press, 1984), pp. 161-162; Robert C. Lucas, *Recreational Use of the Quetico-Superior Area,* U.S. Forest Service Research Paper LS-8, April 1964, p. 9. The Ahlgrens point out that the definition of visitor days changed during this time period. Until 1964, the Forest Service defined it as one person staying up to twelve hours; a ten-minute visit was one visitor day. After 1964, the agency defined the term as twelve hours per person or the equivalent; two people staying six hours each would make one visitor day. This means that figures up to 1964 are higher for the same amount of actual use than are statistics for later years, so the jump from thirty-eight thousand visitor days to six hundred thousand represents an even greater increase in visitor use than the numbers indicate.

[10] Marvin Taves, William Hathaway and Gordon Bultena, *Canoe Country Vacationers,* University of Minnesota Agricultural Experiment Station Miscellaneous Report 39, June 1960, p. 23.

[11] Harmon to Chief, June 17, 1942, Proposed Road Fernberg to Basswood Lake folder, 2320 Wilderness and Primitive Areas files, SNFR [hereafter cited as Basswood Road folder, W Areas files]; F.B. Hubachek, memorandum, March 25, 1952, Quetico-Superior files, SFO [hereafter cited as Q-S files]; J.W. White, memo, January 29, 1964, Data Concerning Change of Name to BWCA file, microfilm roll 17, SNFR-MHS.

[12] Price to John A. Blatnik, August 5, 1948, Mngmt. Plan folders, SNFR; Price to Cram, February 14, 1950, Mngmt. Plan folders, SNFR; Hubachek, memorandum, March 25, 1952, Q-S files, SFO.

[13] Price to Cram, February 14, 1950, Mngmt. Plan folders, SNFR.

[14] Barbara Flanagan, "State Lures Tourists as Year-'Round vacation Spot," *Minneapolis Sunday Tribune,* April 22, 1956. The *Ely Miner* did oppose the appropriation in a four-part series by Lake County highway engineer T.G. Odegard. Titled "Wilderness Problem," it ran in the March 29, April 5, April 12 and April 19, 1956 issues. But the 400-member Ely Rod and Gun Club, which claimed

to be the city's most representative group, went on record in favor of the appropriation. See Arthur W. Anderson and Frank J. Chernivec to Edward J. Thye, February 20, 1956, Background Data Re PL607, microfilm roll 16, SNFR-MHS.

[15] *Ely Miner,* August 2, 1951.

[16] *Ely Miner,* May 31, 1951; [Frederick C. Childers], "The Only Way," *Ely Miner,* October 1, 1953; C. Wilson Harder, "Small Business," *Ely Miner,* June 7, 1951; First National Bank advertisement, *Ely Miner,* May 31, 1951. For photos of FBI-wanted individuals, see the issues for August 16, 1951 and September 6, 1951.

[17] Fred C. Childers, "Humphrey Bill Threat to Ely's Economic Life," *Ely Miner,* July 18, 1957.

In 1966, Interior Secretary Stewart Udall granted International Nickel Co. a twenty-year, renewable lease allowing large-scale mining south of Ely near the Kawishiwi River, just outside the wilderness area. The company projected potential production of nine million tons of ore at a plant that would hire a thousand employees. Further tests, however, indicated that the ore grade was too poor to warrant development. INCO still holds its lease, and is waiting for favorable economic conditions. See "$80 Million Nickel Plant Is Set Here," *Ely Miner,* June 16, 1966; and Walter Butler Co., *Economic Adjustment in Ely, Minnesota* (St. Paul, Minn.: Walter Butler Co., 1968), pp. 23-26.

[18] [Frederick C. Childers], "Will Ely Become a 'Ghost Town'?" *Ely Miner,* July 25, 1957.

[19] Olson to Humphrey, July 17, 1957, Sigurd F. Olson files, Friends of the Wilderness Papers, MHS [hereafter cited as SFO files, FOW]; Olson to Humphrey, August 14, 1957, SFO files, FOW. Howard Zahniser, executive secretary of the Wilderness Society, wrote the bill, with help from Olson and such other conservation leaders as David R. Brower and Ira N. Gabrielson.

[20] "Wilderness Craze," *Ely Miner,* August 15, 1957; "Ely Rod and Gun Club Opposes Humphrey Bill," *Ely Miner,* October 24, 1957. Olson had written to both Humphrey and Zahniser on July 17, the day Childer's first editorial appeared. Both letters are in the SFO files, FOW. On July 22, Zahniser wrote to Sen. James Murray, chair of the Senate Interior and Insular Affairs Committee, and told him of the new special provision for the Superior Roadless Areas. See "Wilderness

Bill Changes," *Living Wilderness,* Autumn 1957, pp. 31-32. See also copy of the bill dated July 22, 1957, with the Superior Roadless Area exceptions handwritten and inserted by Howard Zahniser, along with a request for Olson's opinion. It is in the Wilderness Society files, SFO.

[21] [Frederick C. Childers], untitled editorial, *Ely Miner,* October 9, 1958. Childers' contention that the remaining resorts expanded little was later contradicted by sociologist Robert Lucas, who found that they had expanded by about 15 to 25 percent. He agreed, however, that this probably was not enough to compensate for the total capacity of the resorts purchased by the government. See Lucas, *Recreational Use of the Quetico-Superior,* p. 43.

[22] "Taxes and a Little Bit of History," *Ely Miner,* February 18, 1960; "Chamber Protests Resort Purchases," *Ely Miner,* January 28, 1960.

[23] "Chamber Protests Resort Purchases," *Ely Miner,* January 28, 1960. See also "Ely's Economy Squeezed by Federal Land Buying," *Ely Miner,* February 25, 1960; and "Stoots: 'Land Program to Benefit Community'," *Ely Miner,* March 24, 1960.

[24] Ted Wynn, "Chamber Secretary Asks Public to Act," *Ely Miner,* June 30, 1960.

[25] Ted Wynn, "Outside Interference Is Hurting Ely's Economy," *Ely Miner,* September 21, 1961.

[26] For comments about Childers' refusal to publish pro-wilderness letters, as well as the refusal of his predecessor, John Ainley, see Olson to Hubachek, July 12, 1948, Olson Activities folders, Quetico-Superior Council Papers, MHS.

[27] F.B. Hubachek, memo to Charles S. Kelly and Olson, November 22, 1960, SFO files, FOW.

[28] L.P. Neff to Blatnik, March 11, 1963, Box 9, PE # 2 folder, JAB.

[29] [Frederick C. Childers], "Take It Or Leave It," Ely Miner, July 25, 1963.

[30] One of the chamber's films, *Where the Wilderness Begins,* can be seen at the Vermilion Interpretive Center in Ely.

[31] See Mel Ellis, "Fly In and Fish," *Field and Stream,* July 1957, p. 22.

[32] [Howard Zahniser], untitled editorial, *Living Wilderness,* Summer 1952, inside front cover. Many other articles in this magazine and in the *Sierra Club Bulletin* during the 1950s stressed the spiritual values

of wilderness.

33 See comments by "Mr. Davis," in David Brower, ed. *Wildlands in Our Civilization* (San Francisco: Sierra Club, 1964), p. 162.

34 David R. Brower, "Scenic Resources for the Future," *Sierra Club Bulletin,* December 1956, p. 3.

35 Philip Hyde, "The Uses of Nature," *Sierra Club Bulletin,* November 1958, p. 31.

36 Stephen Fox, *John Muir and His Legacy: The American Conservation Movement* (Boston: Little, Brown and Co., 1981), pp. 266, 279, 315.

37 Olson, note, January 13, 1947, *Lonely Land* files, SFO.

38 Sigurd F. Olson, "The Wilderness Concept," *The Ames Forester,* 1962 annual, p. 14.

39 Sigurd F. Olson, *The Singing Wilderness* (New York: Alfred A. Knopf, 1956), pp. 130- 131.

40 Olson, "The Spiritual Need," p. 218.

41 Olson, *Singing Wilderness,* p. 133.

42 *Plan of Management, Superior Roadless Areas* (Duluth: Superior National Forest, 1948), in Plans of Mngmt BWCA 1948 files, microfilm roll 5, SNFR-MHS; Edward P. Cliff to E.L. Peterson, January 27, 1958, Data Concerning Change of Name to BWCA files [hereafter cited as BWCA Name files], microfilm roll 17, SNFR-MHS; Ahlgrens, *Lob trees,* p. 131.

43 A.W. Greeley to Chief, February 8, 1957; Howard Hopkins to Region 9, February 15, 1957; Cliff to Region 9, January 20, 1958; Cliff to Peterson, January 27, 1958, all in BWCA Name files, microfilm roll 17, SNFR-MHS.

44 See Roy K. Thomas to Editor, *Minneapolis Star,* March 8, 1964, in BWCA files, JAB; and Magie to Neff, January 26, 1964, in BWCA Name files, microfilm roll 17, SNFR-MHS.

45 Lucas, *Recreational Use of the Quetico-Superior,* plate 3, and p. 36.

46 Lucas, *Recreational Use of the Quetico-Superior,* pp. 19-20, 33, 36.

47 Robert C. Lucas, *The Recreational Capacity of the Quetico-Superior Area,* U.S. Forest Service Research Paper LS-15, September 1964, p. 16.

48 Robert C. Lucas, *The Importance of Fishing as an Attraction and Activity in the Quetico-Superior Area,* Lake States Forest Experiment Station Research Note LS-61, July 1965; Lucas, *Recreational Capacity*

of the Quetico-Superior, p. 9. A 1956 survey found that 28 percent of Quetico-Superior canoeists ranked spiritual benefits as a very important reason for taking a canoe trip. See Taves *et al, Canoe Country Vacationers,* p. 14.

⁴⁹ Donald B. Lawrence, quoted in *Naturalist,* Autumn 1964, p. 9.

⁵⁰ Bill Rom, "Latest Threat to the Canoe Country," *Naturalist,* Winter 1963, p. 31.

⁵¹ Sigurd F. Olson, "Wilderness Preservation," *Naturalist,* Winter 1964, p. 10.

⁵² Transcripts of the hearings were published as the *Official Report of Proceedings Before the Boundary Waters Canoe Area Review Committee of the United States Department of Agriculture* (Milwaukee, Wis.: Richard Peppey Reporting Co., Inc.), available at SNFR.

⁵³ [Frederick C. Childers], "Take It Or Leave It," *Ely Miner,* April 16, 1964. Mine employment figures come from "Pioneer Mine to Close on April 1st Next Year," *Ely Miner,* March 31, 1966. Logging employment figures are from U.S. Census data, as published in Walter Butler Co., *Economic Adjustments,* p. 53.

⁵⁴ Henry Larsen to Blatnik, July 28, 1964, BWCA files, JAB. Larsen was from Grand Marais, where logging was much more important than mining. Blatnik's BWCA files also contain many letters from Ely residents protesting the proposed wilderness status. The BWCA Review Committee hearing transcripts also contain many statements voicing the local views about logging, as well as other wilderness uses.

⁵⁵ Clayton G. Rudd, "Boundary Waters Canoe Area," *Naturalist,* Autumn 1964, p. 1. For the photos, see "Finn Lake: The Beauty of a Lake Destroyed — a Wilderness Violated — For What?" *Naturalist,* Autumn 1964, p. 16. For the Forest Service view, see H. Mathews to Forest Supervisor, November 19, 1964; and George S. James to Harvey Broome, November 30, 1964, both in BWCA-Finn Lake Sale folder, 2320 Wilderness and Primitive Areas files, SNFR.

⁵⁶ Boundary Waters resources Committee, *Protect Our Wilderness With Multiple Use* (n.p., ca 1965), in Conservation Printed Materials files, Minnesota Arrowhead Association Boundary Waters Resources Committee folder, MHS.

⁵⁷ Cook County BWRC, *Boundary Waters Canoe Area to be*

CLOSED (n.p., ca 1965), in Conservation Printed Materials files, Boundary Waters Resources Committee folder, MHS.

⁵⁸ Johnson quoted in Izaak Walton League of America, *The Boundary Waters Canoe Area of the Superior National Forest in Northeastern Minnesota: A National Wilderness Heritage for All* (Glenview, Ill.: Izaak Walton League of America, 1965), back cover, copy in Conservation Printed Materials files, Superior National Forest folder 3, MHS.

⁵⁹ [Frederick C. Childers], "Take It Or Leave it," *Ely Miner,* July 29, 1965.

⁶⁰ "A Comment on the Boundary Waters Canoe Area Decision," *Living Wilderness,* Spring 1965, pp. 20, 24; "Quiet Spot in Minnesota," *New York Times,* June 14, 1965; A.W. Greeley to Blatnik, March 21, 1966, BWCA files, JAB. See also Izaak Walton League, *The Boundary Waters Canoe Area.*

⁶¹ Orville L. Freeman, Statement on BWCA Regulations, p. 2, December 16, 1965, 1650 Historical Data files, microfilm roll 17, SNFR-MHS.

⁶² [Frederick C. Childers], "Take It Or Leave It," *Ely Miner,* December 23, 1965.

⁶³ *Your Boundary Waters Canoe Area Wilderness Needs Help, Now!* (Minneapolis: Friends of the Boundary Waters Wilderness, August 1976); Miron L. Heinselman, "Crisis in the Canoe Country," *Living Wilderness,* January-March 1977, pp. 13-24; Gene Kragenbrink, "BWCA vs Exploitation," *Outdoor America,* February 1977, p. 2.

⁶⁴ Quoted in John Murrell, "BWCA Talks Spark Fiery Boos, Cheers," *Duluth News-Tribune,* July 9, 1977.

⁶⁵ Bob Cary, Birdshot and Backlashes, *Ely Echo,* February 23, 1977. Friends of the Wilderness Vice Chairman Bill Cunningham later also said that the group had used BWCA permits for its mailing list. See Doug Smith, "Echo Interviews `Friends of the BWCA,'" *Ely Echo,* May 18, 1977.

⁶⁶ Bob Cary, "Fraser Bill: BWCA Management By Fire," *Ely Echo,* April 27, 1977; Bob Cary, "Citizens Seek Fires Test in BWCA Management," *Ely Echo,* April 6, 1977.

⁶⁷ Bob Cary, "For Sig's Sake Get the Facts Right," *Ely Echo,* March 16, 1977.

[68] Miles Aakhus, "A Sacred Place," *Ely Echo,* June 8, 1977.

[69] Samuel P. Hays, *Beauty Health, and Permanence: Environmental Politics in the United States, 1955-1985* (New York: Cambridge University Press, 1987), pp. 32-33.

[70] "Peace in the BWCA," *Duluth News-Tribune,* January 23, 1977.

[71] "BWCA Unit Told Benefits of Logging," *Minneapolis Tribune,* July 9, 1977; John Murrell, "BWCA Talks Spark Fiery Boos, Cheers," *Duluth News-Tribune,* July 9, 1977. Regarding the hanging, the *Ely Echo* took a neutral approach, reporting that "a supporter of the wilderness concept was hung [sic] in effigy from one of the logging trucks." See Doug Smith, "1200 Attend BWCA Hearings in Ely, *Ely Echo,* July 13, 1977.

[72] Al McConagha, "Environmentalists Say Anderson Has `Stuck Knife' in BWCA Bill," *Minneapolis Tribune,* April 9, 1978.

[73] Quoted in Sam Cook, "Burton Bill Draws Local Comment," *Ely Echo,* March 22, 1978.

[74] [Bob Cary], "Protestors' Roadblocks Stop BWCA Entry Points," *Ely Echo,* August 9, 1978. See also Tom Webb, "Angry BWCA Area Residents Block Roads, Vent Frustration," *Minneapolis Tribune,* August 6, 1978; Sam Cook, "Alliance Stages Protes Parade," *Ely Echo,* August 16, 1978; and Robert Ostmann Jr., "Fear Stalks the Ely `Resistance,'" *Minneapolis Tribune,* August 26, 1978.

[75] Ostmann, "Fear Stlaks the Ely `Resistance.'"

[76] [Bob Cary], "Get On Target," *Ely Echo,* September 27, 1978. See also [Bob Cary], "Why Not a Shootout on Sheridan Street?" *Ely Echo,* August 30, 1978; and [Bob Cary], "Now It's Logical!" *Ely Echo,* September 6, 1978.

[77] Voices, *Ely Echo,* August 3, 1977.

[78] The term "antimodern modernist" comes from T.J. Jackson Lears, *No Place of Grace: Antimodernism and the Transformation of American Culture, 1880-1920* (New York: Pantheon Books, 1981), pp. 310-312.

[79] [Bob Cary], "Everything Is Settled?" *Ely Echo,* October 5, 1981.

Epilogue / pages 158 - 167

[1] Friends of the Boundary Waters Wilderness, "Action Alert," ca

October 1990; "1988 BWCA Visitor Use Study," pp. 4-5, *BWCA Wilderness News,* Autumn 1990.

[2] The plaque and cabin foundations — along with a pile of beer cans and other garbage from the 1950s and early 1960s — are located on Half Dog Island, near the southwestern end of Washington Island.

[3] Paul Summer to L.P. Neff, March 13, 1965, BWCA folders, John A. Blatnik Papers, Minnesota Historical Society Research Center, St. Paul, Minn.

[4] Ibid.

BIBLIOGRAPHY

Primary Sources

Manuscript Collections

John A. Blatnik Papers, Minnesota Historical Society Research Center, St. Paul, Minn. [Location hereafter cited as MHS.]
Camp Charles L. Sommers Canoe Base Records, Moose Lake, Ely, Minnesota
Friends of the Wilderness Papers, MHS.
Governors' Correspondence, Minnesota State Archives, MHS.
Hubert H. Humphrey Papers, MHS.
Izaak Walton League of America, Minnesota Division Records, MHS.
Minnesota Conservation Department Records, State Archives, MHS.
Minnesota Department of Natural Resources, Fisheries Records, Winton, Minnesota.
Minnesota Game and Fish Division Records, State Archives, MHS.
Quetico-Superior Council Papers, MHS.
Sigurd F. Olson Papers, MHS.
Superior National Forest Records, Duluth, Minnesota.
Superior National Forest Records, MHS.
Edward J. Thye Papers, MHS.

Books

Bolz, J. Arnold. *Portage Into the Past: By Canoe Along the Minnesota-Ontario Boundary Waters.* Minneapolis: University of Minnesota Press, 1960.
Brooks, Paul. *Roadless Area.* 1942. New York: Ballantine Books, 1971.
Brower, David, ed. *Wilderness: America's Living Heritage.* San Francisco: Sierra Club, 1961.
Brower, David, ed. *Wildlands in Our Civilization.* San Francisco: Sierra Club, 1964.
Carhart, Arthur H. *Timber in Your Life.* Philadelphia: J.B. Lippincott

Co., 1955.

Cary, E.F. *Whither Away?* St. Paul: Webb Publishing Co., 1949.

Curwood, James Oliver. *Honor of the Big Snows.* Indianapolis: Bobbs-Merrill, 1911.

Douglas, William O. *My Wilderness: East to Katahdin.* Garden city, N.Y.: Doubleday and Co., 1961.

Eliot, T.S. *Collected Poems, 1909-1962.* San Diego: Harcourt Brace Jovanovich, 1970.

Frankel, Charles. *The Case for Modern Man.* Beacon Hill, Mass.: Beacon Press, 1959.

Hoover, Helen. *The Long-Shadowed Forest.* New York: Thomas Y. Crowell Co., 1963.

Jaques, Florence Page. *Birds Across the Sky.* New York: Harper and Brothers, 1942.

Jaques, Florence Page. *Canoe Country.* Minneapolis: University of Minnesota Press, 1938.

Jaques, Florence Page. *Snowshoe Country.* Minneapolis: University of Minnesota Press, 1944.

Kilgore, Bruce, ed. *Wilderness in a Changing World.* San Francisco: Sierra Club, 1966.

Leopold, Aldo. *Round River: From the Journals of Aldo Leopold.* Edited by Luna B. Leopold. New York: Oxford University Press, 1953.

Olson, Sigurd F. *Listening Point.* New York: Alfred A. Knopf, 1958.

Olson, Sigurd F. *Open Horizons.* New York: Alfred A. Knopf, 1969.

Olson, Sigurd F. *Reflections From the North Country.* New York: Alfred A. Knopf, 1976.

Olson, Sigurd F. *Runes on the North.* New York: Alfred A. Knopf, 1963.

Olson, Sigurd F. *The Singing Wilderness.* New York: Alfred A. Knopf, 1956.

Wright, Harold Bell. *When a Man's a Man.* New York: A.L. Burt, 1916.

Magazines

American Forests. 1920 through 1965.

Field and Stream. 1930 through 1940, 1950 through 1965.

Forest and Stream. 1915 through 1920.

National Parks Magazine. 1940 through 1965.

Naturalist. 1950 through 1967.

Outdoor America. 1924 through 1960, 1976 through 1979.

Outdoor Life. 1920 through 1965.

Parks and Recreation. 1922 through 1926.

Sports Afield. February 1923 through May 1924, 1930 through 1939, 1951 through 1965, 1970 through 1980.

For a detailed listing of approximately 400 magazine and newspaper sources please contact the publisher.

Secondary Sources

Books

Centennial Roaring Stoney Days, 2d ed. Ely, Minn.: Ely-Winton Historical Society, 1982.

Ahlgren, Clifford, and Ahlgren, Isabel. *Lob Trees in the Wilderness.* Minneapolis: University of Minnesota Press, 1984.

Aho, Karl N., Rev. *Portrait of the Church in an Economic Eclipse: A Study of the church's role in Minnesota's Iron Range.* Minneapolis: Minnesota Council of Churches [1964].

Baldwin, Donald N. *The Quiet Revolution: Grass Roots of Today's Wilderness Preservation Movement.* Boulder, Colo.: Pruett Publishing Co., 1972.

Bell, Daniel. *The End of Ideology: On the Exhaustion of Political Ideas in the Fifties.* New York: Free Press, 1960.

Berger, Peter L. *The Sacred Canopy: Elements of a Sociological Theory of Religion.* Garden City, N.Y.: Doubleday and Co., 1967.

Boorstin, Daniel J. *The Americans: The Democratic Experience.* New York: Vintage Books, 1973.

Boulding, Kenneth E. *The Image.* Ann Arbor: University of Michigan Press, 1956.

Boyer, Paul. *By the Bomb's early Light: American Through and Culture at the Dawn of the Atomic Age.* New York: Pantheon

Books, 1985.

Brownell, Lee. *Pioneer Life in Ely.* Virginia, Minn.: Lee Brownell and Iron Range Historical Society, 1981.

Butler Co., Walter. *Economic Adjustment in Ely, Minnesota.* St. Paul: Walter Butler Co., 1968.

Carhart, Arthur H. *The National Forests.* New York: Alfred A. Knopf, 1959.

Clawson, Marion, and Held, Burnell. *The Federal Lands: Their Use and Management.* Lincoln: University of Nebraska Press, 1957.

Coatsworth, E.S. *The Indians of Quetico.* Toronto: University of Toronto Press, 1957.

Commager, Henry Steele. *The American Mind: An Interpretation of American Thought and Character Since the 1880s.* New Haven, Conn.: Yale University Press, 1950.

Committee on Land Utilization. *Land Utilization in Minnesota.* University of Minnesota Press, 1934.

Cronon, William. *Changes in the Land: Indians, Colonists, and the Ecology of New England.* New York: Hill and Wang, 1983.

Curti, Merle. *The Growth of American Thought,* 3d ed. New Brunswick, N.J.: Transaction Books, 1982.

Dana, Samuel Trask, and Fairfax, Sally K. *Forest and Range Policy: Its Development in the United States,* 2d ed. New York: McGraw-Hill, 1980.

Dana, Samuel Trask; Allison, John H.; and Cunningham, Russell N. *Minnesota Lands: Ownership, Use, and Management of Forest and Related Lands.* Washington, D.C.: The American Forestry Association, 1960.

Danziger, Edmund Jefferson, Jr. *The Chippewas of Lake Superior.* The Civilization of the American Indian, vol. 148. Norman: University of Oklahoma Press, 1978.

DeVoto, Bernard. *The Course of Empire.* Lincoln: University of Nebraska Press, 1952.

Dulles, Foster Rhea. *America Learns to Play: A History of Popular Recreation, 1607-1940.* New York: D. Appleton-Century Co., 1940.

Eddy, Samuel, and Underhill, James C. *Northern Fishes: With Special reference to the Upper Mississippi Valley,* 3rd ed. Minneapolis: University of Minnesota Press, 1974.

Ekirch, Arthur A., Jr. *Ideologies and Utopias: The Impact of the New Deal on American Thought.* Chicago: Quadrangle Books, 1969.

Flader, Susan L., ed. *The Great Lakes Forest: An Environmental And Social History.* Minneapolis: University of Minnesota Press, 1983.

Foerster, Norman. *Nature in American Literature.* New York: Russell and Russell, 1958.

Folwell, William Watts. *A History of Minnesota,* 4 vols. St. Paul: Minnesota Historical Society Press, 1921.

Fox, Stephen. *John Muir and His Legacy: The American Conservation Movement.* Boston: Little, Brown and Co., 1981.

Garraty, John *The Great Depression: An Inquiry Into the Causes, Courses, and Consequences of the Worldwide Depression of the Nineteen-thirties, as Seen by contemporaries and in the Light of History.* Garden City, N.Y.: Anchor Press, 1987.

Garraty, John A. *The New Commonwealth: 1877-1890.* New York: Harper and Row, 1968.

Gatewood, Willard B., Jr., ed. *Controversy in the Twenties: fundamentalism, Modernism, and Evolution.* Nashville: Vanderbilt University Press, 1969.

Glacken, Clarence J. *Traces on the Rhodian Shore.* Berkeley: University of California Press, 1967.

Glover, James M. *A Wilderness Original: The Life of Bob Marshall.* Seattle: The Mountaineers, 1986.

Graber, Linda H. *Wilderness as Sacred Space.* Washington, D.C.: Association of American Geographers, 1976.

Hackett, Alice Payne. *70 Years of Best Sellers, 1895-1965.* New York: R.R. Bowker Co., 1967.

Hays, Samuel P. *Beauty, Health, and Permanence: Environmental Politics in the United States, 1955-1985.* New York: Cambridge University Press, 1987.

Hays, Samuel P. *Conservation and the Gospel of Efficiency: The Progressive Conservation Movement, 1890-1920.* New York: Atheneum, 1980.

Higham, John. *Strangers in the Land: Patterns of American Nativism, 1860-1925.* New Brunswick, N.J.: Rutgers University Press, 1955.

Hine, Robert V. *The American West: An Interpretive History.* Boston: Little, Brown and Co., 1973.

Hofstadter, Richard. *The Age of Reform: From Bryan to F.D.R.* New York: Vintage Books, 1955.

Hofstadter, Richard. *Anti-Intellectualism in American Life.* New York: Vintage Books, 1963.

Huth, Hans. *Nature and the American: Three Centuries of changing Attitudes.* Lincoln: University of Nebraska Press, Bison Books, 1972.

Innis, Harold A. *The Fur Trade in Canada: An Introduction to Canadian Economic History,* rev. ed. New Haven: Yale University Press, 1962.

Iron Range Resources and Rehabilitation. *Ely and its Resources.* St. Paul, Minn.: Iron Range Resources and Rehabilitation Board, 1959.

Issel, William. *Social Change in the United States, 1945-1983.* New York: Schocken Books, 1987.

Johnson, Elden. *The Prehistoric Peoples of Minnesota,* rev. 2nd ed. St. Paul: Minnesota Historical Society Press, 1978.

Kaufman, Herbert. *The Forest Ranger: A study in Administrative Behavior.* Baltimore: Johns Hopkins University Press, 1960.

Kline, Marcia B. *Beyond the Land Itself: Views of Nature in Canada and the United States.* Cambridge: Harvard University Press, 1970.

Lambert, Richard S. *Renewing Nature's Wealth: A Centennial History of the Public Management of Lands, Forests and Wildlife in Ontario, 1763-1967.* Toronto: Ontario Department of Lands and Forests, 1967.

Landis, Paul Henry. *Three Iron Mining Towns: A Study in Cultural Change.* Ann Arbor, Mich.: Edwards Brothers, 1938.

Larson, Agnes M. *History of the White Pine Industry in Minnesota.* 1949. Use and Abuse of America's Natural Resources, edited by Stuart Bruchey and Eleanor Bruchey. New York: Arno Press, 1972.

Lass, William E. *Minnesota's Boundary With Canada: It Evolution Since 1783.* St. Paul: Minnesota Historical Society Press, 1980.

Lears, T.J. Jackson. *No Place of Grace: Antimodernism and the Transformation of American culture, 1880-1920*. New York: Pantheon Books, 1981.

Lewis, R.W.B. *The American Adam: Innocence, Tragedy and Tradition in the Nineteenth Century*. Chicago: University of Chicago Press, 1955.

Lynd, Robert S., and Lynd, Helen Merrell. *Middletown: A Study in Contemporary American Culture*. New York: Harcourt, Brace and Co., 1929.

Lynd, Robert S., and Lynd, Helen Merrell. *Middletown in Transition: A Study in Cultural conflicts*. New York: Harcourt, Brace and World, 1937.

MacQuarrie, Gordon. *Ole Evinrude and the Old Fellows*. 1947. Milwaukee: Evinrude Motors, 1984.

Marx, Leo. *The Machine in the Garden: Technology and the Pastoral Ideal in America*. New York: Oxford University Press, 1964.

Meine, Curt. *Aldo Leopold: His Life and Work*. Madison: University of Wisconsin Press, 1988.

Mitchell, Lee Clark. *Witnesses to a Vanishing American: The Nineteenth-Century Response*. Princeton: Princeton University Press, 1981.

Nash, Roderick. *The Nervous Generation: American Thought, 1917-1930*. History of American Thought. Chicago: Rand McNally and Co., 1973.

Nash, Roderick. *Wilderness and the American Mind*, 3rd ed. New Haven: Yale University Press, 1982.

Nesbit, Robert C. *Wisconsin: A History*. Madison: University of Wisconsin Press, 1973.

Nute, Grace Lee. *Rainy River Country*. St. Paul: Minnesota Historical Society Press, 1950.

Nute, Grace Lee. *The Voyageur*. St. Paul: Minnesota Historical Society. Press, 1955.

Nute, Grace Lee. *The Voyageur's Highway*. St. Paul: Minnesota Historical Society Press, 1941.

Oakley, J. Ronald. *God's Country: America in the Fifties*. New York: Dembner Books, 1986.

Olesen, David, ed *A Wonderful Country: The Story of Bill Magie*.

n.p., 1981.

Peterson, Theodore (Bernard). *Magazines in the Twentieth Century.* Urbana: University of Illinois Press, 1964.

Piper, Don Courtney. *The International Law of the Great Lakes: A Study of Canadian-United States Co-operation.* Durham, N.C.: Duke University Press, 1967.

Riesman, David. *The Lonely Crowed: A Study of the Changing American Character.* New Haven: Yale University Press, 1950.

Rosenberg, Emily. *Spreading the American Dream: American Economic and Cultural Expansion, 1890-1945.* New York: Hill and Wang, 1981.

Schmitt, Peter J. *Back to Nature: The Arcadian Myth in Urban America.* New York: Oxford University Press, 1969.

Searle, R. Newell. *Saving Quetico-Superior: A Land Set Apart.* St. Paul: Minnesota Historical Society, 1977.

Shi, David E. *The Simple Life: Plain Living and High Thinking in American Culture.* New York: Oxford University Press, 1985.

Slotkin, Richard. *Regeneration Through Violence: The Mythology of the American Frontier, 1600-1860.* Middletown, Conn.: Wesleyan University Press, 1973.

Smith, Henry Nash. *Virgin Land: The American West as Symbol and Myth.* Cambridge: Harvard University Press, 1950.

Steen, Harold K. *The U.S. Forest Service: a History.* Seattle: University of Washington Press, 1976.

Susman, Warren I. *Culture as History: The Transformation of American Society in the Twentieth Century.* New York: Pantheon Books, 1984.

Toye, William. *The St. Lawrence.* Toronto: Oxford University Press, 1959.

Tuan, Yi-Fu. *Space and Place: The Perspective of Experience.* Minneapolis: University of Minnesota Press, 1977.

Tuan, Yi-Fu. *Topophilia: A Study of Environmental Perception, Attitudes, and Values.* Englewood Cliffs, N.J.: Prentice-Hall, 1974.

Turner, Frederick Jackson. *The Significance of the Frontier in American History.* Edited by Harold P. Simonson. New York: Frederick Ungar, 1963.

Van Vleet, J.M. *Johnson Brothers Engineering Corp., 1918-1935: The Four Men from Terra Haute.* Lake Mills, Iowa: Graphic Publishing Co., 1982.

Walker, David A. *Iron Frontier: The Discovery and Early Development of Minnesota's Three Ranges.* St. Paul: Minnesota Historical Society Press, 1979.

White, J. Wesley. *Historical Sketches of the Quetico-Superior.* 16 vols. Duluth: Superior National Forest, 1967-1974.

Wiebe, Robert H. *The Search for Order, 1877-1920.* New York: Hill and Wang, 1967.

Williams, George H. *Wilderness and Paradise in Christian Thought: The Biblical Experience of the Desert in the History of Christianity and the Paradise Theme in the Theological Idea of the University.* New York: Harper and Brothers, 1962.

Williams, Raymond. *The Country and the City.* New York: Oxford University Press, 1973.

Wirth, Fremont P. *The Discovery and Exploitation of the Minnesota Iron Lands.* 1937. New York: Arno Press, 1979.

Wognum, Anne. *Winton Historical Booklet.* n.p., 1976.

Worster, Donald. *Nature's Economy: The Roots of Ecology.* Garden city, N.Y.: Anchor Press, 1977.

Journals and Papers

"History of Outboards." *The Antique Outboarders,* October 1981, p. 59.

Andres, Russell P. *Wilderness Sanctuary.* Inter-University Case Program #13. Indianapolis: Bobbs-Merrill Co., 1953.

Backes, David. "The Air Ban War: Sigurd F. Olson and the Fight to Ban Airplanes From the Roadless Area of Northeastern Minnesota's Superior National Forest." Paper read at the International Conference on Environmental Education, October 1984, Lake Louise, Alberta.

Backes, David. "Places in Time: Changing Images of the Quetico-Superior." Paper read at the Forest History Society annual conference, October 1986, Vancouver, British Columbia.

Betten, Neil. "Strike on the Mesabi - 1907." *Minnesota History* 40 (1967):340-347.

Breckenridge, W.J. "A Century of Minnesota Wild Life." *Minnesota History* 30 (1949):123-134.

Crandall, Willard. "A Short History of the Outboard." *Outdoor Life*, May 1930, pp. 68-70.

Dahlgren, Calvin A. "Fish and Game in the Superior." *Parks and Recreation*, July-August 1924, pp. 629-634.

Fox, Robin. "The Cultural Animal." *Encounter* 35 (1970):31-42.

Inskip, Peter D., and Magnuson, John J. "Changes in fish Populations Over an 80-Year period: Big Pine Lake, Wisconsin." *Transactions of the American Fisheries Society* 112 (1983):378-389.

Jockel, Joseph T., and Schwartz, Alan M. "The Changing Environmental Role of the Canada-United States International Joint Commission." *Environmental Review* 8 (1984):236-251.

Johnson, Fritz H., and Hale, John G. "Interrelations Between Walleye *(Stizostedion vitreum vitreum)* and Smallmouth Bass *(Micropterus dolomieui)* in Four Northeastern Minnesota Lakes, 1948-69." *Journal of the Fisheries Research Board of Canada* 34 (1977):1626-1632.

Kellert, Stephen R. "Historical Trends in Perceptions and Uses of Animals in 20th Century America." *Environmental Review* 9 (1985):19-33.

Killan, Gerald, and Warecki, George M. "Saving Quetico-Superior: The Ontario Perspective." Paper read at the Forest History Society annual conference, October 1986, Vancouver, British Columbia.

Lears, T.J. Jackson. "From Salvation to Self-Realization: Advertising and the Therapeutic Roots of the Consumer Culture, 1880-1930." In *The Culture of Consumption: Critical Essays in American History, 1880-1980,* edited by Richard Wrightman fox and T.J. Jackson Lears. New York: Pantheon Books, 1983.

Lime, David W. *Factors Influencing Campground Use in the Superior National Forest of Minnesota.* USDA Forest Service, North Central Forest Experiment Station Research Paper NC-60, 1971.

Lime, David W. *Large Groups in the Boundary Waters Canoe Area: Their Numbers, Characteristics, and Impact.* USDA Forest Service, North Central Forest Experiment Station Research Note NC-142, 1972.

Lucas, Robert C. *The Importance of Fishing as an Attraction and Activity in the Quetico-Superior Area.* St. Paul, Minn.: U.S. Forest Service, Lake State Forest Experiment Station Research Note LS-61, July 1965.

Lucas, Robert C. *The Recreational Capacity of the Quetico-Superior Area.* St. Paul, Minn.: U.S. Forest Service, Lake States Forest Experiment Station Research Paper LS-15, September 1964.

Lucas, Robert C. "User Concepts of Wilderness and Their Implications for Resource Management." In *Environmental Psychology: Man and His Physical Setting,* edited by Harold M. Proshansky, William H. Ittelson, and Leanne G. Rivlin. New York: Holt, Rhinehart and Winston, 1970.

Lucas, Robert C. *Visitor Reaction to Timber Harvesting in the Boundary Waters Canoe Area.* St. Paul, Minn.: U.S. Forest Service, Lake States Forest Experiment Station Research Note LS-2, January 1963.

Lucas, Robert C. "Wilderness Perception and Use: The Example of the Boundary Waters Canoe Area." *Natural Resources Journal* 3 (1964):394-411.

Sirjamaki, John. "The People of the Mesabi Range." *Minnesota History* 27 (1946):203-215.

Taves, Marvin; Hathaway, William; and Bultena, Gordon. *Canoe Country Vacationers.* St. Paul: University of Minnesota Agricultural Experiment Station Miscellaneous Report 39, June 1960.

Walshe, Shan. "History of the Quetico-Superior country." Mimeographed. French Lake, Ontario: Quetico Provincial Park, 1984.

Webb, W.J. "The Fifty Greatest Years of Outboarding." *The Antique Outboarder,* January 1977, p. 10.

Webb, Jim, and Van Vleet, John. "The Johnson Story." *The Antique Outboarder,* January 1979, pp. 3-27.

Theses and Dissertations

Backes, David James. "The Air Ban War: Sigurd F. Olson and the Fight to Ban Airplanes From the Roadless Area of Minnesota's Superior National Forest." Master's thesis, University of Wisconsin-Madison, 1983.

Backes, David James. "The Communication-Mediated Roles of Perceptual, Political, and Environmental Boundaries on Management of the Quetico-Superior Wilderness of Ontario and Minnesota, 1920-1965." Ph.D. dissertation, University of Wisconsin-Madison, 1988.

Hayden, Thomas Howard. "The Influence and the Accomplishments of the Izaak Walton League of America on conservation in Minnesota." Master's these, Macalester College, 1972.

Pyter, Bernadett. "A Bio-Bibliography of Sigurd F. Olson." Master's thesis, University of Minnesota, 1972.

Warecki, George Michael. "The Quetico-Superior council and the Battle for Wilderness in Quetico Provincial Park, 1909-1960." Master's thesis, University of Western Ontario, 1983.

David Backes

David Backes grew up spending summer vacations in the canoe country of northeastern Minnesota. His encounters with loons and wolves and northern lights led him to seek an outdoor career. After brief stints with the Forest Service in Colorado and a nature center in northern Wisconsin, he completed in 1979 a bachelor's degree in natural resources at the University of Wisconsin-Madison.

He then moved to Ely to work for the *Ely Echo* where he discovered his love for writing. He soon returned to the University of Wisconsin-Madison for graduate work in environmental communications.

His stories for the *Ely Echo* on acid rain and waste disposal earned him a national award in 1982 from the Outdoor Writers Association of America. Mr. Backes completed his Ph.D. in 1988, and joined the faculty of the Department of Mass Communication at the University of Wisconsin-Milwaukee. He is currently working on the authorized biography of Sigurd F. Olson.